Just Smile and Say HELLO

The True Story of Trang Moreland

Love!
Trang
Morel
2019

ISBN 978-0-692-87592-6

Printed by Steuben Press, Longmont, Colorado.

Cover Design by Bill Koch.

THIRD PRINTING

A Note From The Editor

I hate editing. I'm a writer. I have been since I knew how to put words on paper. I've written quite a few articles, stories, novels, and poetry. I've even had a few published.

What stopped me from succeeding with most things I've written, is the fact that I hate the editing process. The first draft is often my last.

But when Trang came to me with her book, I was so captivated by her story, I couldn't resist helping.

Feeling up to challenge, I first read the book straight through, then again making notes, and then again—almost 20 times!

Then I started to change things up a bit. I did all the things I had been taught, and I got rid of all the "LY" adverbs and replaced the verbs with stronger ones.

When I took the finished product back to Trang, she read it and replied, "But this is your voice, not mine."

So, I did it all over again!

I have learned a lot about the writing and the editing process. Did you know that three people can spend over two hours of their lives working on one paragraph?

We have picked this story apart, chapter by chapter, paragraph by paragraph, sentence by sentence, and word by word. And, unfortunately, there are still mistakes.

Therefore, I beg of you, read this book for the story that lies within. A wonderful and true account of a very strong young woman who lived a life that most Americans cannot even imagine.

Try to picture her environment, her struggles, and her determination.

I feel every person in the United States should read this book!

I describe this story as "proof that truth is stranger than fiction", as it has more drama, romance, adventure, and tutelage than any other book you can read in any genre.

I want you to read this and come away feeling inspired. And, regardless of your religious or political beliefs, I hope this story makes you proud to be an American.

—*Cherie Kail, Editor*

Acknowledgments

Writing a book may seem like an individual project, but transferring my memories to paper has taken an entire team—especially when writing in a second language!

I would first like to thank my husband, Jay, for spending the last six years working many late nights helping me. This book wouldn't be possible without him.

To the two most precious people in my life: my son, Rick and daughter, Melissa: thank you for helping me with spelling errors and for just being such great kids!

A very big THANK YOU to my brilliant editor, Cherie Kail, for giving my book so much attention and helping the pages come alive. Thanks also for the friendship you've shown me from the beginning.

Thanks to: Barry Scholls, Courtney Coffman, Colleen Glover, Terry Purdy (you corrected more misspelled words and poorly structured sentences than anyone!) and all my clients for proofreading.

I'm extremely grateful for the artistic skills of Bill Koch and the talented photography of Jim Celuch. Together, they made my book cover look amazing!

Thanks to my sweet employee, Karryn Hickenbottom, who continues to help me not only in the salon, but with book orders and speaking engagements.

No words can describe the depth of my respect for my mother, by brother Dinh (Anh Hai), and my sisters, Phuong (Chi Ba), Diem (Chi Tu), and Quyen. Without them, there wouldn't be a story to tell. The foundation of who I am is built on the love and closeness we shared.

I am deeply indebted to my mother-in-law for always being there for me and making it possible to accomplish what I have.

Special thanks to my Aunt Lien and Uncle Raymond for providing the opportunity to come to America and for helping me start my new life.

Thanks to Jay's family, for all your kindness and support.

Finally, I am forever grateful to all my sponsors and everyone who pre-ordered *Just Smile and Say Hello*. Thanks to your confidence in me, my dream of publishing a book has now become a reality.

Chapter One

"State Highway Patrol! Get your hands in the air!" yelled the angry trooper as he sprang from his vehicle with his weapon drawn.

Oh, please don't shoot me! I thought while obeying his orders.

As I sat, horrified, in the front seat of my Nissan Altima, I wondered, *How could this be happening to me? What did I do that was so wrong? I'm a harmless Asian girl who loves America and would never do anything to offend the country or any of its law officials.*

All through my childhood, I dreamed of living in America. I worked long and hard for many years to get where I am.

So how did I end up with the police chasing me down a highway on such a warm spring day?

I've heard it said that when in fear for your safety, your life will flash before your eyes. That's just what mine did.

Those early days of my life seemed so long ago and far away. Even with the angry trooper's pistol pointed at me, my mind began to wander….

Back to the days of poverty….

The days of my youth….

Back to Viet Nam……..

ᘓ∎ᘔ

It was just a small hut made mostly of bamboo and nipa palms. The dirt floor would turn to mud when rain seeped through the roof. It had a kitchen area where my mother cooked rice and other Vietnamese delicacies three times a day over an open fire. One room served as a living area during the day and sleeping area at night. A small room in the back held a large woven bamboo container used for rice storage. There was no electricity and no running water.

Just a hut, but it was home—until the war came. As fighting between the American soldiers and Viet Cong (VC) intensified, the conflict drew closer each day. The fertile green rice paddies where my family worked and played literally became a battlefield.

To save everyone from the gun fire and exploding bombs, my parents fled their modest country home with my brother and two older sisters in 1968. They moved to the city of Phu Lam, not far from Sai Gon. This was the first of three moves my family would make to outrun the war.

Three years later, Mom gave birth to me and then to my younger sister in 1973.

Dad was an officer in the South Vietnamese army which forced him to be away most of the time, while Mom struggled to help support us by selling food along the streets. Our brother was placed in the care of monks for safe keeping while the war was going on.

I had no real memories of my dad and the only stories I knew were told to me by my family members. My favorite was one my mother told about the day she and my father met.

Like most marriages in Viet Nam, Mom and Dad's was arranged. Keeping with tradition, you didn't move out of your parents' house until you were married. The only exception to this was when the youngest son was married. He and his bride would live with the boy's parents until the parents passed away. I never really knew the reason for this arrangement outside of the fact it gave the parents someone to take care of them as they got older. When a girl was married, she kept her maiden name while the children were given their father's family name.

Mom's name was Nguyen Thi Ba, (Nguyen is the last name and Ba is her first.) She was the second oldest of nine brothers and sisters and was a very innocent young girl who always wore the traditional Vietnamese clothing (long black pants with a long sleeve button down blouse.) Mom never went to school because my grandpa believed that girls had no need to go and felt her time was better spent working in the family's rice paddies.

With just a few days' notice before my father and his parents were scheduled to come, Mom made sure the house was clean and in order. When the day finally arrived, she became really scared and uncertain. She hoped he wasn't a man who was mean or homely.

Her heart was beating really fast. While she was in the kitchen making a pot of tea, she looked out the door and saw three people walking down the path between rice paddies. She heard one of her brothers yelling, "They're coming; they're almost here!" A minute later, "They're here!"

Mom suddenly became even more nervous and then heard someone yell, "Oh, he's handsome. Wow! He's very handsome!"

As my dad and his parents approached the front of the house, Mom's parents met them at the door. They welcomed them into their home and sat down at the living room table.

My Dad remained standing off to one side as a show of respect to the elders.

Mom came walking in from the kitchen with a pot of hot tea, bowed her head, and greeted everybody. She poured tea in the cups and served everyone at the table, making sure both hands were on the cup as she handed it to them. Placing both hands on the cup was a must in order to show respect for someone older than yourself.

Mom kept her distance and didn't say anything to Dad. She walked back to the kitchen and immediately ran out to the canal where the family boat was tied off. This was Mom's favorite spot. There were many coconut and banana trees casting shade over the ground where chickens pecked for food. Mom quietly sat, thinking about everything when all of a sudden, she heard a noise behind her.

Quickly turning around, Mom saw Dad walking towards her with a big smile. He stopped a couple of steps short of where she was sitting and said, "Hello."

Mom was so nervous, her hands were shaking. She didn't say anything, even when Dad reached over and placed a small bottle of perfume in her hand before walking away.

She was seventeen years old when they were married.

Over the years, I asked Mom many times to tell that story again. To this day, it never fails to put a smile on her face each time she recounts those moments.

CR∎SO

One November evening in 1974, the family had gathered around our porch to eat and chat. As Mom held a bowl of rice in one hand and fed my younger sister with the other, she listened carefully to what each one of us said and inserted her words of advice at every appropriate moment.

I sat quietly as my older sisters shared fun stories about our dad. Though I was too young to know what I was feeling at the time, I now know it was jealousy. I only had vague memories of him; I wanted him to come home so I could have stories to tell too!

Everyone was hoping he would be home soon. Little did any of us know, our lives were about to change forever.

Mom finished feeding Quyen and set the rice bowl on the floor. She looked up and saw two police officers approaching our porch. Everyone tensed up because the police never brought good news.

One stepped forward and spoke to my mother. "Are you Nguyen Thi Ba?"

Mom could hardly speak. "Yes."

"And your husband is Tran Van Cuong?"

"Yes," she replied, her voice even weaker this time. Her hands were shaking.

The officer seemed sorrowful from the beginning, but looking at the curious faces of my siblings and me made him even sadder. "I'm sorry, ma'am," he said, "but your husband has been killed."

Before the words were out of his mouth, my mom had collapsed on the ground and began sobbing. My older sisters ran to her and tried to comfort her, but they were crying too.

Though Quyen and I weren't old enough to understand the tragedy, just seeing my mother so upset made us cry as well.

Later, we were told by witnesses that a man Dad considered his friend, shot him in broad daylight to steal his motorcycle. It happened so quickly, there was nothing anyone could do.

They said as he laid in the street, slowly bleeding to death, he called out for his family again and again. Hearing this made everyone's grief even more unbearable, especially for Grandma and Mom.

He was thirty-seven.

Since my mom was so deeply devoted to my Dad, she vowed to never re-marry.

As time went by, I began to wonder if I looked like my Dad. When I asked Mom if she had a picture of him, she walked over to the cabinet in the corner of our hut and opened a drawer where she kept everything important. She returned with a small photograph and said it was the only one she had. The picture of dad was of his upper body in a military uniform. And then she showed me his dog tags.

Whenever I asked about him, Mom repeatedly told me how smart and kind Dad was and that he loved every one of us dearly.

She once told me that when I was born, Dad would proudly ask anyone who came to visit "Do you think she looks like me?"

Everyone said I looked exactly like him. That was all I needed to hear.

My father – Tran Van Cuong

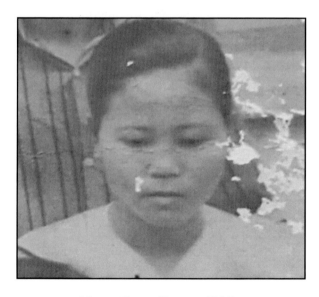

My mother – Nguyen Thi Ba

Chapter Two

My mother worked harder her whole life than any person I have ever known, and she never drew one single paycheck.

Cities and towns in Viet Nam have always had abundant vendors temporarily set up along streets and roads, with each vendor specializing in only one or two kinds of food or merchandise. While living in Phu Lam, Mom would wake up at 4:00 a.m. every morning and begin cooking food she would sell that day. She packed the prepared food into two woven bamboo baskets hooked on each end of a bamboo pole balanced over her shoulder. With the grace of a seasoned worker, Mom carried the two baskets to a section of the city where people knew the vendors would be set up for business.

When everything was sold at the end of a long, hot, grueling day, she would carry all her wares back home to clean up and get ready for the following morning. Before her day was finished and finally being able to sit and relax, Mom would cook our supper and make sure everyone was cleaned up and ready for bed.

Surviving in the city was always hard, but after Dad passed away, it became almost impossible. Since the fighting had moved away from our home and rice paddy, my family decided to return to our home in the country.

We found our little hut still sitting next door to my dad's parents', but it was badly damaged by fire, making it unlivable.

While temporarily living with my mom's parents, we built a new hut where the old one sat. We still had no electricity or running water and did all our cooking over an open fire.

Looking outside our front door, you could see a river less than 100 feet away. Weaving its way from the jungle in the back country, the river was the lifeblood for everyone along its banks.

During the rainy season, three large ceramic pots were set under the downspouts to capture water for drinking, cooking, and bathing.

Whenever the dry season came, water had to be purchased from vendors who traveled up and down the river in boats designed to carry large amounts of fresh water.

Each day required the gathering of wood and rice straw for cooking, as well as catching fish and finding vegetables to cook with our rice. Rice was the biggest part of every meal, three meals a day.

Most people in our area had abandoned their homes during the war, but Grandpa wouldn't leave his hut or rice paddy. He and others like him dug large holes concealed under their houses to hide in and have a safe place to sleep at night.

Grandma stayed with him during the day, but every evening, before dark, she'd walk to a friend's house in a local town of Cho Diem. She felt safer there because the VC would come out at night from wherever they were hiding, and that's when most of the fighting with the Americans would occur.

But Grandpa stayed behind as the war went on around him. I remember him telling us, "The bomb that burned your hut hit so close, it sucked the air right from my lungs! I thought for sure I was going to die!"

Even after that frightening experience, he refused to leave his home.

My grandparents' rice paddy was located next to their house, but my family's paddy was a long distance up the river. When the war ended, most families in our area returned to their homes around the same time we did. Everyone soon discovered their rice paddies were in horrible condition due to the many years of neglect. Our paddy looked like a jungle with all kinds of trees and plants growing all over.

Fortunately, since Grandpa had stayed behind and maintained his paddy, he was able to provide for us while we cleared ours for use again.

Every day, Mom and my oldest sister, Chi Ba, would wake up early in the morning, cook a pot of rice, fry some vegetables and pack it away in our boat. They also filled a bucket with rain water dipped from one of the large ceramic pots. It would then take two hours of paddling before reaching our rice paddy.

With machetes, scythes, and hoes, Mom and my sister put everything they had into the field. Working rain or shine, it took nearly two years before it was ready to grow rice again.

My brother had two years of school remaining and could only help out on the weekends while my next to oldest sister, Chi Tu, was forced to quit school and stay home to watch my younger sister, Quyen, and me.

Chi Tu cried every day because she wanted to go to school so badly. One day, some of her school friends stopped by for a long visit. She was so happy to see them and seemed to enjoy their company more than anything.

When they left, she cried harder than before.

It was difficult for me to watch her stand by the door every morning looking at all those kids walking to school out on the main dirt path. Mom and Chi Ba were always long gone by this time of morning and so there was no chance for her to leave and visit with her friends. So many times, I wished there was something I could do to change things.

When Mom and Chi Ba first arrived at the rice paddy each morning, they would eat half of their rice and vegetables for breakfast while it was still warm. Every so often, Mom would stop working and use her bare hands to catch fish that were swimming in the flooded paddy. She was so good at grabbing the fish that she could catch more than five people put together.

At lunch time, they would build a fire and cook a few fish to have something warm with the cold leftover rice from that morning. Mom also would look for wild fruit and vegetables that were growing in the area and place them in the boat along with any extra fish she might have caught. The fruit she usually picked was called Binh Bat (Custard-apple family). It's close to the size of a pear and has at least a thousand seeds inside, making it a little difficult to eat. Throughout the day, they drank warm water out of the bucket they brought from home.

At the end of each day, both Mom's and Chi Ba's hands were sore and sometimes bleeding. As painful as that was, it was the least of their worries. A bigger concern was the unexploded landmines left over from the war. People were losing their arms and legs, and sometimes worse, every day.

One day, my Grandpa's younger brother was working to clear his rice paddy when he saw part of an American airplane in one corner of his field. Not knowing the VC set landmines all around the crash sites to kill any Americans who might come and investigate, he walked over to look when one of the landmines exploded and killed him. His rice paddy was right next to ours.

Mom and Chi Ba prayed every day that it wouldn't happen to them. Mom always believed Dad's spirit watched out for them.

In the evening, after Mom and Chi Ba returned home and everyone had their supper, we sat around a kerosene lamp on the floor to weave large bags using flattened grass reeds. The process of making the bags is called Duong Bao and required the simultaneous use of your hands and feet. The bags were used for shipping fruits, vegetables and seafood because they would keep the contents inside fresh for a longer period of time by allowing air to circulate. We also made smaller bags called Bao Nhan to be used for protecting the Nhan fruit from birds during its growing season.

Mom was always the last person to finish and go to bed. Yet she would be the first one up again in the morning, starting the fire for cooking rice and preparing for another hard day's work.

Weaving the bags was the easy part. First, Mom and my two older sisters would spend three days and two nights paddling our boat upriver to reach a place in the jungle where there were plenty of grass reeds growing. It was in the middle of nowhere and there weren't any people living around that area.

I had heard so many scary stories about people getting malaria from the jungle and I was really afraid for them. It was always a scary trip for them as well, but they were careful about protecting themselves from mosquitos and always made it back okay.

Sometimes, if other responsibilities prevented Mom and my sisters from making the trip to the jungle, Mom would stop one of the vendors on the river and buy some reeds. She tried her best to avoid doing that because it really cut into our profit.

The grass reeds were naturally round and needed to be made flat for the purpose of weaving. We tied several grass reeds into a small round bundle and laid the bundle on top of a four foot length of train rail. One of my uncles had given us the rail after he received it from a worker repairing a section of tracks in the city.

Using a heavy wood tamper cut from a hardwood tree limb, one of us tamped along the entire bundle length as someone else held it steady on the rail. The bundle would be turned over and then tamped down the entire length again.

We repeated this process until all the reeds were flat. If the reeds were still young and green, they were fairly easy to flatten. It was always the older ones which were dryer and harder that gave us trouble. We had to soak those reeds in water for a whole day before tamping.

After risking our lives to collect the material and spending endless hours in preparation, the entire family weaved bags deep into the night, every night. It took about three weeks to make 100 bags.

Since they were in high demand, they sold quickly. Our profit: $0.59 (US currency) per day for the whole family.

Chapter Three

Conserving water was a must when the rainy season ended; then it was time to start buying fresh water again. The purchased water was stored in the ceramic pots and was to be used for drinking only. Water used for cooking and washing clothes was taken from our grandfather's pond.

**My brother – Anh Hai (Tran Chung Dinh)
Carrying water from pond.**

As a last resort, we would use river water, but we tried not to since it was heavily polluted with sewage. But when the pond dried up, we were left with no other choice.

Wanting to have more fresh water at a cheaper price, Mom decided to try buying at wholesale prices from a vendor who was farther away. So she and Chi Ba loaded three large ceramic pots between them on our boat.

After paddling hard for a very long way, they came to a place where the river emptied into a much larger one. The vendor they were looking for was located a short distance downstream on the other side of the larger river.

The negotiated price for the fresh water was far less than what Mom had expected and it took very little time for the vendor to fill all three ceramic pots.

Feeling extremely happy with the great bargain they made, she and my sister turned their boat around and began their return trip home.

Ten minutes after leaving the vendor, the wind started to pick up and soon began blowing extremely hard. The river became choppy and started pushing their boat towards shore.

Mom and my sister were both getting scared because the ceramic pots full of water made the boat top heavy and very unstable. Before they knew what was happening, the boat flipped over.

Mom had no idea how to swim and almost immediately disappeared under the water.

Chi Ba barely knew how to swim herself and had a difficult time reaching the river bank. Feeling scared and helpless, the only thing she could do was start screaming.

"Help! Someone! Anyone! Please help! My mother is drowning! Help us!"

She couldn't see Mom anywhere. She was so worried about her dying, she continued screaming while hoping someone would hear her.

After what felt like an eternity, a fisherman in a boat appeared from nowhere. "Get in," he ordered. "I can help you."

He helped my sister in his boat and asked, "Where did she go under?"

With the wind blowing, the beating waves, and the stress of her own struggle to survive, Chi Ba was a bit disoriented. Guessing the best she could, she pointed to a spot in the river. "There! Right there—I think."

The fisherman tied one end of a long rope around his hand and dove into the water where she pointed.

With just one attempt, the fisherman returned to the surface with Mom in his arms. She was unresponsive when he placed her in the boat. Chi Ba thought for sure she was dead.

My sister didn't know anything like CPR, so she just kept rolling Mom back and forth while the fisherman maneuvered his boat to the other side of the river and tied off to a tree in front of his house.

Wasting no time, he grabbed Mom's body and placed her face down with her midsection centered over his shoulder. He bounced her up and down by running around his house.

After seeing Mom wasn't responding to his efforts, he ran over to a large ceramic pot with a broken top that was sitting next to his house. Showing the confidence of a professional rescuer, he placed Mom inside the empty pot, gathered up some straw from the kitchen area and built a fire around the base of the pot.

All my sister could do was trust him. As she was crying and doing her best to hold herself together, she began pleading with the fisherman; "Please, sir! Please! I no longer have a Dad; please don't let my Mom die. She's all we have!"

She fell to her knees and began praying.

The fisherman placed his hands on Mom's shoulders and started moving her around inside the pot. After a few short moments, her eyes suddenly opened.

Chi Ba jumped to her feet in joy and later recalled that it was the happiest moment of her life.

Mom didn't feel well at all, and by that time, it was getting dark. The fisherman and his wife thought it was best if they waited until morning before leaving and asked them to spend the night.

While there was still enough light, the fisherman went out to retrieve their boat from the river. When he returned with their boat in tow, Chi Ba rushed out to help tie it off and see if there was any damage.

It was at that time, she learned the fisherman had an argument with his wife earlier that day after coming home from fishing. Becoming angry, he went back out on the river to clear his head and that was when he heard my sister's screams for help.

When morning came, Chi Ba went up to the fisherman and knelt on the floor before him. With her hands placed together, she bowed her head to the floor several times. (This is a Vietnamese custom to show gratitude, especially when it's something of great importance.) "Thank you for saving my mother's life," she said. "My whole family thanks you."

The man stopped Chi Ba from bowing and told her, "I'm just happy she is okay."

He let her keep the blanket and clothes they'd given her the night before.

After following them to the mouth of the smaller river where he knew they would be safe, he said goodbye and wished them well.

With no way for Mom and my sister to contact us, my family and I had worried all night. We had the feeling that something really bad had happened. While we were making plans to go out and look for them, my brother noticed their boat coming up the river.

Mom should have gone to the hospital, but didn't. She was very sick and extremely weak. It took at least a month for her to become strong enough to get out of bed.

One evening, as we were sitting around Mom's bed talking, she began telling us everything she could remember when their boat flipped over. Right after being forced under water, she began thinking that she was surely going to die because no one was around and the river was so big. All she could think about at that moment was leaving us behind.

As she lay on the bottom, she suddenly remembered she had her earrings on. She wished she would have left them at home so we could have them. They were the most valuable thing she owned and didn't want them lying on the bottom of the river forever.

Listening to Mom talk about those moments on the river forced me to look at something I never wanted to think about. Just knowing how close we came to losing our mother that day was almost too much to bear.

For many years, my sister, Chi Ba, would pause at times to talk about the fisherman, and whenever anyone in our family came across someone in need, we never failed to honor him by passing on his kindness.

Chapter Four

Vietnamese culture forbade dating before marriage. Chi Ba respected this tradition. Besides, she was always too busy helping our mother to meet anyone. At the age of seventeen, she had an arranged marriage with a boy serving in the military. After her wedding, she moved away with her husband to live in his family's home.

A few months later, my brother, Anh Hai, was forced into an arranged marriage with a girl he didn't know. Following tradition, the new bride moved into our family's home after their wedding.

One day when my sister, Chi Tu, returned home from town, she walked over to me and quietly remarked, "Hey! Guess what? I saw Anh Hai's old girlfriend today."

"Girlfriend? How do you know that?" I asked.

"I know a lot of things. Come with me," she replied.

I followed her over to the large wood cabinet sitting in one corner of the house. She opened a drawer on the bottom and handed me a stack of letters written to my brother.

Looking up at me, Chi Tu said, "There's fifty-one of them. Make sure you go in order and be sure to start with number one."

"You put numbers on them! Anh Hai will kill us if he finds out!"

"Just read them!"

All of the letters were very neat, fully written pages. Her hand writing was beautiful! I learned her name was Thao and she was smart, sweet, and very kind. It was plain to see that she and my brother were madly in love. They first met while in high school and instantly became best of friends. When my brother graduated, he had to work full time in our family's rice field but managed to sneak off once in a while to visit with her.

When a couple of years had gone by, Mom informed my brother that she wanted to have grandchildren and his thoughts naturally went to the only girl he ever loved, Thao.

Following tradition, a woman living in our area who knew both families was chosen to approach Thao's mother and father with the proposal of marriage. Thao's mother disapproved of my brother and promptly dismissed any idea of him marrying her daughter.

Chi Tu concluded while placing the letters back into the drawer, "The only reason her mother disapproved of Anh Hai was because our family is so poor. She was looking for someone who could provide her daughter with a *good life*. To make sure Thao stayed far away from our brother, she made arrangements to have her sent off to college. Before leaving, Thao and Anh Hai said their good byes with broken hearts and tears."

Knowing that Anh Hai was unable to marry Thao, a girl was chosen for him by other members of our family which led to his arranged marriage.

My heart ached for my brother and the girl I'd never met. I prayed then and there I would find true love like theirs. But for me, there would be a happy ending.

Chapter Five

Four years had gone by since we moved back to the country. Mom had to work hard but she was very happy with how things were going. We were extremely poor but always managed to have plenty of rice to eat. However, everything was about to change.

The government began a program called "Tap Doan," which gave them the authority to take control of all rice paddies. The way the program was designed, people were required to work in a field selected by the government and earn points for each day's labor. At the end of the season, they could trade their accumulated points for rice. The more points you accumulated, the more rice you would get.

Tap Doan didn't work so well and it didn't take long before many of the people became angry. Most wanted everything to go back to how it was before the government takeover and be responsible for their own rice paddy. They became frustrated after working hard all day and ending up with the same amount of points as someone who was lazy and barely did anything. The rice fields also did poorly because the people in charge didn't have experience in growing rice and there was an enormous amount of stealing. The end result was a shortage of rice and people going hungry, including our family.

My sister Quyen and I didn't know any better and gave Mom a hard time by crying every time we didn't have enough to eat. Over time, I began to sense that something was very wrong, just by the look on Mom's face when she didn't know I was watching.

Mom didn't want us to know how bad everything really was and tried to hide the truth as long as she could. One day, I overheard a conversation she was having with my grandma about a man from a neighboring village. "They found him, dead in his bed. Starved to death."

"Rumor has it, he's the third one this week, and it's getting closer all the time." The concern in Grandma's voice was frightening as she added, "I'm afraid one of us might be next."

I wondered if it was true and could it happen to my family? After looking around our home and seeing what little we had (the storage room was almost empty) and how many mouths there were to feed, I realized we were closer to starving than I ever imagined.

For the next few nights, I lay wide awake, worrying that someone in my family might die. Maybe my mom, or grandma, or brother or a sister----

Maybe it would be me!

To make what little rice we had last longer, Mom began cooking smaller amounts and mixing it with a lot of sweet potatoes (Khoai Lang) and cassava (Khoai Mi).

To help prevent starvation, Viet Nam imported a grain from other countries called "sorghum" (Bo Bo). It looked a little like puffed wheat and cooked the same way as rice, only it took a lot longer. Anyone wanting Bo Bo had to use points earned working in the rice paddies.

During the off season, when no work was required, Mom and my brother would earn money by buying and selling sweet potatoes and cassava. Every night at about midnight, they would leave in our boat and paddle for two hours before reaching a floating market located on one of the larger rivers.

Once their boat was fully loaded with potatoes and cassava, they returned home to pick me up before continuing on to the open market near Ho Chi Minh City. At that time of the morning, I was barely awake. Mom would lay a blanket on top of the potatoes and let me continue sleeping while she and my brother paddled as hard as they could, making sure we arrived at the market before the sun came up.

After tying off our boat along the market shore, Mom and Anh Hai each filled a large bamboo basket with potatoes and headed into the market along with a set of hand scales. My job was to stay at the river bank and watch the boat so no one would steal anything. Anh Hai's job was to constantly keep Mom in supply throughout the day.

During one of his trips away, I grabbed a line that was hanging low along the bank of the river and started swinging.

When Anh Hai returned to the boat for more goods, he looked over at what I was doing and began screaming, "Get off! Get off! Do you know what you're swinging on? That's an electric line!"

I screamed and jumped back. "I didn't know! I didn't know!" I shouted. "I've never seen one before!"

"Well, now you know," he scolded. "So don't *ever* go near one again!"

The incident scared me so much, from that day on I stayed away from anything that looked like an electric line.

A few days after following the same routine, Anh Hai began putting me to work. He told me I needed to switch jobs with him and start carrying potatoes over to Mom.

"I can't do that! They're too heavy for me!" I hollered.

"Then just carry half a basket!" he snapped back.

Throughout the day, I noticed how Mom really knew what she was doing. A lot of the buyers kept trying to negotiate the price lower, but most of the time, Mom managed to make a sale.

One day when Mom had all her potatoes sold and returned the baskets and scales to our boat, she asked me to follow her but wouldn't tell me where we were going.

We stopped at a street café where she bought a soda drink for me. It was the first time in my life I had tasted one and continually took one sip after another. I was so happy and felt like I was in heaven.

Mom smiled at me and said, "Save a little for your brother."

Mom always set aside the worst looking vegetables that people wouldn't buy and took them home for us to eat. If there were any saleable potatoes remaining at the end of the day, we would find buyers along the river on our way home. To make a sale, Mom used a loud, clear voice so people could hear her from their homes. She shouted, "Khoai Mi! Khoai Lang! Lam on, mua vo, mua vo." Translated, "Cassava! Sweet potatoes! Please buy, please buy."

People interested in buying would walk out to the river bank and signal us to stop with a motion of their hands. Just as the women at the market, they always tried to negotiate a lower price which sometimes resulted in us not making a sale. At the end of the day, we rarely had any good potatoes or cassava remaining to keep for ourselves.

As soon as we arrived home and unloaded the boat, Mom wanted me to take a bath right away because the bath towel needed time to dry in the sun before the next person bathed. The towel didn't take long to dry because it was so small and thin, I could see through it.

One time, rather than taking a bath, I ran next door to my grandparents' and jumped into their rain filled pond surrounded by coconut and banana trees. It felt so cool and relaxing. I swam around and tried catching a fish but they kept sliding off my hand.

A short while later, Mom made me get out because it started to rain along with thunder and lightning. I felt really bad because without the sun, Mom had to use my wet towel when she took a bath.

After supper, just before we began weaving straw bags, Mom would always burn incense. She bowed her head with her knees on the floor and prayed: "Nam Mo A Di Da Phat." These were words of respect offered to Buddha. She believed in him and always prayed a lot, especially when one of us was sick. Whenever we got better, she set out flowers and some fruit on a tray as an offering for an answered prayer.

Mom also prayed while burning incense as a way to honor my Dad. She started talking to him like he was right beside her.

I grew up without much fear believing Dad's spirit would protect me from all bad things.

Mom always included the wish of good health for the family in her prayers and to have our rice paddy returned to us.

One day, we all received the good news. There was no more Tap Doan. It had been about two years since the government started the program and now they were giving the rice paddies back to the people.

Everyone, including our family, thought it was one of the greatest days ever. We would never have to go without rice again. Thank God!

Chapter Six

One evening when I was nine years old, I came home after visiting my grandma and overheard a conversation between my younger sister, Quyen, and our ten year old cousin, Xuan. They were talking about how our older sister, Chi Tu, had a boyfriend. I was in shock!

Rushing over to them, I asked our cousin with an air of disbelief, "How do you know all this?"

"I just heard it. But I don't remember who told me!" Xuan quickly replied before running off.

I immediately turned to Quyen and said with a stern voice, "Don't you tell Mom! If she finds out, she'll kill Chi Tu!"

"I won't!" She snapped back while also trying to get away from me.

"Not so fast!" I shouted. "Who is he? What's his name?"

"His name is Muoi and he's short, I mean really short. Everyone knows him as the guy who likes to play guitar."

"Where does he live? Who's his parents?"

"He lives not far up the road from us, in the house with all the coconut trees in front of it. I don't know who his parents are or anything else."

"I knew it, I just knew it!"

"Knew what?" Quyen asked.

"You know how I like to skip, jump and swing my arms all over the place while walking? Well, every time Chi Tu and I walked by that house, she'd smack my arm and tell me to act like a normal person. As soon as we were out of view of the house, she'd let me be myself again. Now it all makes sense to me."

"She must have worried they'd think you weren't right in the head."

"Shhh! Quiet! Someone is coming!" I whispered.

"It's Mom!" Quyen said as we put distance between us and acted like nothing was going on.

A week later, while I was visiting my second cousin's wife, she asked me in a low voice, "Did you know your sister, Chi Tu, has a boyfriend?"

"Yes, and I was really surprised! Who told you?" I blurted out.

"Not too loud, Trang! I'm not going to tell you who said this, but your mom also heard the rumor and asked your sister if it was true. She said 'no'. A few days later, your mom found a picture of him under your sister's pillow."

"That's got to be the dumbest place in the world to hide anything!" I said in disbelief.

My cousin's wife agreed and continued, "Your Mom waited for a day when your sister and she were the only ones home and then ordered her to come into the house. She was holding a large stick and angrily closed all the doors before making her sit down.

"She then gave your sister a long lecture on the proper behavior of a young woman. Knowing she could get a beating at any moment, your sister was smart and didn't talk back. I really feel bad for her."

I felt scared for my sister after listening to the part about Mom closing the doors. I couldn't believe I didn't know all of this was going on.

On the way back home, I started thinking about what would happen to me when I got older. I didn't blame my sister for doing what she did; I would have done the same thing myself. I just couldn't understand why it was so wrong to have a boyfriend.

Chi Tu wanted so much to be a good daughter, but she couldn't cut the ties with Muoi. They managed to keep their relationship a secret for a while before Mom eventually learned what was going on.

Through a mediator, Mom immediately demanded the boy's mother (his father was killed during the war) come to talk about accepting my sister. If she wouldn't accept Chi Tu, Mom would find a husband for her.

Parents in Viet Nam think it's their responsibility to find a good wife or husband for their son or daughter. When a girl reaches the age of twenty–five and isn't married, parents begin to be concerned. If the daughter is not married by the age of thirty, she's considered to be an old maid and will no longer be wanted. They will be the talk of the neighborhood. If you're not married, no matter what your age, it's unacceptable to move out of the family home.

A girl is also expected to remain a virgin until she's married and a husband can divorce her if he discovers she's not. Most women know to keep all past relationships a secret, a secret they will carry to the grave.

Muoi's mother refused Mom's demand. By tradition, her only son would remain in the family home with his new bride and she preferred to be the one that decided who the bride would be. His mother wanted a girl that would listen to her. Girls like my sister who sneaked around were considered wild and uncontrollable.

Another reason for the mother's refusal was Mom being a lot younger than she. Most parents of the bride and groom always approached each other as equals. If they weren't close to being the same age, the older parent usually objected because they believed they wouldn't receive the respect their older age entitled them.

After receiving word of the mother's rejection, Mom began watching my sister like a hawk. Mom informed the boyfriend through the mediator that if someone else came along and asked to marry my sister, she would accept the request and it would be too late for him to do anything.

Every day for the following two months, Muoi pleaded with his mother to change her mind. Realizing her son was never going to give up, she finally agreed and began making arrangements for the marriage. He and Chi Tu were in heaven.

Mom went to a Buddhist Temple and spoke with the spiritual leader about the proper date for the wedding. After checking the birthdates of my sister and her boyfriend in his book, the leader remarked, "There's no way these two people should ever get married; it would be a death sentence."

Chi Tu and Muoi were devastated.

Watching her son suffer from the heartache of having his world torn apart was painful for the boyfriend's mother. Wanting to find a way to help, she came up with the idea of trying a different Buddhist Temple to see if they would say the same thing. She asked the spiritual leader of the other Temple to look closely at the details of their birthdates before giving his opinion. The leader studied his book for a short while before declaring everything to be just fine, and suggested when the proper wedding date should be.

Hearing the good news, Chi Tu and Muoi were back on cloud nine again and finally became married four months later.

I thought about the heartache my brother had gone through when he couldn't marry his girlfriend. Seeing Chi Tu and Muoi together made me smile, knowing that true love could exist in our culture.

Chapter Seven

After my brother and older sisters were married, Mom was determined to keep my younger sister, Quyen, and me in school for as long as possible. The elementary school was usually a twenty minute walk away, but when the monsoon season arrived, it took quite a bit longer. The heavy rains turned the dirt path into a trail of mud and created an endless number of water puddles to walk around.

Each day before classes began, students would take turns sweeping the floor in the classroom. Local vendors set up their stands in front of the school and sold fruit, sugarcane, candy, and sticky rice wrapped in banana leaves.

There were no trash cans and the students would throw wrappers and banana leaves everywhere on the ground. It took a lot of time and work to clean up the mess by sweeping the trash into a pile outside.

With more students than chairs in the classroom, we always made sure to do a good job of sweeping because we never knew whose turn it would be to sit on the floor.

On the days when it was my turn, I found writing in a thin notebook on my lap very difficult and uncomfortable. Keeping my pants clean was almost impossible.

Even with conditions being as they were, I felt lucky to be in school. Some kids had to stay home every day because their parents didn't have the money to send them. Mom always managed to find a way to pay for my sister and me, even if it required our family to cut back expenses in some other area.

We both loved the book bags weaved by our mom and carried them every day. The only problem was that every time it rained, we either had to quickly get out of the weather or cover our bag up to keep the books from getting wet.

I went to school in the morning, Quyen went in the afternoon. I loved my sister, but I was more than happy our schedules ended up being that way. I didn't want her running back and telling Mom anything about my social life.

To save money, I learned to get the most use from my notebook by writing small and using tightly packed words that covered every blank spot on the sheet from top to bottom. I had a pen and pencil but no crayons. Whenever we had art class, I was fortunate and grateful to have a friend who allowed me to borrow her crayons when she wasn't using them.

One time, when she handed me the small box containing three colored crayons, I sat looking at them for a long time while thinking how great it would be to have a set of my own. Noticing I was lost in thought, my friend shook my arm and reminded me there wasn't much time to finish our project.

Crayons weren't the only thing at school I wished for. I wished we had a restroom. I quickly learned the girls go on the left side of the school building, and the boys go on the right side.

The school was located in a very busy place. Out front was the ferry landing, which was always busy with people coming and going to market. There were often large crowds waiting for the next ferry, leaving no privacy for our outdoor bathroom. Scared of getting caught with our pants down, we usually just waited until we got home.

One day, Quyen came home from school crying really hard after having an accident in her pants. The poor girl had diarrhea that day and was wearing thin, white pants. Without a phone to call home or a restroom to go to, all she could do was start walking. She cried the whole way home while being surrounded by a large group of kids screaming, laughing and making fun of her.

The following day, Quyen was feeling too embarrassed to go back and face all those kids, so Mom allowed her stay home for a couple of days. The extra time off helped my sister feel better about herself, but the kids at school did their best to never let her forget. Seeing what happened to Quyen, I became nervous every time I had a stomach ache.

The school didn't provide any food or water. Students who had enough money would buy snacks during break time from the vendors set up near the ferry landing. All the food sold was so yummy. I especially liked the one called "xoi". It was sticky rice with yellow beans in the middle, topped with fresh shredded coconut and sugar, all wrapped in a banana leaf. I was never able to buy any of those treats because Mom couldn't afford them. She always made sure I ate a good meal before leaving the house.

Two of the houses beside the school also sold food, snacks and candy. Both houses sold the same products which created fierce competition between the two. One of them began offering, "Free water if you buy from us."

One day, my best friend, Ha, decided to buy something from the house offering free water, so I went along. Ha bought a small amount of candy and we both walked out to the front of the house to get a drink. I didn't buy anything so I wasn't supposed to be drinking, but I was going to try anyway.

The water was the color of iced tea and had small dead leaves and mosquito larvae floating around on top. It was stored in five large different looking ceramic pots, each filled from downspouts connected to the gutters of the house's palm leaf roof. Water caught from this type of roof was especially bad when the roof was new.

Not wanting to get yelled at, I carefully tried to avoid getting caught by the owner of the house. In one of the pots, I took the provided cup and swirled the water all around to push aside the larvae and leaves. When there was a clear spot in the water, I hurried to dip a cupful and quickly drank it all before handing the cup over to Ha. The water tasted terrible, but being so thirsty, I was happy to drink it anyway.

As I wiped the water from my lips, I noticed out of the corner of my eye the owner (his name was "Sang") walking towards me.

Sang came over and, instead of yelling at me like I had expected, he said in a low voice, "I just want you to know that it's okay to drink water with your friend, but when you do have money, make sure you buy your snacks from me."

"I promise. Thank you," I said.

When the rainy season was over and the days were getting hotter, we noticed the water was beginning to taste really weird. We kept wondering if there was something wrong with it and if it was even okay to drink. A woman living in the community told us one day she saw Sang getting water from the river and mixing it with the good water.

We all figured that the reason he did that was because everyone was drinking more water and he wanted to keep his costs down. My friends and I agreed that what he did was horrible, and we'd never drink his water again. It didn't take very long before we found ourselves so thirsty, we began drinking it anyway.

Not only did we have to drink dirty water, we also had to share a cup with hundreds of other kids. The cup was never washed in between uses and every time we had a stomach ache—and we often did—we always blamed it on the bad water or the dirty cup. I just prayed my discomfort wouldn't lead to an incident like my sister's.

Chapter Eight

Quyen and I were always looking for ways to help Mom pay for our education. Some days when Quyen came home from school, we went out and picked up broken glass and plastics wherever we could find it. We kept everything collected at home in plastic bags until one of the recycling people came by to buy from us.

Other times, we'd go into our Grandfather's rice paddies to catch fish with our hands and pick a few vegetables growing on the dikes. We had so much fun doing that, especially during the monsoon season.

Sometimes it rained for twenty-four hours nonstop and the paddies would be flooded with water up to our knees. Fish would move from one paddy to the next as the water flowed over low points in the dikes and were easy to catch as they swam through the shallow water.

Whenever it was raining, small crabs came out and we could see them crawling around under the water. Most of the time, we'd reach down and catch them with our bare hands, but occasionally, when there were plenty of them to get, we'd use my brother's seine.

One day when our basket was only half full, a severe thunderstorm moved into the area. The rain started coming down so heavily that we had to constantly brush the water from our eyes.

We ran toward the bamboo trees until I remembered Mom saying to never do that when there's lightning.

Quyen insisted it was okay, but I disagreed.

We ran a little farther to an abandoned brick building that was badly damaged from the war. So many bullets went through the walls that half the building had fallen in.

We went over to a corner where the roof was still on. About five minutes later, our cousin, Be Lon, showed up with the same idea of getting out of the rain. Because it wasn't too hot or cold, we all felt very good even though we were completely drenched.

Be Lon asked me about school. She wanted to know about a boy who was called "My Lai", (pronounced "Me Lie") which means he had an American father and a Vietnamese mother. I never knew his real name or anything else about him, except that his dad went back to America after the war.

My Lai got into fights often because he always acted like a snob, but everyone liked the way he looked. He was tall, had light brown hair and beautiful white skin that everyone in Viet Nam would die for. I had a class with My Lai for only one year, and then never saw him again. I heard that he went to live in America.

Quyen thought that was "so cool", and asked, "Do you think we could go to America someday?"

"I don't think so, but I wish I could go there just to learn how to speak English. That'd be pretty cool," I said.

Be Lon responded, "You wouldn't survive in America."

"Why?"

"Because people in America don't eat rice, and they don't use chopsticks or fish sauce. I heard they eat lots of canned food and lots of meat with bread and butter. I also heard that American people will be really mean to you."

"I don't believe that. Whoever is telling you all this is either lying or don't know what they're talking about. Mom told me she saw American soldiers giving candy to kids many times."

As we talked, the thunderstorm moved on and the rain slowed.

"Want to help us catch fish for supper?" Quyen asked.

Seeing some boys in the next paddy, Be Lon declined. "No, thanks. I think I'm going over there and say hello; you know, just to be polite."

Quyen and I knew the truth; Be Lon was always boy crazy.

We went back to catching fish until late afternoon before deciding to quit for the day and go home.

Standing off to one side of the path leading over to our house was a water buffalo grazing in a large patch of grass.

Our cousin named My (pronounced "Me") was responsible for the buffalo's daily care and stood nearby, closely watching it at all times.

Grandfather's water buffalo

Looking at him instantly took my thoughts back to the conversation we had earlier with Be Lon about America, and why I didn't believe the stories she repeated. How My was given his name was one of those reasons.

One day in 1968, my aunt, Co Ba, ("Co" means aunt on the fathers side, "Ba" is the number three) caught a bus out of Saigon to go visit her parents living in the country. She was almost nine months pregnant and believed there was enough time to make the trip before the baby was born. Women in Viet Nam are required to remain in bed for at least thirty days after giving birth. Not wanting to expose her baby to the harsh traveling conditions, Co Ba knew it would be a long time before she made this trip again.

To reach her parents' house, Co Ba would ride in the back of a small three wheel bus until she reached the village of Cho Dem. From there, she'd walk through the local market until reaching a small wooden ferryboat powered by one man with an oar. Once she was on the other side of the river, it was a good twenty minute walk before reaching her parents.

Upon reaching the ferry crossing on this particular trip, American soldiers had a check point set up preventing a long line of people from crossing the river. The soldiers were telling everyone it was too dangerous on the other side because of fighting and no one could go over until it was safe.

As Co Ba was standing in line, her water broke. One of the American soldiers who saw what was happening, picked her up, put her in a truck, and took her straight to the hospital. He was very kind to her the whole time, but she didn't know any English and couldn't talk to him.

Arriving at the hospital, the soldier carried her into the labor room. He waited until her baby was safely born and then gave her some money before saying goodbye. My aunt was so touched by his kindness, she decided to name my cousin "My", which means "America".

Chapter Nine

After talking with our cousin, My, we rushed home and started gathering supplies for supper. When I realized we needed a vegetable that we hadn't picked earlier in the day, Quyen and I ran back out to our garden. Afterwards, we decided to visit our father's grave which was close by.

While standing in front of the stone with our Dad's name on it, a hundred thoughts went racing through my mind. The only thing I knew for sure was, I wished he were still alive. Quyen looked like she was going to cry, so I suggested we go back to the house.

Guessing at the time of day, I decided it was time to start cooking. After working all day in our rice paddy, Mom would be coming home very tired and hungry. Not having a watch or clock of any kind around the house, my only way of knowing the time was by looking at the position of the sun in the sky. Mom was the best at telling the time this way. She could even tell the time in the morning by listening to the chickens.

Mom taught me how to prepare good rice by cooking it over an open fire with rice straw. Before beginning, I would run out to our straw tree and pull an armful of tightly packed straw from the bottom of the stack. Because I was so small and skinny, it took every bit of my strength to pull the straw out.

A straw tree was built close to our house as a way of storing straw for cooking while keeping it as dry as possible. After harvest, three foot lengths of rice straw were tied into small bundles with the flowered end of each stem pointing in the same direction.

When the bundles were brought home, an eight foot diameter circle was formed on the ground by laying bundles tightly against each other with the flowered ends pointing toward the center of the circle. After the circle was complete, a second layer of bundles was laid on top of the first in the same manner except that the finished circle was a little less than eight feet in diameter.

This process was continued until you ended up with an eight foot high, cone shaped stack. A few bundles were stood on end at the top to bring the cone shape almost to a point.

The flowered end of each bundle was always larger in diameter, and by placing that end toward the center of the stack, the bundles would slope downward from the inside toward the outside and help keep water out. The weight of all those bundles stacked on top of each other is what made it so hard to pull straw out from the bottom of the stack. Also, straw always had to be pulled from a different place around the stack each time to keep the whole thing from falling over.

The straw burned very fast compared to wood. When the rice was almost done, Mom taught me to roll straw into two balls and then put them under the rice pot one at a time in order to slow the fire down. The tighter the ball, the slower it would burn. By the time the two balls were done burning, the rice was ready to eat.

I also learned how to cook a large pot of sour vegetable soup with fresh crabs and fish. It always tasted so good; the flavor was amazing.

One time, just before scraping fresh green onions and herbs into the soup from the chopping board, I saw a worm float to the top. I became very upset and was undecided about what to do.

I finally reached for my chopsticks, picked the worm out and never told anyone. That was the one thing I didn't learn from my Mom. I felt even guiltier when everybody made comments about how great the soup was.

After supper, I hopped, skipped and jumped my way over to our grandma's house to return a kettle I'd borrowed earlier. Her doors were always open during the day, so I ran through the front door and straight to the back of the house where I found my grandma sitting in her favorite place in the kitchen.

My grandpa passed away a couple years earlier when I was ten years old. What I remember the most about him was how much he looked like Uncle Ho (Ho Chi Minh) and the attention he received everywhere because of it.

I also recalled how he and Grandma never would eat any meat as part of their religious beliefs; their lives were all about the church and helping people.

I started to spend a lot of time with my grandma after Grandpa was gone. Since she never went to school and never learned to read, I'd spend evenings reading scriptures for her from the Cao Dai religion.

I loved being around her; she was so kind and shared every-thing she had. She would cut her last banana into equal parts so everyone who was present could have a piece to eat.

Grandma was kind and helpful to strangers also. Many times, people would come through our area begging for food, and she would be the first to give them some uncooked rice so they could take it home and cook it themselves.

Once in a while, people with leprosy would show up and all the kids in the neighborhood would run in their houses and close the doors. We didn't understand the disease and worried it was contagious.

Grandma never turned anyone away and always treated the lepers with kindness while giving them a bag of rice. Even though I always felt bad for avoiding them, I never could get over my fear.

One day, Grandma asked me to help her with drying some rice in front of her house. The rice, which still had the hulls on it, had to be scattered all over a small area on the ground that was prepared just for this reason. While stirring the rice every hour or so, it usually took a couple days for the sun to dry it completely, providing it didn't rain.

As I was busy stirring the rice by moving it back and forth with my feet, I looked up and was shocked to see a pregnant woman who looked like a skeleton walking towards me. There were two small children walking in close step behind her as she approached to beg for some rice. I couldn't move or stop looking at her; I'd never seen anyone that skinny before.

After giving the woman a bag of uncooked rice, Grandma decided to invite them into the house. She gave each of them a bowl of cooked rice with tofu, green beans and soy sauce.

They swallowed the food like they hadn't eaten for days.

When they were finished, the woman thanked Grandma many times and got up to leave.

Grandma told her they could stay for a couple more hours if she wanted. The sun was at its highest point and it was very hot out, especially since her baby was about due and her two little children were so young.

While they waited in the kitchen, Grandma went outside and picked several fruits and vegetables to give her to take home.

As I watched them walk away, I couldn't help but wonder if the same thing could possibly happen to me when I grew up!

Helping people by giving them food wasn't the only thing Grandma did for them. She also knew how to combine different types of plants and herbs to make medicines. She treated a lot of people, especially the ones who were too poor to afford a doctor.

One morning, I came home early from school feeling very sick. Feeling like I was freezing, I went straight to my grandma's kitchen, laid down on the hammock and closed my eyes.

My grandma – Ba Noi

Moments later, I heard Grandma walking towards me and felt her hand being placed on my forehead. She told me I had the flu and fixed me a home remedy of hot water with ginger, orange peelings, and a few other herbs.

It smelled really good but tasted terrible. She wouldn't leave my side until she was sure I drank every drop. She then had me go to her bed and lie down while she prepared a hot oil treatment.

Grandma rubbed a medicated oil on my forehead from my temples to the middle of my eyebrows and then massaged it in for several minutes. She then pulled the skin on my temples until it became completely red.

After rubbing the oil on my neck, shoulders and entire back, Grandma began scraping the skin on my neck with the edge of a metal coin until it was red. She then proceeded to do the same to both shoulders and my back, paying special attention to my spine and ribs.

The process took an hour and after she was done I wasn't so cold anymore. My body felt so good from the oil, but at the same time, extremely sore from the scraping.

Grandma covered me up with a blanket and told me to sleep.

After taking a long nap, I woke up feeling so much better and noticed Grandma had prepared a pot of rice soup for me.

This was one of many occasions Grandma helped me that I'll never forget. I felt so grateful that Grandma spent the whole afternoon just taking good care of me. I might have grown up without a lot of things, but the love I received from my Grandma was overflowing.

Chapter Ten

When I was a kid, there was nothing I loved more than the Vietnamese New Year, the biggest holiday in the country. I loved every second of it and counted down the days and hours until it came.

Marked by the new moon, some years it fell in January and others in February. We used the lunar calendar mainly for social events and the solar calendar for government and businesses.

Most people were very superstitious about the New Year and believed certain things either brought you good luck or bad luck. That always worked out great for me because no one would yell and make me cry during this time of year. Crying was considered to be bad luck.

Mom also believed it was bad luck to wear old clothes with holes or patches on them. This was the only time I could buy new clothes. Not wanting people to know just how poor I really was, clothes became one of the most important things to me.

Before we could go New Year's shopping, we had to work in our rice paddy nonstop for almost two months. The rice was ready to harvest at this time of year, so we worked hard and as fast as possible. The quicker we finished, the more time we had to prepare for the New Year. I always hated when we got behind and I'd end up watching my friends go shopping while I was still working.

I would always get extremely excited whenever I saw a group of people practicing the dragon dance. Someone pounded on a drum as they danced and I could feel the beat go through my entire body.

All I could think about was the New Year!

One time, I stopped working for a minute to complain about not getting done on time and how the hot sun was making my skin dark and ugly. Also, my legs, feet and toenails were getting stained from too much iron in the water and I needed time to get it cleaned off of me.

Hearing my long list of complaints, my brother stared at me with such a look of disgust while snarling, "Why don't you just shut up! You're acting like a city girl!"

"I'll tell you one thing, I'm not going to be working like this in the rice fields when I grow up!" I snapped back.

My younger sister chimed in, "You better hope Mom doesn't make you marry a country boy."

"Very funny! Now you shut up."

During the afternoon, Mom's back began hurting so badly, she had to lay down on the dike between rice paddies. She always pushed everyone, including herself, to work long, hard twelve hour days. As long as there was work to be done, she never let any of us go home before dark.

I continued working bent over for a while longer until I had to stand up straight and give my back a break. Looking out over our rice paddy, I noticed a girl walking by on the main path wearing a t-shirt and jeans. I'd never seen anybody wearing jeans before; she looked like a model!

I started yelling to my brother and sisters, "Hey look! Look! Wow, aren't her jeans so cool looking?"

Almost in unison, everyone shouted back, "Don't even think about it! They cost *way* too much money."

"Maybe they sell some that are cheaper."

I didn't dare ask Mom to buy me jeans that day because she was tired and in pain. I decided to wait until she was in a good mood and then tell her how badly I wanted them. I didn't care if they were the only thing I got for the New Year.

We finally finished our work in the rice paddy after a couple more days and harvested enough rice to last us for the whole year.

Everyone was happy, especially me. Having plenty of free time before the New Year was what mattered the most to me at that moment.

The following morning, Mom told us she was going to the market to sell some of our chickens and use the money to buy outfits for Quyen and me. I jumped at the opportunity to tell Mom I didn't want anything this year except a pair of jeans, and I didn't care if they were the cheapest ones.

From that moment on, I nagged Mom about the jeans every chance I got. To my surprise, the following evening she approached me with a smile and said we'd be leaving early in the morning to catch a bus into Ho Chi Minh City, the biggest city in South Viet Nam. Without me knowing it, Mom had already been asking around and learned that none of the local markets sold jeans.

I felt like I was in heaven; I jumped up and down and ran all around the house. I couldn't wait until morning to get the jeans I'd been dying for. Also, just to go shopping in the big city was one of the most exciting things I could think of. I tossed and turned in bed all night.

When I heard the rooster crow the next morning, I tried waking Mom up to get ready.

"Go back to sleep, Trang!" she scolded me. "Wait for the rooster to crow for the third time!"

Mom and I walked into town just before daylight. We crossed the river on the ferry and boarded the first of two buses needed. The first took us to the central station where a large number of buses were continuously coming and going from everywhere inside and outside the city.

The second bus we boarded went deep inside the city and took us through the center of the shopping district. We got off in the section where vendors appeared to be selling mostly clothes.

I felt like I was in another world. The city was alive with shoppers and New Year decorations. Food vendors shouted out their menus trying to make a sale; they even stopped people on the streets and walked down the aisle on buses when they stopped. The atmosphere was amazing and it seemed like everybody was in a good mood, including Mom.

The majority of the traffic was bicycles, motorcycles, and "xich lo" (pronounced "sit low", a three wheel bicycle taxi). There were very few cars—only rich people could afford them.

Mom took my hand after getting off the bus to prevent us from getting separated in the large crowd of people. She told me to watch out for bad guys who would try to pick our pockets. It happened to a lot of people, especially the ones from the country like us, so Mom walked very fast. With my short legs, I had to almost run to keep up with her.

We walked for a long time before finally finding a street vender that sold what we were looking for. My face lit up with excitement when my eyes first caught sight of all those jeans hanging neatly in a row.

Mom looked at me and smiled. I didn't know if I had ever been that happy before. They let me try on a pair and I thought I looked so cool, just like that girl I saw walking by our rice paddy. I was thinking this would be the best New Year's ever!

While listening to Mom work at negotiating a price, I started to get a little nervous. She kept trying her hardest but couldn't come to an agreement. We moved down the street to the next vendor and many more after that. Mom couldn't make a deal with any of them because she had less money in her pocket than what the jeans cost.

I was devastated and quietly stood, staring at the ground.

Reaching down with both hands to lift my head, Mom made me look at her. She said, "I'm sorry, the jeans cost too much and are more than we can afford. I want you to know that you are beautiful and smart, and when you grow up and make a lot of money, you'll be able to buy as many jeans as you like."

I took a deep breath and softly replied, "It's okay, Mom, I understand."

"I knew you would. Now let's go home. There's plenty of nice clothes for you to choose from at the local market, and they're also cheaper."

I held onto Mom's hand as we started to work our way to one of the bus stops. Out of the corner of my eye, I saw a car come up the street from behind us and then pull over to the side-walk. I stopped walking to see what the rich person inside the car looked like.

Mom yelled and told me to keep walking.

I turned my head and continued staring over my shoulder as we kept going. I saw the car door open and a man stepped out wearing a clean black suit, dark sun glasses and shiny shoes. I was so impressed. It made me think about my Dad because Mom had told me many times he always dressed well.

I tugged on Mom's hand and said, "Mom, look! That man is going into the building carrying a briefcase! He must be rich, right?"

"I think he's a business man, so yes, he's probably very rich. Especially since he's riding around in that car."

"Mom, you watch me. When I grow up, I'm going to be a business woman, and I promise that someday I'll build you a dream home, and it will have a refrigerator! I'll also make sure you have enough money and never need to work so hard again."

Mom smiled and said nothing.

Every few minutes, a different Xich Lo would slow down beside us and the operator would ask, "Where are you going? I can take you there for the cheapest price. Come on."

Mom always shook her head and firmly said, "No!"

When we finally reached the bus stop, both of us were tired and so happy to sit down for a while. The long bus ride back to the station seemed like it took forever and we were very hungry and thirsty after arriving.

Food vendors were everywhere and I quickly spotted one that sold "pho", the famous Vietnamese rice noodle soup prepared with strips of beef. Anything sold with beef as one of its ingredients was always more expensive and I knew better than to even suggest buying a bowl.

Mom and I decided to share a small loaf of bread and a cup of unsweetened iced tea. The bread was so amazingly fresh that it must have just come out of the oven, and I loved anything to drink if it had ice in it. We didn't have a freezer at home, so ice was always a luxury.

Just before boarding the bus, Mom bought three more loaves of bread to take home and share with the rest of the family. While we waited for the scheduled departure time, beggars stepped through the front door of the bus, walked down the aisle asking for help, then exited the rear.

There was a man with no arms, one who was blind, a husband and wife with leprosy, and a woman with a large tumor on her neck.

Mom gave each of them some change as I slid back in my seat and cowered behind her.

Even after being reminded many times to always treat the less fortunate with respect, I continued having the hardest time getting past my fear of leprosy.

Just the first few minutes of the return trip home seemed like they took forever! The driver constantly stopped the bus to pick up more people who were standing along the road. He even stopped when the bus was already full. People were almost sitting on top of one another and some were even hanging out the doors with one foot on the step.

Mom made sure I found a window seat when we were back at the station because she knew I suffered from motion sickness and the fresh air always helped. When I would stick my head out the window, I could see chickens and ducks hanging upside down over the side of the bus. They had one end of a rope tied to their feet and the other tied to the rack on top of the bus. I always felt sorry for them. The vendors carried them that way to get more birds to the market at one time.

When the bus made its next stop, a lot more people got off this time than got on. It felt good to be able to move my arms and legs again. Soon after, several vendors came rushing in and worked their way up the aisle trying to sell their products. I saw a pregnant woman carrying a basket of bread while running after another bus and almost tripping on the sidewalk.

Mom and I were so happy to get off when we finally reached our stop.

On our way back to the ferry, we stopped in the clothing section of our local market so I could find a nice outfit for the New Year. The one I selected wasn't as nice as a pair of jeans, but it was very beautiful and perfect for the occasion.

Once we were back in the country, I no longer needed to hold Mom's hand as we walked home.

All the kids in our family were excited and waiting at the house when we arrived. They knew Mom would sometimes bring back fresh bread from the city as a special treat.

With a big smile, Mom reached into the bag she was carrying and pulled out one of the loaves. Two of my little nephews ran toward her so fast, she almost dropped the bread on the floor.

But Mom didn't mind. Everyone was filled with the excitement of the New Year, and nothing, *NOTHING* could make us sad!

Chapter Eleven

Four days before the New Year

There were only four days left until the New Year and I was so excited I couldn't sleep, eat, or sit still. I ran around the house singing and got on everyone's nerves, especially my brother's.

He sat on the floor in the front of the house polishing the candle and incense holders. When finished, he set them back on top of the large wooden cabinet (armoire), where the family altar was set up. It was the most important place in practically everyone's home and where everyone in the family could come and burn incense to honor family members who had passed away.

Quyen and I became more excited when Mom asked us to help with "Ta Mo", cleaning up a family member's grave. This was one of the traditional activities most people performed before the New Year.

When we finished our cleaning and all the neighbors completed theirs, everyone stood around socializing to share feelings of good cheer.

Three days before the New Year

I tossed and turned all night long. Mom, Quyen, and I had to share a hard wood bed with no mattress and my restlessness kept waking them.

The house didn't have any screens in the windows or doors, so mosquitoes came in for an easy feast every night. Before sleeping, we always hung a mosquito net over our bed to avoid being bitten. With my eyes wide open and unable to sleep, the only thing I could keep myself busy with was watching all those mosquitos trying to get inside the net, and listening to their little noises.

Eventually, I managed to fall asleep, but not for very long. With our house being so close to the river, I woke up again and again to the sound of boat motors and the voices of people in the boats. The ones loaded with ducks on their way to the market were always the noisiest.

I woke up that morning feeling like I was in heaven; I knew Mom would let me go to the market as many times as I'd like. This was a part of the New Year deal. At this time, the markets would remain open around the clock until the actual holiday when they would then close down for three solid days. This gave everyone a good reason to stock up on food.

Even knowing I could never buy much, I loved going to the market just for the excitement alone.

As soon as we left the house, Quyen and I started skipping and jumping while Mom and a neighbor lady slowly walked behind us. As we approached the river, we got in the rear of a long line of people waiting to cross over on the ferry.

Once we were on the other side of the river, we finally reached the edge of the open market. A couple minutes later, I found myself in the middle of a large crowd of people. I started feeling an excited, "happy-energy-all-around-me" feeling and for a few moments, I didn't move, talk, or even blink. I just wanted to soak it all in.

Waking up from my trance, I had to walk as fast as I could just to catch up with Quyen.

We spent hours wandering around the market, watching people negotiate prices with the vendors and just enjoying the atmosphere. There weren't set prices for anything and the vendor could tell the people whatever price they wanted. Some people were very good negotiators, and Mom was one of the best. It was always fun to watch when she bargained a little too hard and the vendor would get angry with her.

The highlight of our day was when Mom bought us something to drink and we could watch the excitement while sitting comfortably at a café table.

Two days before the New Year

I woke up wanting to go to the market again, but Mom had other plans. She wanted me to help her and my sister-in-law clean the entire house on the inside and also sweep up all around the outside. We had to get all this cleaning done before the New Year because for three days, starting on New Year's Day, no one was allowed to sweep anywhere. Most people believed you'd be sweeping away good fortune. Mom even went so far as to hide all the brooms for those three days.

A short while after finishing the house cleaning, my sister, Chi Tu, came by to visit. She brought several coconuts that she picked from trees in front of her house. She stayed for the afternoon, helping us make a Vietnamese New Year's assorted candy dish containing treats like coconut, ginger, tangerines and so much more.

Many nights during the year, a group of singers would come to town and perform Cai Luong (Vietnamese opera). More than anything, we always wanted to go watch, but Mom refused to let us; she always insisted we be home before dark. We could have asked her a hundred times, but her answer would always be the same. However, with the approach of the New Year, Mom became a lot less strict.

This year, she let me go to the market after dark with my cousin, Be Lon, and the neighbors. Five minutes after leaving the house, Be Lon pulled me off to the side and whispered in my ear, "I have something really cool to show you, but we have to wait until we're alone."

When the neighbors were far enough ahead, Be Lon reached into her pocket and pulled out a jar of face cream.

"Check it out! This cream will make the skin on your face white in just a few days."

"That's amazing, but where did you get the money to buy this?" I asked with an excited look.

"Open the jar and you'll see."

I opened it quickly to find there was only one-fourth the normal amount of cream in the jar.

"That's all I had the money for."

"I didn't know you could buy only a small amount!"

"Sure, you can even buy one-eighth of a jar if you want!"

"I wish you would have bought the cream a little sooner so our faces could have been white and pretty for the New Year!"

"I wanted to, but I didn't have enough money until today. At least we'll look good for school." We were getting close to the market and Be Lon quickly put the jar back in her pocket.

After spending hours at the market having so much fun, we completely lost track of time. There were still a lot of people shopping, but the majority of them lived in town. Everyone living out in our neighborhood had already gone home.

Stepping off the ferry on the other side of the river, Be Lon and I soon found ourselves alone and scared on the unlit dirt path leading back home. Tall, skinny trees lining both sides of the path swayed back and forth making the strangest noise every time the wind blew.

As we approached a graveyard sitting closely to the path's edge, Be Lon began talking about people who claimed to have seen ghosts around those graves at night.

We became so terrified we couldn't talk anymore and almost peed our pants. Neither one of us wanted to walk in front of or behind the other, so we began walking side-by-side and picking our feet up in unison to focus our attention away from the graveyard.

We remembered how our grandma, Ba Noi, taught us to pray whenever we became scared. Tightly holding each other's hands, we prayed out loud for the rest of our walk home.

One day before the New Year

I woke up very early and full of excitement. The birds were singing louder than any other day, the tide was in and the river was high. All the "Hoa Mai Vang" bushes around the house were getting ready to bloom as they always did around this time of year.

The Altar was all set up with beautiful flowers and a variety of fruit. The fruit was so fresh that it still had branches and green leaves on it, and great care was given to the way everything was arranged and stacked, similar to the care given to a beautiful bouquet of flowers.

When selecting fruit to be placed on the altar, we *always* had to make sure that none of them were ever sour. People believed a sour fruit set out on the New Year would make your life turn sour. We were also never allowed to set out a mango because the Vietnamese word for the fruit is "xoai", which also means "spending". Money would be going out instead of coming in.

My brother made sure there was a full bottle of rice whiskey, a new box of playing cards, and plenty of firecrackers. Every year, we had a fireworks competition with people living on the other side of the river. After losing last year's contest, my brother wanted to make sure this year would be different. He asked everyone in the family to bring firecrackers with them on New Year's morning.

While my brother worried about winning the competition, Mom was more concerned about getting food prepared and making sure we had all the traditional New Year basics. There was plenty of hot tea, a New Year's candy tray, roasted watermelon seeds, pork cooked in coconut juice and fish sauce... just to name a few.

Everyone believed having plenty of food and treats during the New Year's celebration would set the stage for having good fortune the entire year.

The one thing Mom and many others wouldn't do without during the New Year was "Banh Tet" (pronounced "bun tat"). They're made with sticky rice, coconut, yellow beans and pork. Each one is prepared by first mixing some of the coconut in with the sticky rice, then spreading a thick layer of the rice onto a banana leaf. A layer of yellow beans is then spread out on top of the rice, followed by a narrow row of pork laid down the center of the beans. Everything is then tightly wrapped inside the banana leaf and held together with a cord cut from a plant growing along the river. The finished product is approximately one foot long, three inches in diameter and then cooked for several hours in water. With so much time and labor going into making it, Mom reserved Banh Tet for special occasions only and prepared at least a dozen of them each time.

Along with Banh Tet, Mom would also make Banh U' (pronounced "bun ooh") for the New Year. They were made with sticky rice and yellow beans only and wrapped in a coconut leaf folded in the shape of a three sided, three inch high pyramid. Mom started cooking them at the same time as the Banh Tet, but the Banh U' was always done much sooner because of its smaller size.

I couldn't wait until midnight for the start of the New Year, which most people called "Dao Thua" (pronounced "yal th-ua"). It was a big deal because many people believe all the spirits of family members who've passed away come back to visit at that time.

Dao Thua also meant everyone became one year older, instead of celebrating our own individual birthdays.

At exactly midnight, Mom would walk outside and set a tray of fruit and cookies on a pedestal located in front of the house. While holding three burning incense out in front of her, she would bow her head several times before placing the incense in a holder beside the tray of fruit. All of this was performed as a way of welcoming the spirits home.

As hard as I tried to stay awake for Dao Thua and help Mom make preparations, I fell sound asleep.

The New Year

Finally, it was New Year's Day! The moment I woke up, I could hear firecrackers going off everywhere. When I stepped into the kitchen, Banh Tet and Banh U' were hanging everywhere from the bamboo poles used in constructing the ceiling. While standing motionless, staring at the beautiful sight in front of me, I wished everyday was the New Year and felt so grateful for all the food. Life was good.

The celebration lasted all of New Year's Day and for the two days following. Most people believe the first visitor a family receives on New Year's Day determines their fortune for the entire year. For that reason, only family members would usually visit on the first day. No one outside the family ever wanted to take a chance on being blamed for someone's bad luck.

Beginning on the second day, we could go visit family, friends, and neighbors at any time without notice. We were always invited to eat and drink at every home visited. If we couldn't eat, we at least made sure to drink what was offered so our hosts didn't feel insulted.

If someone in your immediate family had died during the previous year, it was never acceptable to visit anyone during the three day celebration. If for some reason you *tried* to visit someone at that time, people in the home would become really upset and sometimes turn you away.

After breakfast on New Year's Day, the firecracker competition between my brother and the neighbors across the river began. With help from the extra firecrackers provided by family members, my brother claimed victory and was in a good mood for the remainder of the day.

Someone tipped the neighbors off about how my brother was able to win the competition and at the same time, my brother was informed the neighbors were being tipped off. The end result of someone's devious plan was the "almost out of control" growth of the competition every year. I would never know what kind of mood my brother would be in. It always depended on who got the upper hand.

My job on the New Year was to make sure the pot of hot tea was always full, all day long. While sitting in the kitchen preparing to boil a pot of water, I heard the other kids out by the river yelling, "Mua lan! Mua lan!" which means, "The dragon dance is coming!"

I immediately dropped what I was doing and rushed outside to be with the others along the river bank. We were all so happy and could barely contain our excitement as the slow moving boat with a flat top inched its way toward us. After what felt like an eternity, we finally had our first good view of the dragon dance and became mesmerized by the performance.

Dancers hidden inside a bright red and yellow costume represented an animal that's a cross between a lion and a dragon. Always performing alongside the dragon is a dancer wearing a red suit and mask, dressed as a man with a big belly. The dancer constantly waved a hand fan all around while the dragon and him were weaving and jumping to the beat of a drum. We loved the music and their costumes were so silly. We always laughed so hard.

If we were lucky, sometimes we could watch the dance twice in one day. There was another group of dancers who walked through our area on the main path and would perform at people's houses. Once in a while, they would pick a random house to stop at, but usually they only performed at the homes where people requested them. Wherever the dragon dance was being performed, you could be sure there was a large group of kids following closely behind.

Mom really enjoyed watching everyone have so much fun, but all the while couldn't keep from worrying about New Year superstitions and traditions. She reminded us again not to sweep the floors and made sure everyone was wearing new clothes. She continually checked to see if there was plenty of hot tea and treats set out for visitors.

Out of all the traditions we faithfully followed, the two I loved the most were having a lot of good food to eat and "li xi" (pronounced "lee-see", meaning "lucky money"). In keeping with the li xi tradition, money was placed inside a small red envelope and given to children by an elder. In order to receive the money, children were required to bow their heads while crossing their arms over their chests. They would then wish good luck, prosperity, happiness, good health and a long life to the person giving the envelope.

By early evening, I had accumulated a stack of Vietnamese paper money that was equal in value to roughly one dollar and fifty cents in U.S. money.

Several of my family members had gathered to play cards for money and were sitting in a circle on the dirt floor in our living room. Knowing I had received li xi money that day, one of my cousins said, "Join us!"

A couple others taunted me. "Yeah! Join in! It will be fun! Come on!"

"No way!" I answered. "I'm not taking a chance of losing any of my money!"

But after seeing how everyone was laughing and having a good time, I decided to sit beside one of my cousins and just watch for a while. As soon as I sat down, his luck improved and he began to win money. Between hands, he turned toward me and pleaded, "Please, whatever you do, don't move. Just sit there and watch. You're bringing me good luck."

A short while later, I had to get up to use the restroom and a neighbor lady sat down in my place. My cousin started to lose money again, so he turned to the lady and said with a smile, "I really like you, but you need to go sit on the other side with those guys."

After a couple of hours, the group got smaller when some of the players ran out of money. The ones that were remaining tried really hard to get me to play. They continued pestering me for the longest time until somehow, I finally gave in.

I won a lot of money at first, but as the evening went on, my luck changed and I ended up losing everything.

My brother-in-law, Anh Tu, finished the game winning everyone's money.

I waited until the other players went outside before going up to Anh Tu and asking, "Can I please have my money back?"

Giving me a funny look, Anh Tu laughed and then replied, "You're kidding, right?"

I shook my head no and looked down at the floor as a tear rolled down my cheek.

Anh Tu freaked out and quickly whispered to me in a panicked voice, "Don't cry! Don't cry! You know it's bad luck!" He immediately gave all my money back and looked around to make sure Mom wasn't listening or watching. Anh Tu knew he would be in big trouble if she saw me crying, especially since I was a twelve year old girl and he, being an adult, had taken all my money.

From that time on, even long after the New Year, every time Anh Tu came over for a family gathering, he would always tease me with a mocking voice, "I want my money back!"

Even with losing my money, begging to get it back, and suffering a lifetime of torment from my brother-in-law, that New Year's is still one of my favorites. Then again, they're all my favorite.

Chapter Twelve

After the New Year celebration, our lives gradually returned to normal. Quyen and I went back to school and Mom tended to her garden.

One day, I returned home from school to find Mom staring at a coconut tree. She seemed very upset.

"What's wrong?" I asked.

"This tree is infested with beetles. It's in bad shape and I'm afraid it's not going to live."

I knew this was a bad situation. The coconuts and their juice were used in preparing so many different dishes that the loss of a tree was a really big deal. The rhinoceros beetles had taken over this one, and it was obvious there was nothing that could be done to save it.

The beetles had bore into the tree's crown to feed on developing leaves, which is what caused all the damage. Eggs were laid in dead and decaying parts of the tree and then hatched into larvae.

Mom wanted to kill all the larvae before they became beetles, but wasn't exactly sure of the best way to get it done.

Chi Ba and her husband came by for a visit that afternoon and joined Mom and my brother in looking the tree over. In the end, everyone was in agreement that the damage was too far along and there was really no hope for saving it. Anh Ba talked my brother into chopping the tree down and removing all the larvae for a cook out.

Taking turns with an axe, Anh Ba and my brother worked up a heavy sweat as they slowly cut into the base of the tree.

When the neighbor kids heard the chopping, they all came running over to see what was happening. After learning why the tree was being cut down, the kids jumped around with excitement and pestered my brother constantly by asking how long it would take.

Word about what we were doing traveled fast to my brother-in–law, Anh Tu, and he immediately came over to help. With the three of them taking turns, the tree came down quickly.

Everyone gathered around, watching with great interest, as my brother began cutting into a decayed section of the tree.

Catching first sight of the larvae sent the kids into fits of excitement as they all began pointing with their fingers while yelling, "Duong duong! Duong duong!"

Anh Ba was just as excited as the kids, if not more. With his eyes all lit up and a huge smile, he used his fingers to pick out the larvae one by one and place them in a large bowl. Each larva was about one and a half inches long and one-half inch in diameter. They were white, which meant they were still young.

Trying to make the treats as delicious as possible, Anh Ba came up with the idea of stuffing a whole peanut inside each larva while they were still alive. He then rolled each one in rice flour before frying them in peanut oil.

The kids were given the first finished batch and squatted down in a circle around the bowl. They each reached for a larva using their fingers, then ate quickly and silently. The faster they ate, the sooner they could reach for another one.

In Viet Nam, most children learned to be aggressive when it came to food. Because food hadn't always been plentiful, everyone understood if you stood in line waiting for your turn to eat, the last person usually ended up getting very little or nothing at all.

As soon as the bowl was empty, the kids stood up rubbing their bellies while saying, "Ngon qua, ngon qua," meaning, "very good, very good." Some of them spoke in English, saying, "Number one!" They kept repeating the words again and again.

My brother gave the kids a hard time by pointing out they were only repeating what they heard, and they had no idea what "number one" even meant.

The kids argued that they did and said it meant "the best." For the rest of the day, the kids all ran around teasing my brother by calling him, "Number ten! Number ten!"

The kids also knew how to say, "Hello," "Good bye," "Good morning," and "Thank you." Those were just about all the words they knew. Most people had learned the words from American GIs and passed them down to their children.

When the remainder of the larvae had finished cooking, my brother and the rest of my family gathered around to enjoy their little feast. I sat close by just watching.

"Why didn't you eat with the other kids?" Asked Anh Tu.

"Because those things look too disgusting!" I replied.

He kept insisting on how delicious they were and how I should at least try eating one.

Not wanting to feel like an odd ball, I closed my eyes and let my sister put a cooked larva in my mouth.

Everyone complimented me by saying, "Good job! Good job!"

I tried to focus on their words and ignore the sick feeling in my stomach. It felt like the larvae was wiggling around in there and trying to crawl his way back out. I couldn't stand it anymore; after about a minute, I threw up.

Looking at me in total disbelief, my brother responded, "Ahh! Number ten!"

Everyone went on and finished eating the larvae without me.

"You know, you're too skinny to be picky," my sister, Chi Ba, remarked as she licked her fingers and smacked her lips with enjoyment.

Unable to resist joining the discussion, Chi Tu added, "She's so picky, she won't even eat 'hot vit lon.'"

Hot vit lon is a boiled duck egg with a partially developed embryo inside. It's one of Quyen's favorite treats. She always preferred eggs with younger embryos because the older ones were beginning to develop feathers.

I always considered hot vit lon to be as disgusting as the larvae.

CR■SO

When I was very young, I thought that the chickens were the dads and the ducks were the moms. One day when we were having a discussion about baby chickens and ducks, I mentioned to Mom what I thought.

"What made you think that way?" Mom asked.

"Because a man looks so different than a woman and a duck looks so different than a chicken, it all just seemed to make sense to me".

Mom gave a brief explanation about how chickens and ducks each had boys and girls, and how each had their own unique way of surviving. While I understood everything she was saying, I couldn't help but feel a little sad about having my naïve view of the world shattered.

When the chickens were full grown, Mom would take them to the local marketplace and use the money she received for clothes, medicine, and school supplies. She always kept the mother hen for laying eggs and raising more chickens, and the smallest one of the group for us to eat.

We all protested, especially my brother. He complained that we had to wait for months for the chickens to get big, and then we only got the smallest one. There were seven of us, so he worried that there wouldn't be enough to go around.

"Don't worry. There'll be enough," Mom promised.

Mom was a very good cook but we all knew her tricks. She would make the chicken really salty, so that we would eat less of it and more rice. She cooked all the parts of the chicken, the head, neck, feet, gizzard, liver, heart, and even the blood. She would drip the blood on a plate of un-cooked rice, which kept it sticking together before being steamed, and then cook the rest of the chicken in fish sauce.

Our kitchen at that time was in a small hut, built a few feet off from the side of our house. It sat on the edge of a small canal that connected to the river running nearby. The family boat was always tied to a small tree growing in front of the hut. Our stove was a fire built on the floor with bricks stacked up in three columns to hold the cookware above the fire.

Before the chicken was done cooking, my sister, Quyen, and I, along with our nephews, Tri and Kha, waited excitedly around the fire with a bowl of rice in our hands.

Mom used her chopsticks to pick off a few fully cooked pieces of meat from the chicken. She placed them in a small bowl and instructed me to run next door and give it to my great grandma.

I immediately ran back home as fast as I could without anyone had a chance to start eating without me.

Quyen asked for the chicken's feet, Tri and Kha got the legs, and Mom made sure I got the gizzard. My brother requested the head while Mom and my sister in-law didn't care what part they got.

Everyone was happy, and we even had some broth left over to eat with rice and vegetables the next day. We loved it all, even though it was salty. It was one of the best meals that I can remember.

ೞ ▪ ೞ

Early one morning, I heard someone knock at the door. I rushed over to open it and was surprised to see my sister, Chi Tu. With her feet covered in mud from all the rain on the dirt paths, she stepped into the house. Her bamboo hat was so old, it was ready to fall apart.

I was so happy when she handed me a container of soup. When I opened the lid, it smelled really good. I took a big sip and it tasted so delicious that I could have eaten the whole thing right then, but I knew I had to share it with my younger sister and two nephews.

Chi Tu asked, "Do you know what kind of soup that is?"

"No," I said while shaking my head and setting the container on the table.

"It's rice soup with dog meat," she whispered.

I covered my mouth with my hands and stepped away from the table while saying, "Troi oi! (Meaning, Oh my Goodness.)" I thought to myself, *I shouldn't have even tasted the soup. I don't want to go to hell.*

Many people in Viet Nam believed that killing and eating dog was a big sin.

Chi Tu explained, "You just eat the soup. You're not the one who killed the dog, so there's no need to worry." She believed the soup was good for our bodies and would take care of sickness and make us stronger. She also told me she got the soup from her neighbor who cooked it late at night because so many people were against eating dog.

Even after listening to my sister give all her reasons why it was OK, I still couldn't do it.

My grandma was especially against killing them; she believed that it was evil to do so. She compared the dog to a human.

Dog meat could usually be found at street bars where all the whiskey drinkers went. I always heard that more people from North Viet Nam ate dog than people from the South. However, there was no one I knew that ever treated dogs and cats as pets. Dogs were only used as watch dogs, and cats as mousers.

I remember when Quyen and I were little, every time we touched a dog or cat, we always got yelled at. Everyone said they were dirty and diseased. (We had never heard of veterinarians or a special food just for them. No one had the money to give animals that kind of care.)

Still, it just didn't seem right to eat them.

Chapter Thirteen

Getting to school on time was always an adventure, starting at home.

"Stop looking at yourself in the mirror and come get a bowl of rice! Don't keep Ha waiting!" my mother would yell.

My middle school was just across the river from the grade school, so every morning, we had to wait for the ferry to cross. There was always a long line of people waiting, especially in the morning. Many of the local people went to the market at the same time students were going to school and the ferry could only carry a small number at one time. Most students worried about being late for school and tried their best to crowd ahead of everyone to avoid the wait for the ferry's next return.

There were several times when I saw the ferry sink in the water, so every time it became overloaded, I really started to worry. Whenever it sank, everyone screamed and only a few knew how to swim. Most had to be rescued and the students' books and notepads were ruined.

Because of that, I always avoided being among the first ones on the ferry. If it became overloaded, you couldn't get back off without jumping in the water.

Mom always told me to leave the house early when I went to school so I could avoid the big crowd, yet somehow, I always managed to be late for one reason or another.

Ha was my best friend. She lived with her grandma in a small hut with dirt floors, located about half an hour walk up river from me. I never knew exactly why she didn't live with her parents; I just assumed it was because her grandma had lost her husband and Ha came to help.

Every morning she would meet me on the narrow dirt path that ran past our house. I always ended up making her wait and she would yell for me. Ha and I were inseparable.

ෆ▪ළ

There were a lot of students in middle school that were from the city, and they always had nicer clothes than I did. I only had two outfits to wear and they were starting to get very old and worn.

One day, Mom showed me a beautiful robe that had belonged to my brother, Anh Hai. She started telling me the story of where the robe had come from.

"Your brother was about twelve years old," she began. "The American-Viet Nam war was going and we felt the safest place for him to be at that time was in the Buddhist Temple called Chua Phap Hach Tu.

"When he turned seventeen, the war ended and Dad had just passed away. I needed him to come home with us to the country and help work in the rice paddies. So your brother had to say 'goodbye' to all the people at the temple. But to this day, he has faithfully returned every year to visit and pay his respects."

Mom stopped a moment and I started to worry she wouldn't finish. I knew Anh Hai had stayed at the temple, but I had never heard the whole story. I hoped she would continue without me asking.

"It wasn't long after, the war with Cambodia began and the Vietnamese Government started to draft young men into the army. A couple of our relatives had lost sons during the startup of the war, and I was beside myself with worry. I'd just lost your father; I couldn't bear to lose my son!"

I listened silently as Mom relived her worst fears. She was very good at keeping her emotions to herself; I had only seen her cry twice. She didn't even let it show how worried she was when our food was running low and we were near starvation. So I felt honored that she would open up and share this story with me.

"A few months went by and I received a letter from the government stating that your brother was exempt from the draft because he was my only son. I felt so blessed!

"Eventually, after the conflict with Cambodia ended, the draft was finally cancelled and everyone breathed a sigh of relief."

She paused again to collect her thoughts since she had gotten a little off track.

"Anyway," she started again, "while staying at the temple, your brother had to wear this robe. I've kept it all this time."

I took the garment and ran the material through my fingers to feel the texture. As I did, an idea started forming in my head.

Grey wasn't my favorite color, but if I added a second color on the collar, pockets, and around the trim, I thought it would look pretty good.

After receiving permission from Mom to use the robe, I wasted no time in taking it over to a local woman who made clothes. She was very good; not high priced and very quick.

When I reached the woman's front door, I saw her sitting at the sewing machine working on something. She looked up and smiled when she saw me.

Her house had a dirt floor with a metal roof but was very clean and neat. In her living room, I could see she had a few new shirts hanging for display and some new material stacked on the table.

I stopped at the door and she got up and walked toward me. She looked to be a little younger than my mom and had beautiful, pale skin.

Her name was Tuyet, but since she was close to the same age as my mom, I called her "Di"; the same as I would call my aunt.

I crossed my arms and bowed my head to say "hello."

Instead of, "hello," she asked, "Are you Trang?"

"Yes," I answered.

She knew me because her daughter was in my class. She directed me over to the table with a motion of her head. When I laid the robe down, she looked surprised.

I told the story of my brother and asked, "Can you use the material to make me a button up shirt?"

She took a long look at it by flipping it over and over on the table and finally said, "Yes, I can do that." She then took all my measurements.

"Do you think you could have it done by tonight?" I asked in an excited tone. I wanted it finished that night so that I could wear it to school the next day. A girl wearing a new shirt at our school always got a lot of attention.

Studying the clock on the wall for a second, she replied, "It's already a little after 1:00 in the afternoon. I really don't think I can get it done that fast. Not with all these other projects that need to be finished."

"Well, OK. I'll stop back tomorrow then." Looking a little sad, I turned towards the door and started to leave.

"But you can come back around 7:00 tonight to check and see," she suddenly added.

I smiled and thanked her from the bottom of my heart.

After I was back home, I couldn't do anything but think about the new shirt being made. When it was finally time for me to go pick it up, I arrived at her house ten minutes before 7:00.

Looking up and seeing me standing at her door, Di Tuyet remained sitting behind her sewing machine and spoke in a firm tone, "It's not done."

My heart sank in my chest because I thought for sure I'd be wearing it the next morning.

"If you'd like to wait, I can have it done in about an hour," she added.

"I'll wait! Oh, thank you a million times," I replied, while feeling such relief.

When it was finished, the shirt fit me perfectly. I couldn't stop smiling because I was so full of joy. I paid and thanked her again before rushing through the door to get home.

The next morning, Ha was surprised to see me standing on the road waiting for her this time. After noticing I was wearing a new shirt, she immediately understood my sudden change of behavior.

I was the talk of the school that day in my beautiful new outfit. I was so grateful to have it. And though I liked the attention and all the compliments I got, my favorite part would always be sharing a moment with my Mom when she gave it to me.

**Shirt made from Buddhist robe,
I'm still wearing seven years later**

છ ▪ ૪૦

I loved going to middle school. Ha and I would walk by the market almost every day and do a lot of window shopping. The place I loved to stop at the most was a beauty salon named Tien Uoc Toc Thu, translated - Thu's Salon. We loved watching the beauticians and students doing hair.

The owner was very young and stunningly beautiful. She was tall, had white skin, trendy hair, and her clothes were always the latest style. Ha told me it was rumored she was married to a rich guy, and that was how she had money to open a salon. Most people knew her because of her beauty and very nice personality.

One day, as we stood in front of the salon watching the beauticians, the owner looked out at us and smiled. With her hand, she signaled us to come in and we quickly entered with huge smiles. I got so jealous of the white skin on her face.

While Ha and the owner were talking, I took advantage of the opportunity and wandered around her shop. I loved everything, from the smell of the salon, to the hair posters and the mirrors. I even got to watch the beauticians cutting hair up close.

As we were leaving, the owner asked us to come back sometime and get a haircut. We both said we would and thanked her for being so gracious.

During our walk back home, I mentioned to Ha how I wanted to do hair someday. I knew Mom couldn't afford to send me anywhere to learn, and I heard that students working at a salon had to pay the owner a lot of money to train them. I didn't know what to do.

"You need to marry a rich guy or keep buying lottery tickets," Ha said half-jokingly.

I glared at her, not seeing the humor in the situation. "Rich guys are very picky, you know, and only marry beautiful girls."

After getting home, all I could think about was the salon and how great it would be if I could cut someone's hair.

My younger sister, Quyen, who had long hair all the way down to her hips, came walking in the house at that moment.

That's when a light went off in my head.

"Can I cut your hair?" I asked.

"No way!" She quickly replied, flashing an indignant look.

Thinking fast, I said, "You know, short hair is in style now, and I know how to cut it because I just came back from watching the girls at the salon do it."

I followed Quyen all around the house for the next couple of hours, nagging her nonstop until she finally gave in. Convincing her to make a big change in her look, I told her I was giving her "a short bob haircut".

The only thing around the house I could use for cutting hair was mom's sewing scissors and a very large comb. I grabbed a short stool for my sister to sit on and began taking several large cuts out of her beautiful long hair. It didn't take long for me to realize that I was in over my head and her hair wasn't turning out anywhere near the way I wanted. There was no way I could let my sister know just how worried I was getting. I kept on cutting like nothing was wrong, though my palms were so sweaty, I could hardly hold on to the scissors.

When I got down to the point where the entire length was almost cut off, it looked horrible. There were giant gaps everywhere. I was beginning to panic and tried really hard to get it fixed before someone walked in and told my sister how bad it was.

As I continued working with the rough areas by making several smaller cuts, it actually started to look pretty decent.

Finally, after I made the finishing touches on what started out being a complete disaster, Quyen jumped off the stool to get a look at her new hair style.

Standing motionless with her mouth hanging wide open, she stared into the cabinet door mirror sitting against the back wall.

Suddenly, she screamed, "I like it! Wow, you really did a good job! I can't believe how great it looks!"

"Really?" I asked. I tried not to let her see how shocked I was.

My sister was so pleased with her hair, she couldn't wait to run over to the neighbors' house and show off her new look.

I breathed a sigh of relief. Some way, somehow, my first haircut was a success.

Chapter Fourteen

Coming up with the money for school became more difficult each year, but Mom remained determined to keep Quyen and I going as long as she could. As we moved into higher grade levels, the fees charged by the schools also went up. We were constantly on the lookout for different ways of coming up with the money.

Mom planted as much rice as our paddy would allow her to grow and, each year, increased the size of our vegetable garden. We picked vegetables directly from the garden each day to eat with our meals and sold everything else that was ripe.

Once in a while, when the growing season of a certain vegetable would peak, there'd be so many of them ripe that it was impossible to sell them all. When that happened, Mom would pickle many of the extras to carry us through the off season. Her pickled vegetables were the best, and I loved eating them.

One day, when I was helping her pick some mustard greens, the idea of trying to sell the pickled ones came to me. I said to Mom, "Pickle as many of those as you can and I'll go door to door and sell them."

Smiling back, she said, "That's not a bad idea. You might end up making a lot of money."

"When do you think I can get started?"

"You'll have to wait at least five full days before they'll be ready to sell."

After five days had passed, the vegetables looked really good. They had turned from green to a golden brown and tasted sour, just the way we liked them.

It was raining outside, but I didn't care. I rolled my pants up to my knees, put on a bamboo hat and went into the kitchen after washing my hands. I pulled handfuls of the vegetable out of the large crock, filling a large metal bowl with as much of it as I could carry.

I started out walking, holding the metal bowl against my hip with one hand, and carrying a set of hand scales inside a woven shopping bag with the other. Heavy rains during the past couple of days had made the paths all muddy and very slick in some places. Walking very slowly, I carefully avoided all the spots I knew from experience would make me slip and fall. (Many people fell on their butts trying to walk too fast on those muddy paths, especially students on their way to school.)

A short distance down the path, I crossed a narrow stream using a bridge built to be used by one person at a time (Cau khi, monkey bridge). It was made with three or four logs tied together end to end and had a rickety hand railing tied off to the supporting legs. Crossing the bridge wasn't an easy thing to do, especially if you were carrying anything in your hands. You always considered yourself lucky if you made it across without falling in the water.

Twenty minutes later, I stopped at the first house to try to make a sale. They were very nice to me but said they didn't need any.

When I stopped at the second house, five or six little kids came running out toward me. A couple of the kids didn't have shirts on, the others had no pants. They stopped a few feet in front of me and stood there just staring. The constant noise of a dog barking was coming from somewhere behind the small, broken-down hut. A moment later, the mother came walking out to see what I was selling.

"They look so good, but I don't have any money," she said. "Maybe next time."

The lady at the third house said my vegetables were overpriced. I tried negotiating, but it didn't make any difference.

The people who lived at the fourth house were the richest in the neighborhood. They had a beautiful brick house and two very mean dogs, but nobody was around.

As I was walking back out to the main path, the bowl on my hip felt like it was getting heavier by the minute. There were dark clouds all the way across the sky and it was getting ready to rain again. The wind was picking up and blew extremely hard at times. Being so small and skinny, it felt like the wind could have blown me off the path several times.

When I reached the main path, I could either turn left to go home and call it quits, or continue going further down the path and keep trying. I turned right.

The very next house I stopped at was the smartest choice I made. Not only did the lady buy some vegetables at my asking price, she also yelled for family members living beside her and the neighbors next to them to all come over. They ended up buying every vegetable I had in the bowl.

I was so happy and felt very grateful for my good fortune. I safely tucked the money I earned into my pocket and prepared to leave by bowing my head and telling the lady, "Thank you."

At that very moment, the rain began pouring heavily and the lady immediately dragged a chair over to where I was standing.

"Sit down and stay here until the rain slows down. It's not good to be out there when it's thundering and lightning," the lady said with a concerned tone in her voice.

As I gladly obeyed her request, she sat on the dirt floor and began working on woven bags. I got down on the floor to help. She began talking about the new shrimp factory in the area that everyone had been gossiping about. A lot of people, including myself, were excited because there were very few factories anywhere near where we lived.

Many people tried to get a job there, but it was very hard to get hired. The rumor was that you either had to know someone in charge at the company, or you needed to slip money under the table to someone in management to get a job. The company also had a policy of only hiring people between the ages of eighteen to twenty-five years old. I was too young and knew there wasn't any hope for me, at least that's what I thought.

The lady explained that some days, more shrimp was delivered to the factory than their employees could peel during the scheduled amount of time. The factory was extremely careful about how long the shrimp could sit out in the warm air, and if it wasn't peeled, sorted, packaged, and frozen within a certain amount of time, it all became unsellable. On the days when an extra amount of shrimp was delivered, the factory paid women and children to help with the peeling.

The lady, along with a group of women and children in her neighborhood, had been peeling shrimp at the factory for about two weeks. She said some days they would stand around all day waiting for work and end up doing nothing. Other days, they were very busy. It all depended on how many shrimp were brought in off the boat that day.

"Would you like to go to the factory with us tomorrow?" the lady asked.

I could feel my face light up as I replied, "Yes, I would! Oh, thank you so much! Can I bring my younger sister with me?"

"Sure you can. Make sure you bring a large metal bowl with you and meet us out on the path at the break of dawn."

"I will. Thank you."

The rain had slowed down quite a bit and it looked like the worst of the storm was over. I stood up, bowed my head and said, "Good bye."

Rolling my pants up as high as I could, I began walking through the puddles of water that were impossible to avoid. The heavy rain had turned the water flowing in the streams and river into a dirty brown color.

Realizing how late in the day it was getting, I started walking a little faster while paying extra attention to avoid slipping and falling. I didn't like the thought of going anywhere near that horrible bridge when I was alone and it was close to getting dark. Many soldiers were killed in that area during the war and people always talked about seeing ghosts around there.

Approaching home, I saw some kids laughing and having the time of their lives playing along the edge of the path. Getting a little closer, I could see they were taking turns sliding down the bank into a drainage ditch. I was thinking that some of the kids must have decided sliding was more fun than catching fish when I saw the row of baskets sitting along the path. The minute

I noticed my sister, Quyen, was among the group, I couldn't resist running over and joining the fun.

I only had enough time to slide down the bank a couple of times in order to get back to the house before dark. After feeding the chickens and ducks, I started a fire under a pot of rice, hung up the mosquito nets, closed the house doors, burned incense, and said a prayer to keep evil spirits away (Mom believed that evil spirits always came after dark).

Most nights, Quyen and I waited for Mom to get home before eating supper. That night, however, we knew she wouldn't be back until long after dark. She needed to wait for low tide before opening a drainage pipe to let water from the rice paddy flow into the river.

After supper, Quyen and I went out by the river and sat with our backs against a tree to wait for Mom. We worried she wouldn't see a tree branch when paddling in the dark and would get knocked into the river. If she did, would she be lucky enough to have someone save her like the last time?

One boat after another came down the river and each time, we thought for sure it was Mom. After watching with worry and disappointment as so many boats came and went, we both fell asleep.

Mom woke us up when she returned and told us to go in the house. She always said, "Stay in the house after dark," but we never listened.

I eagerly told her about selling the vegetables and the job at the shrimp factory. "Can we go work there, Mom? Please?"

Mom always thought things through very carefully before giving an answer. My sister and I began to worry that she would say no.

At last, she replied, "I guess you can go."

Quyen and I were so happy, we jumped up and down.

Then I remembered something that made me worry. "Oh, but, Mom, we were supposed to help you in the rice paddy tomorrow. Will you be okay by yourself?" We knew it was too much work for her to do on her own.

Mom smiled. "Don't worry; your brother has the weekend off from his job and he's coming to help me."

Quyen and I started jumping again. We were thrilled to have the chance to help our family and help ourselves stay in school.

Chapter Fifteen

Mom got up the next morning extra early to cook some rice and woke us up when it was ready. She made us eat well before allowing us to leave the house.

When finished, I ran out on the porch to get a drink from the large ceramic pot filled with rain water. Sitting on a ledge beside the pot was a metal cup from a GI mess kit which I used to get a quick drink. Normally I would take time to avoid the leaves and mosquito larva, but I was in such a hurry, I didn't care about any of that.

We left the house just before daylight and the air was a little cool. Mom worried we would get sick and made us both wear an extra long-sleeved shirt and a bamboo hat. Rice plants covered with dew were bent over the narrow path and quickly drenched our pant legs, adding to the chill.

Mom insisted on walking with us until we met the 'kind lady' that bought my vegetables the day before. She worried about us walking alone in the dark and also wanted to see who was in the group that we were going with.

As we approached the lady's house, I was so happy to see everyone, (especially the lady) standing around with large bowls in their hands.

The group was waiting for more people to join them.

Mom approached the lady who had invited us and said, "Hello, I'm Trang's mom. I appreciate you telling her about this job. I was just wondering if you could keep an eye on her and her sister?"

The lady smiled. "Of course I will. They look like sweet girls. I'm sure we are going to have a lot of fun together."

Mom thanked her and turned to us with a serious look and said, "You both be careful."

We rolled our eyes at her and answered, "We will, Mom."

I still felt a little guilty for not staying to help in the rice paddy as I watched her walk away.

Even with the short cut we took, we walked for what seemed like miles across many rice paddies before reaching the main road. When we did, I was surprised to see several other groups all headed toward the factory. There were small groups and large ones, and everyone carried a bowl in their hands. We really enjoyed walking with all those people.

I couldn't wait to see what the building looked like. As we got closer and it finally came into view, I could see how new and fancy it was. There was a little security house sitting at the front gate with a large group of people already waiting to get in. The majority of them were women and children and I was surprised at how young some of them were. The youngest looked to be only nine or ten years old. Then again, Quyen was only twelve and I was fourteen.

At the start of every morning, two or three trucks would bring in loads of shrimp which the factory employees would peel, sort, and pack. If any more trucks showed up after that, they let the people standing outside the gate come in and peel shrimp under a pavilion built on the side of the factory.

While waiting at the gate, everyone watched with anticipation as one truck after another approached the factory, only to be disappointed when each one continued on. We waited the entire day and no other trucks with shrimp ever showed up.

The following morning we returned and began waiting again for what seemed like hours. I was almost ready to fall asleep when I heard some kids cheering and saw them jumping up and down. Everyone stood up as a guy walked out of the security house. While everyone gathered in front of the gate, each wanting to be the first let inside, the security guard managed to get the area cleared enough to allow the truck to come through.

As soon as the truck unloaded its shrimp, two other security guards joined the first to help with letting us workers come through the gate. I recognized one of the guards as someone who was very interested in my cousin, Be Lon. After letting half of the people in, the guards motioned for the rest of us to stop and started to close the gate.

My sister and I were at the cutoff point but were allowed to go on through after I quickly mentioned to the one guard that Be Lon was my cousin. The remaining half of the people outside the gate became upset and began yelling and screaming. It was total chaos until security told them another truck was coming, and then they all started to calm down.

We followed the crowd to the pavilion and everyone found an empty spot and squatted down. Everyone was supposed to fill their bowls from the large basket of shrimp and return for more only after peeling their entire bowl. Because everyone got paid by the kilo, some of the workers who were first through the gate peeled only a small amount of their shrimp before running back to the basket to top off their bowls again. This created some fights between them and the workers who were filling their bowls for the first time.

Wanting to avoid getting in the middle of any fights, I waited for the ones who were squabbling to move out of the way. When I walked up to the basket, it was already empty. I sadly walked back to our spot and saw my sister had some water ready for us to peel the shrimp.

When the security guard I knew walked by and noticed we had no shrimp, he grabbed our bowl and went over to the women who took more than their share. The guard took shrimp from several of their bowls and placed it in ours. When he walked away, some of the mean women really gave us nasty looks.

We peeled all the shrimp in our bowl as quickly as possible so we could be ready when the second truck came. Because this was our first time, it took us a little longer than most of the other workers. We took extra care to keep from breaking any of the tails off or else the factory would make us pay for any damaged shrimp. As it turned out, there was no need to be in a rush that day. Everyone sat around waiting for a second truck that never came.

Working at the factory was always a mixture of busy and slow days. Busy days made everyone happy because we could come in and peel shrimp all day. Many of the women didn't even want to take a break. I became very quick at peeling and on good days, I could earn almost twenty cents.

"Twenty cents!" I remember hearing one woman complain. "I hear in America, a person can make over $3.00 an hour! And I'm working for twenty cents a day!"

I didn't know what she was complaining about; I thought twenty cents was a lot of money; it would certainly help our family a great deal.

Two weeks went by fast and we finally had our first payday. We couldn't wait to go home and give Mom the money because we knew how much she needed it.

Before starting back, we went over to the coffee shop across the street from the factory and shared a glass of soda. We loved the ice in the glass as much as the soda and made sure to eat every piece before leaving.

Eating the ice that day brought back a fond memory:

I remember one time when Mom came back from the market and surprised us with a small block of ice. We broke off pieces to put in our glasses of rain water and added some squeezed lemon for flavoring. For some reason, that day, Mom decided to let us have some sugar to mix in with the lemon juice. We were so grateful because Mom could afford only a few spoonfuls of sugar at one time and normally used it only for cooking. It turned out to be one of the most delicious drinks I ever had and was a moment I'll always remember.

We did really well at the shrimp factory during the first year, and we were so happy to be able to help Mom with money. By the second year, the factory was getting less and less shrimp delivered until it got to the point where we stopped going. It wasn't very long after that the factory closed down.

I was sad to lose the job and was praying for new opportunities to come.

Chapter Sixteen

At age sixteen, I was finishing the ninth grade. Everyone in my class was required to pass a very difficult test before being allowed to move on to high school. Many students failed. A week into summer break, the school posted the test results on a bulletin board.

My best friend, Ha, and I were very nervous as we waited in line, especially after seeing some students cry when they looked at the posting. When it finally came our turn to step up to the board, we jumped up and down and screamed at the same time after seeing both our names on the passing list.

The high school was a lot farther away than the middle school. Walking, it took us about one and a half hours to get there, but once in a while, we took a bus if we had the money. Sometimes the bus was so full, they wouldn't stop to pick us up, so we ended up walking anyway.

Before school started, Ha and I made sure we signed up for classes where none of the students knew us. That way, no one in our families would ever know what we were doing.

The first day of high school was fun and exciting with all new teachers and new students. After school, Ha and I wandered around the city and visited the big market that was just around the corner.

On the second day, during lunch break, Ha and I were standing together on one side of the courtyard as hundreds of students gathered in small groups.

As we were talking, I noticed a boy working his way through the crowd and coming toward us. He had short hair with long bangs, and when he flipped his hair, I could see his eyes looked Chinese. He was so handsome and I could tell he was a city boy just by the way he carried himself.

He stopped in front of me, smiled really big, handed me a letter, and then disappeared into the crowd.

I hurried to put the letter in my pocket before any of the other students had a chance to see it, but I wasn't quick enough. A couple of girls did see and walked over and asked, "Is he your boyfriend?"

"No!" I replied. "I don't even know his name."

"His name is Loc. He's half Vietnamese and half Chinese. He's kind of a bad boy and everyone in town knows him. So good luck!"

When the break was over, we all went back to our classrooms for two more hours. The 120 minutes felt like forever because I wondered about the letter and couldn't wait to read it on my way home.

When school finally ended, Ha and I ran out of the classroom as fast as we could and made sure to take a different road where not too many people knew us.

Respecting Vietnamese culture, we knew that having a boyfriend, or even accepting a letter from a boy, was not allowed. Any girl who did this was considered wild, bad, and unruly.

I was so excited and got the biggest smile as Ha and I read it together. It was a very cool letter from a guy named Tung and he was asking me out on a date.

Ha asked, "Who's Tung?"

"I have no idea, but I need to find out!" I said as we both giggled uncontrollably.

We stopped walking and squatted down on the side of the road to read the letter once more. I suddenly remembered that two months earlier, I met a guy named Phu at my cousins' house. Phu told me he had two younger brothers named Tung and Loc. It all started to make sense to me.

I learned later that while Phu and Tung were out for a drive the day before, they had seen Ha and me walking. When Tung got home that night, he wrote me the letter and had Loc give it to me at school.

"He's a good writer. This is the best letter I've ever read," Ha said, and I agreed. "Are you going to go out with him?"

"No! Mom would kill me if I did."

"Just keep it a secret, then."

I was in the best mood when I got home from school. I did all the house work and started cooking supper. I didn't know Quyen was standing behind me while I was cutting up okra until she asked, "What's wrong with you?"

"What do you mean?"

"You've been singing the whole afternoon!"

"I like singing! What's wrong with that?" I responded with a huge smile.

While I liked Tung's letter a lot, I wanted to play "hard to get" so he would respect me. Ha agreed and suggested I should ignore his letter for a while.

A week later when school let out, I was walking toward the front gate. I saw a good looking guy sitting on a motorcycle across the street. He caught my eye because he had Chinese features and wore a very expensive outfit, especially his jeans. Not many people could afford that brand.

I kept an eye on him while pretending to not be paying attention and noticed he was looking at me. When I reached the sidewalk outside the gate, he started his motorcycle and took off.

I kept my eyes on him and I was surprised when he circled back and stopped beside me. He looked at me with a big smile and I grinned back at him.

"Are you Trang?" he asked.

"Yes, and who are you?" I asked in return.

"My name is Tung."

I didn't let him finish talking before turning my head away with a hand covering half of my face. My heart began pounding really fast and I could feel my face starting to turn red. I wanted to look my best so I pressed both of my lips together as hard as I could so they would turn nice and red. (You learn to do that when you don't own any lipstick).

He waited until I turned my head back and asked, "Would you like to go to the café down the street and let me buy you something cold to drink?"

"No," I said.

He asked again and I said, "Maybe."

The third time he asked, I said, "Okay."

I did that on purpose because my sisters and cousins told me it's a rule for girls to always wait until a guy asks at least three times. They said by doing that, you would get more respect and be better appreciated by the guy.

I made sure Tung went to the café before I did so no other students would know, especially the ones who lived close to my house. Ha came running through the gate a couple of minutes later and I told her everything that had just happened. She didn't want to go along with me, but said she'd wait at the ferry so no one would know we hadn't always been together.

I felt so guilty for letting Ha walk without me, because I knew I'd be sad if she did that to me. I could also hear Mom yelling at the top of her voice in my ear, but nothing could stop me from going to the café that day. I already liked Tung.

Reaching the café, I was nervous and excited at the same time. Tung was four years older than I and lived with his family in a two-story house about five minutes from the high school. That would only be a dream for most people. His family owned a knife shop and also baked Chinese cookies to sell to the vendors.

Tung had an unsweetened iced tea while I had a clear soda. Normally, I ate all the ice after finishing my drink, but that day I left it in my glass so Tung wouldn't know how poor I was. I was so nervous I couldn't remember anything we talked about.

When I stood up to leave, he asked, "Would you like to go to a movie some time?"

"Maybe," I said. He then offered to take me home and right away I said, "No, thanks."

I thanked him for the drink and said goodbye after agreeing to meet again tomorrow.

Rushing back to the ferry, I found Ha patiently waiting just as she had promised. She was very understanding and asked for all the details as we walked home.

"Tell me everything!" she demanded.

"He is so wonderful!" I began like a crazy, love-sick school girl. I then shared all the details of my afternoon.

"What a great first date!" Ha said.

"It wasn't a date!" I snapped defensively.

"Yes, it was!" Ha teased. "Trang's a bad girl!"

Though it was true and I knew my mom would kill me if she found out, I was too excited to stop. I liked Tung and would continue seeing him.

Tung caught on quickly that he had to ask me more than once before I would agree to anything. He asked me every day of the following week if he could take me home before I finally said yes. I agreed not only because I liked him, but I also wanted to know what it felt like to ride on a motorcycle.

When I was little, every time we heard a motorcycle go by on the main path, all of us kids in the neighborhood would stop whatever we were doing and watch it go by until we couldn't see it anymore.

When Tung and I walked out of the café, I took a rubber band from around my wrist and tied my long hair up in a ponytail. I left some short pieces down to frame my face, trying to be cute.

Once I was on the back of the motorcycle and Tung took off, it felt like I was in heaven and I loved every second of it. Both of us had the biggest smiles on our faces and I wished the ride could somehow go on forever.

Trying to avoid anyone who might know my family and see me with a boy, I made Tung stop and let me off a long distance from the ferry.

By this time, Ha had grown tired of waiting every day and told me I was on my own.

From that day on, Tung waited every day at the café to buy me a drink and take me home. Every time I got on the motorcycle, students from my school and women selling vegetables along the street would give me dirty looks. It wasn't long, before I was labeled a wild, bad girl in that area. But I was still having too much fun to care.

Five months later, word about Tung and me worked its way back to Mom. She was very upset and almost made me quit school. For half the night, she preached to me about boys and life in general. She told me having a boyfriend was a big "no, no" and completely unacceptable.

"If he really loves you, he'll wait until you finish school and then have his parents come over and talk to me." Mom went on to explain, "I'll give you permission to marry him, so it's not me you have to worry about; I'd worry about *his* parents. They might not allow their son to marry you because they have money and will most likely look down on us because we're very poor. That happens a lot and I don't want you to get hurt."

I felt bad for adding more stress on Mom. She already looked older than her age and her skin was three times darker than anyone who didn't work in the rice paddies. The shirt she had on was so old that it had several patches that didn't match. Having a total of three shirts and three black pants, Mom always kept her best outfit set aside to be used for shopping and weddings only.

The entire time I was growing up, I never saw Mom go to a salon, not even once. She always kept her hair clean and used coconut oil each time she washed it to make it look shiny. Her black hair was so long, it needed to be wrapped around several times into a large bun and held in place with a metal pin. She never owned or wore any makeup, not even lipstick.

When Mom finished her preaching, I tried to smooth things over by saying, "The reason I rode on the motorcycle with Tung was because I was tired of walking and he was just helping me get home quicker. I wanted to have plenty of time to do house work and get my homework done." I could tell Mom didn't believe a word of it.

The next day after school, I had to tell Tung how upset Mom had gotten the night before and I needed to stop seeing him for a while.

Looking sad, Tung said he understood and would stay away.

I had explained everything to Ha during class and we began walking home together the same as we did at the beginning of the school year.

When I came home from school one day about a month later, there was a bicycle sitting on the porch. "The bicycle is yours and from now on you don't have to walk to school anymore," Mom said with a big smile.

I ran over to the bicycle, threw my book bag on the ground and jumped on.

I ended up with scratches head to toe from falling down so many times. Mom constantly tried to get me to stop and eat supper but I wouldn't listen and kept on riding.

It wasn't until it became too dark to see anything that I finally quit and took the bike inside the house for safe keeping.

Mom said she got a good deal on the bicycle from one of the neighbors up the street and paid for it with the money earned from selling the pig she was raising. She wanted me to know she tried to get the bike at the start of the school year but couldn't after the pig became sick and its growth was slowed.

Riding my bike to school for the first time was a big deal for me. Ha made sure I stayed on the edge of the road in case I fell. She got her bicycle a few days before I did and had more time to practice and get better at it. I fell a couple of times before reaching the school and thanked her for making me stay out of the way of traffic.

A couple of months later, as Ha and I were standing in line to pick up our bikes after school, Tung showed up with a friend of his named Sang. Ha and I stepped out of the line and walked across the street to see them. They asked us to go to the movies with them and we immediately said, "No."

Not wanting to take no for an answer, they continued asking until I pulled Ha over to the side.

"There's no way I can go because Mom would kill me!" I whispered.

"We'll just make sure we get home before dark and come up with an excuse for why we're late. I don't think we'll get into any big trouble," she said.

With everyone else wanting to go, I quickly warmed up to the idea, in spite of a nagging feeling in my stomach. I really liked Tung, and the chance to watch a movie and sit next to him over-rode that bad feeling.

When I was younger, a neighbor told me about the time he and his cousin went to the movies for the first time. He said he couldn't believe how real everything looked on the huge screen and how the sound was so amazing. During one of the scenes, when a car looked like it was coming toward everyone in the theatre, his cousin got so scared, he jumped out of his seat and ran outside screaming. My neighbor swore it was a true story, but we didn't believe him. I always hoped one day, I would see for myself.

Tung and Sang were both riding bicycles and we decided to leave ours at the school before climbing on the back of theirs. The closest movie theatre was one hour away in a section of Ho Chi Minh City called Cho Lon.

As we entered the city, everything seemed to come alive with people walking everywhere on the streets and sidewalks. Many were going in and out of tall buildings with business signs on their doors and windows.

When we reached the theater, the first thing that caught my eye was all the large pictures of movie stars hanging up outside the building.

While Tung and Sang walked over to pay someone to look after their bikes, I asked Ha, "So, do you like Sang?"

"He's really nice, but we just don't click. It's OK, though. He's kind of funny and it's been a lot of fun so far!"

I was impressed and relieved when Tung walked up to the counter and paid for all four tickets. I didn't have enough money to even buy one. The moment I stepped inside the theatre and got my first look at how large the movie screen actually was, I couldn't help but let out a, "Wow!"

"Shhh!" Ha quietly scolded me. "Don't do that! People will know you came from the rice paddies!"

The movie was amazing! So amazing, we lost track of time. As soon as we walked out of the theater and saw how late it was getting, Ha and I began freaking out. It would be way past dark by the time we got home.

Tung and Sang saw the worry on our faces and pedaled their bikes as fast as they could.

After picking up our bikes at the school, Ha and I rushed to get home, but we knew it was already too late.

As we were getting closer to home, I could see in the moonlight, from a long distance away, Mom standing in the middle of the main path waiting for me. To make things worse, Ha's grandma was standing beside Mom, waiting for her.

Ha and I instantly jumped off our bikes after seeing them, and frantically tried to make up some kind of story. I'd never seen fear on Ha's face like I did that night.

Without giving it much thought, I picked up a big rock and started smacking my bike's rear fender to make it look broken. Mom didn't know anything about bicycles and I thought it would be an easy story to sell her.

"Don't smack it too hard," Ha said. "It might cost you a lot to fix it."

"I know, I know!" I told her. "I just want to cry!"

As we got a little closer, we could see Mom and Ha's grandma holding long sticks in their hands and there was no way we could avoid them.

Before Mom had a chance to say anything, I blurted out, "I'm sorry we're late, but my bike broke down and we had to push it a long way, and...."

I went on and on, but, knowing my flair for telling stories, Mom didn't believe a word of it.

After we both got our butt smacked really good with their sticks, Ha followed her grandma home on the main path while I listened to Mom yell at me all the way back to our house. For the next two weeks, I felt like I was in boot camp and Mom was the drill sergeant.

It took me a month to save enough money to fix my bike.

Ha and I had learned our lesson and never again did we come home after dark.

Chapter Seventeen

Having a "problem child" such as I, was only one of the many hardships my mother had to bear. In her late 40's, she began slowing down quite a bit, constantly suffering from female problems. She went to a local doctor off and on when she had the money, but her condition wasn't getting any better. As time went by, Mom started looking very pale and becoming skinnier by the day.

The day came when her condition got so bad that Mom knew something was seriously wrong and needed more help than the local doctor could offer. Getting on a bus at our local market, I went along with her to a hospital called Hung Vuong, specializing in female problems. It was located in a section of Ho Chi Minh City called Sai Gon and required taking two buses to get there.

During the entire ride, I could tell Mom was in a great deal of pain.

After walking through the front doors of the hospital, Mom stepped to the back of a long line of female patients, while I stood off to one side. As the line slowly moved forward, I kept moving along with it to stay close to Mom.

When she finally reached the receptionist's desk, she had to pay before being allowed to see the doctor.

Two hours later, a nurse called Mom's name and directed her through a door while making me stay behind to wait in the lobby.

The entire time I was waiting, I kept hoping the doctor wouldn't find anything seriously wrong with her and would just give her a prescription that wouldn't cost much money. Maybe on our way back home, we'd have enough money to buy a loaf of bread and a glass of ice water we could share. I didn't like being in the hospital and couldn't wait until Mom came back out so we could leave.

When Mom finally came walking out, I could see the distress in her face. "I'm sorry, Trang," she said, the pain showing in her voice. "I have to stay and get treated immediately." She cradled the lower part of her belly with her hands.

Mom said she asked the doctor, "Can I take my daughter home, pack some clothes and come right back?"

"No!" the doctor replied. "I don't want you going anywhere! You could bleed to death before you make it back! You might need an operation, but only as a last resort."

I panicked after hearing the word *operation*. There were a lot of people who died after getting an operation. People had always complained that Viet Nam was behind in technology and the doctors didn't have good equipment or training.

You could see the stress all over Mom's face as she said, "I pray I won't need an operation, I don't have enough money for that."

Hospitals in Viet Nam didn't allow you to make payments. If you didn't have the money, you would not get treated. Many people went home in pain or simply died; that's just the way it was.

Normally, Mom wouldn't let me travel alone to go home, but on that day, she didn't have a choice. She had to let me find my own way back so I could inform our family what was happening. Mom was so worried about me traveling in the city and kept telling me over and over which buses to take.

I was also instructed to have my brother prepare to sell some of our rice if an operation was needed.

While waiting for the nurse to call Mom back, I remembered a movie I watched at a neighbor's house a week before. It was about a young, beautiful girl who worked for a very rich couple. The old and ugly husband offered the girl money for sex often, but she always replied, "I'd rather die than do that."

Later in the movie, the girl's mother became seriously ill and wasn't expected to live unless an operation was performed immediately. Needing to come up with the money fast, the beautiful girl had to swallow her own tears and accept the man's offer of money. Some of my friends were crying after that scene and it took me by surprise. "What's wrong with you? It's just a movie!" I said with a smug tone in my voice.

Remembering my comment while looking at Mom suffering in pain, I suddenly felt small and uncaring.

When Mom was finally called back in, I walked out to the street in front of the hospital and waited for a bus having the name Binh Chanh on the front. It seemed like a hundred buses had gone by before the one I wanted came into view. I signaled with my hand for the bus to stop, but it was full of passengers and kept on going.

I waited for another thirty minutes before the one I needed stopped. It was already packed with passengers and the driver's assistant jumped down to help me squeeze in the door. I said to him, "I need off at Binh Dien. Can you tell me when we're getting close?" He didn't say anything so I repeated it.

"I heard you the first time," he snapped.

I felt better that he knew where I wanted to get off, but I didn't trust him to tell me. I had no idea how far it was to my stop and kept watching out the window with the hope I'd recognize a building or some other landmark that was close to it. Every five to ten minutes, the bus would stop to either drop people off or pick more up.

Each time it stopped, I would get shoved so hard, I'd almost fall onto sitting passengers. Vendors were always waiting out along the street; they tried to make sales through the bus windows or come on the bus if there was room.

Adding to the chaos was a young girl sitting in the back with motion sickness. She threw up all over the floor and on people sitting next to her.

Everyone was trying to push their way out of the mess and I got shoved to the point of almost falling out the bus door. I couldn't wait to get off.

Just when I thought I couldn't take it anymore, the driver's assistant repeatedly banged on the side of the bus with his hand to signal the driver to stop. With a movement of his head, he motioned that this was my stop and I quickly jumped off the step.

I took a second bus to the local market at Cho Dem, crossed the river on the ferry and rushed home.

Nobody was around when I reached our house. I went straight over to the large ceramic pot holding rain water to get a drink and wash my face. Feeling refreshed, I ran over to the kitchen where I found some left over rice from that morning.

There weren't any vegetables or fish to eat with it so I grabbed a small jar of lard sitting on the cabinet shelf. The jar was almost empty and I had to turn it upside down and let it drip on my rice. Mom always wanted us to save the lard for cooking, so I took only a few drops. Normally, I would eat my rice with fish sauce, but mixing a little bit of lard with some soy sauce made a great combination and gave it an even better taste.

The last bus of the day going into the city was at 5:00 and I had to quickly get all of Mom's things together. There wasn't enough time to go over to my sister's house or my brother's place of work and tell them about Mom. I prepared a pot of rice before running next door to my Grandma's to let her know about everything. I also asked her to relay Mom's instructions to my brother when he came home.

Grandma panicked when she heard me say, "Mom might need an operation." She gave me what money she had for my bus fares and the hospital before walking into the living room to burn incense and pray.

I ran back home to pack Mom's clothes and some rice into a bag before rushing back to the hospital.

I couldn't wait to see Mom and find out how she was doing. A nurse directed me to the recovery room. I jogged there, excited to see Mom, but nothing could have prepared me for what I was about to see.

Blood was everywhere! There were about twenty patients in the room and only ten small beds. Mom was lying beside a strange woman I'd never seen before. Most of the women, including Mom, couldn't move, and some of them were moaning very loudly. The white linens were stained red while fresh puddles of blood stood on the floor. The room looked like a place in hell filled with women who had come back from the dead.

Mom told me she had just had a procedure called "dilation and curettage" and they did it without putting her to sleep or giving her a sedative. She thought she was going to die because the pain was so bad.

After I was there for an hour, Mom's pants were soaked with blood and it started to run all over the bed sheets. I didn't know what to do.

A woman who was there taking care of her sister handed me a few old newspapers and told me to lay them under Mom's bottom to soak up the blood.

The hospital didn't take care of any personal needs (food, water, going to the bathroom, etc.) It was left up to family members to take care of that and to also pay for any drugs, tests or procedures performed. Most of the other patients' family members were female, except for a couple of men who were there taking care of their wives.

When it was getting late in the evening, I began wondering where I could sleep. I didn't want to be kicked out onto the street, so I looked around for a clean, safe place to lie down without being in the way.

I was relieved to see other people that were in Mom's room picking out places to sleep along the wall in the hallway. Most of the people spread out old newspapers or extra clothes to cover the dirty floor before lying down, and they slept in a curled up position to keep from taking up too much space.

The ones who didn't have anything to cover the floor with had to sleep sitting with their backs against the wall. Both sides of the hallway were almost full, with only a few spots left, so I hurried and took a place next to a guy who seemed very kind, although old, worn out and skinny. His skin was dark from long hours in the sun and half of his hair had turned grey.

I learned from talking with him that he had been there for over a week taking care of his wife. He lived out in the country, far from the city, and was too poor to afford the several hour bus ride back and forth to see his three small children. I felt bad because he didn't have any family members nearby that could bring food or any other necessities for his wife and him. He said he always bought the cheapest food out on the street and most of the time, his wife and he ate plain bread.

I kept praying for Mom to get better until I fell asleep. I must have slept well because when I woke up the next morning, the hallway was completely empty except for a couple of older ladies sleeping along the opposite wall.

Anxious to see Mom, I grabbed my bag and quickly ran into her room.

She was awake and looking much better, but I felt sorry for the woman lying beside her. She was still moaning from the pain.

Mom asked me to help her move her body around so she could lie on her side for a while. We struggled for some time to get her into position while trying to be careful she didn't take more than her half of the bed. She then asked me to go buy her a small glass of hot milk and I immediately ran out the door.

Half way down the hallway, my eyes lit up when I saw my older sister, Chi Tu, walking toward me. I was so happy to see her!

"How is Mom?" She asked.

I gave her all the details of everything that had happened and said that I was on my way to get Mom some milk.

Chi Tu was carrying a bag that had rice soup, a can of sweet milk and a thermos full of hot water inside.

I felt so relieved that she came prepared and would know how to take better care of Mom than I could. Caregiving was such a huge responsibility for anyone, especially a teenager like me.

Five days later, Mom was far enough along with her recovery that the doctor allowed her to go home.

I was relieved that she was going to be okay, and felt really happy just to be a kid again.

Chapter Eighteen

At the end of my tenth grade year, I was so glad I had passed and would be able to move on to the eleventh grade. Mom was very happy because I was the first girl in the family to ever advance that far. But just as before, we were faced with the problem of needing extra money. The fees continued to climb.

One evening, while I was weaving tote bags under our porch roof, my sister, Chi Tu, came over for a visit. She smiled, said, "Hello," and asked if she could help.

She reached over and took one of the bags I had already woven and used it to sit on so she wouldn't get her pants dirty.

As we were talking and working on the bags, we watched a dozen or more boats go by, one right after another. Each boat had two people in it, one sitting in the front and one in the back, both of them paddling in unison. Their oars created a distinctive loud noise cutting through the water with fast, powerful strokes.

Chi Tu said they were on their way to a floating market where large boats were anchored in the river close to the Ong Lanh market. The people in the small boats would buy produce straight from the anchored boats and resell it at smaller markets or to people living along the river.

I remembered when Mom and my brother did the same thing, except they always went to a smaller floating market in the opposite direction from our house. I now assumed the market

Mom always bought from must have purchased their produce from the large boats anchored near Ong Lanh.

Thinking if we bought directly from the large boats ourselves, I reasoned my sister and I could make a lot more money.

Jumping to my feet with excitement, I voiced my thoughts to Chi Tu and added, "Why don't we follow that group of boats over to the floating market when they come by again? We'll be safe making the trip at night if we stay close to them, and we could sell the produce to people living along the river on the way back home. I'm sure we'll earn a lot more money than sitting here making these bags."

"That's not a bad idea. We should do that sometime," Chi Tu said.

"Not sometime! I was thinking more like tomorrow!"

"We can't do it tomorrow!" Chi Tu snapped back. "First, we need to save some money; it takes money to make money. We'll need about 150,000 Dong (around $15.00 USD) to buy enough pineapple and cassava root to make the trip worthwhile."

Every night for the next month, my sister and I stayed up late weaving as many tote bags as we possibly could. After selling all the bags to a local vendor for 100,000 Dong, we ended up $5.00 USD short of what was needed. Understanding our situation, some of our family members got together and loaned us the rest.

On the day we decided to make the trip, Chi Tu and I got an early start on gathering all the basic supplies we would need. We loaded into our boat a small cement fire pit, rice, water, a blanket and a few other small items. I couldn't wait to go and kept walking back and forth from the house to the river, just to make sure we didn't miss the group of boats.

At about 7:00 PM, we could see them coming. I hurried and jumped into the front of our boat while my sister quickly got in the back. "Oh boy! Here we go!" I said with a big smile.

"Paddle as fast as you can so we can keep up!" Chi Tu kept telling me.

An hour later, we had fallen far behind the group but could still see them off in the distance against the moonlit sky. We kept paddling as hard as we could but continued getting further and further behind.

It finally dawned on us that the people in the other boats had probably been doing this every day for many years and there was no way we could ever keep up. I thought if there was ever a competition for paddling, they'd be champions.

Thirty minutes later, they were completely out of sight and we found ourselves alone on the river.

The sound of muffled voices along with the dim light of oil lanterns came from houses sitting along the banks on both sides. Just knowing there were other people nearby gave us a feeling of safety. The farther down the river we traveled, the larger it became and the number of houses was getting less and less. A short while later, we went into a long stretch of the river that was completely desolate.

I remembered a story about robbers who always worked in this kind of area and how important it was for anyone traveling to stay in a large group. I knew Chi Tu had heard the same story and that was the reason she kept insisting we keep up with the rest of the boats.

With the help of darkness and the eerie sound of the wind, we became very scared and had goose bumps all over. We paddled faster.

Not only was I scared, I needed to go to the bathroom. I didn't want to add more stress to my sister by complaining, so I remained quiet. I could hear her beginning to pray and I started doing the same.

As soon as we saw the first house on the side of the river, we both breathed a sigh of relief. I immediately shouted to my sister, "I have to go pee!"

"Ok, just pee in the river," Chi Tu said after stopping the boat.

I did what she said, but it wasn't easy. "I wish I were a boy!" I told her.

"Me too," she said while laughing. "It sure would make it a whole lot easier."

Sometime around midnight, we got our first glimpse of the floating market. From a distance, I could see the whole river lit up from all the anchored boats. When we finally got close enough, the sight of so many different sized boats and all the activity going on at this time of night was truly amazing.

Vendors selling different kinds of snacks were shouting out their product name while paddling in-between and around all the anchored boats that had just arrived. I loved most of the snacks they were selling and made a comment on each and every one as they were shouted out.

"You can buy one," my sister said, making my day, "but it has to cost no more than ten cents."

I was happy but had the hardest time deciding which one I wanted to buy. Finally I chose a sweet banana dish that had coconut milk and chopped peanuts on top. I shared it with Chi Tu and ate my half slowly to enjoy every bite.

Knowing how busy we'd be in the morning and wouldn't have any time to cook, my sister tied our boat off to a tree on the bank. She unpacked our portable fire pit and started a fire while I prepared the rice. We had to wait until the rice was done before going to sleep.

Without the mosquito net we forgot to bring, we had to cover ourselves with a blanket and use our bamboo hats to cover our heads. There wasn't enough room for us to sleep side by side, so my sister lay with her head at one end of the boat and I lay at the other. The ribs on the boat weren't covered with floor boards and poked us in the back the entire night. We had a terrible night's sleep.

The market came to life around 4:00 AM, waking us up. The lights were turned way up, making the river appear almost as bright as it would be during the day.

Vendors like the ones we followed from home were surrounding the large anchored boats that sold produce. Everyone was shouting back and forth trying to make a better deal.

My sister untied our boat and we paddled over to join in the chaos. We worked our way around several of the large boats trying to negotiate a good deal, but everything was priced too high that day.

"People make many trips to this market and sometimes when the price is low, they make good money," Chi Tu said, looking frustrated. "Other times when the prices are high, like now, they make very little."

After a moment's pause, she continued, "Since this is our first trip and we can't afford to not make money, I was just wondering if it would be better to go home with an empty boat."

"No!" I quickly replied.

"But the prices are too high; we'll have a really hard time reselling everything."

"Maybe it'll take more time to sell, but we should at least try," I responded.

After a little more coaxing, Chi Tu agreed to not go back empty. We filled half of our boat with pineapple and the other half with cassava root.

Wanting to eat breakfast before starting out, we tied our boat back off to a tree and ate the cold rice we cooked the night before. Forgetting to bring along some fish sauce to eat with our rice, we cut up the smallest pineapple in the boat and used it instead.

After breakfast, we paddled up one of the tributaries my sister heard was a good place to make sales. Both sides of the smaller river was lined with houses sitting side by side and looked to be very promising.

I began shouting out the names of the items on our boat while trying to sound professional like other vendors I had heard. My voice sounded really terrible at first but slowly improved as I shouted the same thing over and over again.

After ten minutes of shouting nonstop, a lady walked out from her house and signaled for us to stop with her hand. She stepped on our boat, picked out a few pineapples and asked, "How much?"

My sister told her the price.

"Your price is too high! You might as well take it home and eat it yourself! Nobody is going to buy it for that price!" She complained.

The lady offered us a really cheap price and we refused to sell her any. Rather than get mad at her, we both laughed because she reminded us of our mother. I could remember one time when Mom stopped ten different boats before buying anything.

All through the next hour, my sister and I took turns doing the shouting. We had many people stop us but we still couldn't make any sales. It wasn't until we finally decided to drop our price a little bit before our luck began to change.

By noon, we were completely worn out. The sun was at its highest point and the heat was almost unbearable. The tide was going out and we paddled hard against the fast moving water just to keep from moving backwards. I wanted to complain that my arms hurt, the stupid boat was barely moving, the sun was burning hot, and I was hungry. I thought we should just tie the boat to a tree and walk home. When I turned around and saw the determined look on my sister's face, I decided to keep my mouth shut and try a little harder.

When both of us became too tired to keep the boat moving forward, we tied off to a tree and took a much needed break. The bucket of rain water for drinking was hot from the sun and the left over rice from breakfast was ready to spoil and beginning to smell badly. Lunch that day was quick and yucky!

By 4:00, the sun was lower in the sky and the air was cooling off. With the tide completely out and the river standing still, paddling became much easier. Life was good again.

We continued working our way up the river into an area where the people were much nicer and we started to make more sales. One lady invited us up to her house to wash our faces and get a cool drink of water.

When the sun was beginning to set, we stopped selling and headed for home. We arrived around 7:00 and were greeted by my younger sister along with my nephews, Tri and Kha. They'd been sitting by the river waiting for our return and were jumping around with excitement, thinking they could eat all the pineapple they wanted.

Chi Tu said, "Yeah, right." We were worried about losing money on the whole deal and gave them the smallest pineapple in the boat to share between them.

Later on, a few of my neighbors showed up thinking we were going to give them a big discount. We let them buy for the price we paid.

Mom was just happy we made it back safely.

Early the next morning, Chi Tu showed up ready to go up the river with me to make more sales. By 4:00, we sold everything on the boat except for a few pineapples and five kilos of cassava root. Everything was picked through many times and nobody wanted what was left. We decided to take what was remaining back for our family to eat rather than give it away for almost nothing.

Once we were back home and had our boat unloaded, my sister and I sat down and counted all the money. We made a profit of just over $3.00 USD's. I was expecting a little more than that but was still happy when I received my half.

After that trip, we never looked at the vendors on the river the same way again, and we asked Mom to never beat their prices down too much. With a new found respect for this form of business, my sister and I agreed there must be better ways of making money.

Chapter Nineteen

Grandma's house sat next to ours and her doors were always wide open. Each time I went anywhere on foot, it was quicker and more convenient for me to walk straight through her house than to walk around. One day while passing through her kitchen, Grandma stopped me with a motion of her hand.

"I have some good news for you," she said. "Yesterday Ba Tu (a neighbor) came by for a visit and mentioned that her daughter, Hanh, was going to open a massage therapy business in her home very soon. She said Hanh is looking for someone to work at the front desk and must be someone who is trustworthy."

"Did you tell her I needed a job, Grandma? Did you?" I asked, unable to contain my excitement.

"I sure did, but you better go to her house and let her know you're interested."

"Is Hanh the one who lives in the city, Grandma?"

"Yes. She and her husband are both doctors now and have three children. They're the ones who paid for Ba Tu's new home."

I wanted to wait until Mom came home before going to Ba Tu's, but I worried other girls in the neighborhood might beat me to it. Deciding I could talk to Mom afterwards and not take a chance by waiting, I ran over to see Ba Tu.

When I was approaching her house, some dogs were running around outside and started coming toward me. They stopped advancing but continued to bark loudly until Ba Tu came out and yelled at them.

I crossed my arms, bowed my head, and said, "Hello."

"How are you, Trang?" Ba Tu asked.

"Great, thank you. Grandma told me about the job at your daughter's house and I wanted to let you know I am interested."

"Oh, that's good to hear, Trang. Hanh needs someone she can trust and I know she'd be happy with you. She was like a sister to your dad and enjoyed hanging out with him. The business won't be ready to open for another two or three weeks and I'll get back with you as soon as I talk to Hanh."

"Thank you for everything, Ba Tu! This means a lot to me," I said before turning to leave.

"Just a second, Trang," she said. "I'm going up to my daughter's house tomorrow to do housework. She always has me do it because she doesn't trust strangers in her house. If you would like to take care of her housework as well, I'll talk to her about that. There's plenty of room for you to stay at their house if you want and you'll save the cost of traveling back and forth every day. Hanh always pays once a month."

"That all sounds great! Thank you!" I felt so grateful for the opportunity and especially loved the word "pay". "I need to ask Mom first when she gets home, OK? I'm almost certain she'll let me because she knows you and your family."

"That'll be fine. Just let me know one way or the other first thing in the morning."

I waited for Mom to get home from the rice paddy later that night and gave her a chance to relax before I told her about the job offer. I then asked, "Can I go? Please, please, please!"

Mom didn't say yes or no. The longer she waited before giving me an answer, the more I worried she'd say no.

An hour later, I asked again.

This time, she looked directly at me for a moment and quietly said, "OK."

I was beyond excited. Having a chance to live in the city and experience how people lived there was a dream come true. Every time I saw someone from the city, they always seemed to have lighter skin and I couldn't wait until mine was the same. Everyone around here would be so jealous. The best part was, I'd get paid to do it.

The next morning, I rushed over to Ba Tu's house to tell her I had Mom's permission.

Ba Tu was happy to hear the news and promised to get back with me as soon as she returned from Hanh's late in the afternoon.

I spent the entire day close to home just in case she came back early. My thoughts went back and forth between worrying about not getting the job and imagining how nice it would be to live in the city.

Late in the afternoon, just before supper, I saw her walking toward our house. I ran out to meet her and immediately knew I had the job by the huge smile on her face. She said Hanh was thrilled to have me work for her and asked if I could start tomorrow.

I quickly answered, "Yes!"

"Great! Just come to my house early tomorrow morning and we'll leave for the city!"

I was humming and skipping all the way home and went straight to the back room of our house.

My younger sister followed me and just stood there, watching me pack. I was taking only my newest outfits so I would look my best. Looking sad, she asked, "Are you going to be a maid?"

"Shhhhh! Be quiet! Make sure you don't tell people that. Okay? I don't want people to look down on us." I added a stern look to make sure she understood me.

Quyen nodded her head.

"Okay. But when are you coming back?" she asked.

"About one month. As soon as I get paid, I will come home for a visit."

Quyen stood there with her head down and didn't say anything.

I lowered my head and turned it sideways to look at her. "When I get paid, I will give you some money. Make sure you help Mom and be good to our nephews. Make sure they don't fight."

She nodded her head again while continuing to look down at the floor.

"What's going on?" I heard Mom ask as she walked in.

"Oh nothing, just packing."

Mom stood there watching for a couple of minutes and then asked me to look at her. "You be smart!" She said in a firm voice. "Take good care of yourself and stay away from strangers! Remember the story I've always told you!"

While I was growing up, Mom always told me a story about young girls from the country who went to the city to work and live. Sometimes, many of those girls would fall into a trap used by madams at prostitute houses. "I would rather see you eating dirt than being a prostitute," Mom would always say.

The next morning, Mom woke up extra early to cook me rice for breakfast. Normally, she would yell my name several times before I'd actually wake up and get out of bed. That morning, she only had to yell once.

It was still dark outside and the roosters were taking turns crowing while I brushed my teeth. I walked into the kitchen and sat on the floor next to Mom. Since I was the only one eating, I ate right out of the pan sitting on the fire pit.

Mom lectured me again and again about the story of young girls working in the city.

Walking with me over to Ba Tu's house, Mom told me again to be smart and stay away from strangers.

As soon as we reached the house, Ba Tu came walking outside after hearing the dogs bark. Mom greeted her with a worried smile and began asking her about the job I was hired to do.

"Will you please keep an eye on her and make sure she is safe?" Mom asked.

Ba Tu gave her a reassuring smile and replied, "Of course I will!"

I still worried she'd change her mind and not let me go. I felt a wave of relief when she said goodbye and walked home.

With my woven bag stuffed with clothes and personal belongings in hand, Ba Tu and I headed off to the city. We rode two different buses and then traveled a long distance along the streets on foot.

As we were walking, I couldn't keep my eyes from wandering around while trying to pay attention and follow Ba Tu. Food vendors would sometimes take over the sidewalk with tables and chairs, forcing us to walk on the street. The traffic was very heavy and constantly beeping their horns.

About ten minutes later, she suddenly stopped and pointed to her daughter's home on the other side of the street.

The house was so tall, I had to tilt my head back to see the top of it. *Wow!* I thought, *It's true, they really are rich people.* I couldn't wait to go inside!

The door was unlocked and we walked right in. No one was in the living room and we continued walking into a long hallway that lead toward the back of the house.

Half way down the hall, I inadvertently voiced a, "Wow!" after seeing a refrigerator sitting in a room at the end of the hallway.

My mind went wild. *Ice! I love ice!* I thought with much excitement.

I didn't know how things were going to work out for me here, but at least I'd be able to have some ice every day.

The next thing I saw was a sink with running water! I couldn't believe someone could be so lucky.

Moments later, a woman wearing a beautiful long dress walked in with a big smile. "Hello, there!" she said while looking directly at me.

"Hanh, this is Trang. Trang, this is my daughter, Hanh," Ba Tu said.

"Trang! Welcome! You're such a pretty girl! You look just like your Dad. He was such a good man and I really miss him."

I felt a warmth in my heart the minute she mentioned my dad. I was so happy to meet someone who had known him so well! I was really going to like living with Hanh.

I crossed my arms, bowed my head and said, "Hello."

"Please, make yourself at home," Hanh said. "I'm really glad to have you here. When we're ready to open the business, I'll get with you and explain what I want you to do at the front desk. In the meantime, Mom will give you a tour of the house and help get you started on your other duties."

I stood there grinning and said nothing.

"Where is everybody?" Ba Tu asked Hanh.

"The kids are at school and my husband had to go to work early this morning, so I'm the only one home." Looking at the watch on her wrist, she softly exclaimed, "Oh! Look at the time; I'd better leave for work myself."

Hanh looked nothing like the women I saw in the country every day. She wore make up, her hair was short and styled, and she had beautiful light skin. The perfume she had on smelled so good, I breathed slowly through my nose to take it all in.

I hoped and dreamed that one day I could experience the good life. Watching Hanh get on her motorcycle, I thought how cool it was she owned one. I would never allow myself to dream that big!

When Hanh left for work, Ba Tu showed me around and pointed out all my daily responsibilities, including what kind of food to cook.

My favorite part of the tour was when she opened the freezer section of the refrigerator. She showed me how ice was made and let me know I could have some any time I wanted. To add to my excitement, she pointed to a group of containers on the counter that held different flavored powders for making soft drinks.

"Go ahead and make yourself a drink," she told me as she walked away. "I'll be back in a little bit."

I mixed a glass of the best lemonade ever. I wished I could have shared it with my younger sister and nephews. They'd be just as happy as I was.

Before supper, Ba Tu showed me where they kept the rice. I was instantly worried after seeing how small the bag was.

Noticing the look on my face, she commented, "Unlike everyone in the country, people in the city eat only one small bowl of rice, twice a day. There's no need to cook very much for each meal."

I knew I was in trouble. The amount of rice I was told to cook was enough for me alone. My family and I always had three or four small bowls each for every meal. We never had snacks to eat between meals and learned to stuff ourselves with rice before going about our day.

At supper time, Hanh introduced me to her husband and their three young boys. The husband was very nice and the kids were cute. They asked me all kinds of questions about life in the country and what I thought of the city so far.

"Life in the country is very difficult; you have no idea how good you've got it here!"

They laughed like I was joking, but I knew they would never survive in the country.

Ba Tu was right, people in the city didn't eat much rice. I was the last person to finish eating and scraped every bit of rice left in the pan without anyone seeing. I worried they'd make fun of me.

The next morning, I woke up early because I was so hungry, but then remembered the family didn't eat rice for breakfast.

They instead selected from one of many different food choices sold by vendors on the street. I needed my rice.

As soon as Hanh and her family left for work and school, Ba Tu had me follow her to the front door so she could show me which vendors were the best to buy from.

"Take your time choosing what you want. I'm going back in the house because I already had a cup of hot milk and don't need anything else."

I stood there looking at all the vendors and wished that I could eat all the food I liked. Having very little money in my pocket, I walked around checking out the prices and made sure I picked one thing from the best of the cheapest.

Later that morning, Ba Tu left to go back to her house in the country. I was home by myself with a freezer full of ice and it felt like I had just won the lottery.

After making a large glass of lemonade and drinking it very fast, I made another one, then another and another. I began feeling guilty for taking advantage of the situation, even though they said I could have as much as I wanted.

The feeling of guilt came to an end rather fast after I became sick from drinking too much. I learned a valuable lesson.

When my stomach settled down and I was feeling a little better, I went on to do the laundry. There was a large pile of dirty clothes sitting in a metal bowl on the laundry room floor. After opening a valve, good water came out from a pipe sticking through the wall and I let it run straight into the bowl. It was so clean and such a convenience! Back home, I had to go out to the river or pond and bring back water in a bucket before doing laundry.

As I was scrubbing all the clothes by hand, I remembered watching a movie and feeling sorry for a poor girl working as a maid for rich people. Even though I ended up in the same position as the girl in the movie, I didn't feel sorry for myself. I liked what I was doing a lot more than working in the rice fields. Not only was I being paid, I was looking forward to having lighter skin by not being in the sun all day.

Ba Tu returned from the country three days later. She and I spent the whole afternoon cleaning the second floor to get ready for the massage therapy business.

"Do you know what day the business will be opening?" I asked.

"The room will be ready in a few days, but my daughter believes she must wait until a Buddhist Monk gives her a specific date that will give her the greatest chance for good fortune. I'll let you know as soon as I hear anything," Ba Tu replied.

Ten days later, at about 10:00 A.M., the noise made by the front door opening caught my attention. I stopped ironing the shirt I was working on and looked down the hallway.

A woman wearing a bamboo hat and dressed in a country outfit was walking down the hall toward me but I couldn't see her face.

"Trang! Trang! Where are you?" A loud voice rang out.

It was my mother! I was worried as much as surprised when I heard her voice. I didn't have a chance to say hello or ask her anything before she yelled, "I want you to pack your clothes and leave here immediately! Hurry!"

"Ok, I'll go get my things. What's going on?

"Let's just get going! Right now! I'll tell you what's going on later."

I followed Mom outside, feeling very guilty for not letting the family know I was leaving.

Once on the bus, Mom calmed down enough to tell me why she ripped me from the house.

"I went to visit Ba Tu last night, but she wasn't home. On the way back, I got to talking to one of her family members who lived nearby. The lady leaned in closely and whispered, 'Do you know what's *really* going on at Hanh's house?'

"I told her that I thought it was a business for massage therapy, and she answered, 'That's just a front. Your daughter is in danger, great danger! You need to get her out of there as soon as possible before she's sold as a prostitute!'

"I was so scared for you, I couldn't move!

"'Go now!' the lady told me."

Mom stopped a minute to catch her breath, then continued. "This woman isn't always serious, so I didn't know what to do. I couldn't stop worrying about it and soon, I was in a panic.

"I caught the first available bus to the city."

With Mom telling this, I began to wonder. I didn't *see* anything wrong during my brief stay there, but I remembered Ba Tu telling me one time, "When the business is open, don't ever go up to the second floor, even if someone asks you to. When no one needs you at the front desk, just stay in the back."

She repeated the sentence a couple more times until I said, "OK". I never asked her why, but I did feel that something was odd.

One thing I know for sure; I didn't get any pay and went home with nothing, — except having a few cold glasses of lemonade.

Chapter Twenty

A few months into my twelfth grade year, government officials began requiring high school girls to wear an all-white, traditional, Vietnamese dress called ao dai (pronounced "ow die"). All boys were to begin wearing dark blue pants with a white shirt. No one was happy to hear the new rule and teachers gave us two weeks to comply or we wouldn't be allowed back in school.

One ao dai dress cost five times more than a normal outfit, plus you had to wear special pants that complimented the dress. I needed to have at least two complete outfits so I could wear one while the other dried after washing. (Clothes would seldom dry overnight, especially during the rainy season.) Imagine wearing a long white dress with white pants while riding a bicycle on a dirt path. It would cost a lot of money just to buy soap.

I knew Mom couldn't afford the extra costs; she already had a hard time buying school supplies and paying the school fee. As it was, I already skipped lunch most of the time to avoid asking for money and seeing her all stressed out.

School was over for me and I never returned after receiving the two week notice. Mom was just as disappointed as I was, but we both understood, that was the way it had to be.

Since I was no longer in school, I had no choice but to go with Mom and work in the rice paddy. To make things worse, sneaking off to see my boyfriend would now be almost impossible. Tung and I were still meeting up every afternoon. How would I see him now?

During the rainy season, we planted rice, but in the dry season, we worked on vegetable gardens planted on the edge of dikes running between the paddies. Using a hoe to break up the dirt, we spent days getting the garden ready. Mom ended up doing most of the work and her hands would be sore by the end of each day. As hard as I tried, I was never able to keep up with her.

Among all the things I ever wanted to do, working in the rice paddies was at the bottom of my list. Not only was it back breaking work, most of the time the sun was so hot that the mosquito larvae swimming in our bucket of drinking water would die. I always tormented myself by wishing for a little bit of ice.

During one of those hot days, I kept wanting to take a break, but Mom repeatedly said, "No, just wait a little bit. We'll be taking a lunch break soon."

An hour later, I commented, "I thought you said we would take a break soon."

Again, she said, "Soon." Moments later she added, "It took us two hours of paddling to get here, and it's going to take another two hours to get back home. Losing all that time makes our day short and we need to get as much done as we can."

After digging a large furrow for planting vegetables, we placed rice hay in it and covered it with loose dirt using our bare hands. We then burned the hay to help enrich the soil which created so much smoke you could see it from a mile away.

Finally, I heard Mom say, "Time for lunch."

Hearing those words made me happy but upset at the same time. I didn't understand why we didn't stop sooner.

To get out of the sun, we went inside a tiny hut Mom built using bamboo and leafed branches cut from the banks of the river.

The hut was located between our paddy and a large path that ran along the river. Mom made sure it was large enough to build a fire for cooking and have a place to sleep. The bed was built up off the floor using four large bamboo sticks acting as corner posts. The bed frame and sleeping surface was made with many smaller bamboo sticks fastened to the corner posts and each other using nails and strips of bark cut from a tree growing along the river. (The bark was cut into long slivers and laid out in the sun to dry. When the bark dried, the edges curled in together which made the slivers look and act like a rope).

We built our fire pit close to the hut's door by using three rocks laid out in a circle and placing a wire grate on top of them.

After lunch, the sun was close to its highest point and it was torture to go back to work. "It's too hot," I complained.

"You can wait and come out later," Mom said.

I wanted to stay inside, but after thinking about Mom needing to work harder without my help, I was overtaken with guilt. Taking a deep breath, I stepped out into the scorching hot sun.

Most days, as evening approached, I would start feeling better knowing we were that much closer to going home.

Mom always wanted to work as late as possible and on evenings when it wasn't raining, she'd stop the boat on our way home and cut nipa palm trees (cay dua nuoc) growing along the river for firewood. Mom wouldn't go home until the boat was full, even when I continued to complain about being hungry and too tired to paddle.

At home, when time permitted, we cut the trees into short lengths to use for cooking along with the rice straw. Sometimes I wondered if Mom was a machine. She'd work seven days a week, year after year from morning to night, and not once did I ever hear her complain.

The beginning of the rainy season marked the time to prepare the rice paddy for planting. Mom paid people with water buffalo to come and plow our field, and afterward, we spent days pulling weeds out of the broken soil. Most of the weeds were long rooted and grew in clusters which made for a slow and difficult process. Mom always yelled if I just pulled the tops off.

Every day, by late afternoon, our backs were hurting from hours of working bent over. We often sat on one of the dikes between paddies to take a break and our butts would get muddy from sitting in dirt with wet pants.

Once in a while, Mom's back would be hurting so badly that she needed to lie down. All the time we were resting on the dikes, we worried about snakes that were around or bugs getting in our pants. As soon as our backs felt better, we would stand up and get off the ground.

After we had all the weeds pulled from the field, Mom would again hire the people with water buffalo to go over the field with cultivators and break up the soil into a workable condition. Before planting the rice, we went back and pulled any new or regrown weeds.

All rice fields are not treated the same. Depending on their location, some could be planted twice a year. Our field could only be planted once each year, which made it extremely important we got our planting right. Mom would spend all her time and energy in the field because rice was our main source of food for the entire year.

We always saved all the best looking grains of rice from the year before and used them to grow the next season's crop. To get the rice started, Mom soaked three large bags of rice (with the hulls still on) in water all night and then removed them the following morning. The bags of rice were then covered with empty bags or leaves and set out under the sun all day.

Each day for the next three days, Mom soaked the bags in water just long enough to get the rice wet and then placed them back in the sun. After the third day, we could see sprouts coming out through the bags and we knew planting time had come.

Once we were back in our field, Mom filled a bamboo basket with the sprouts and carried them over to one corner of the rice paddy. While holding the basket against her hip with one hand and grabbing a handful of sprouts with the other, Mom began sowing the sprouts thickly and evenly in a large, confined section of the corner. In two and a half months' time, the rice would grow enough to be ready to transplant throughout the remainder of the field.

One of the most important things involved in growing rice is to make sure the water level in the field is just right. When first sowing the sprouts, care had to be given that they remain in contact with the soil by only allowing enough water in the field to keep everything damp. If it rained extremely hard and water covered the sprouts before they developed roots, the sprouts would float to the top and require us to start over. To prevent that from happening, twenty-four hour care was required for the first two weeks after planting.

We controlled the water level by connecting the field to the river using a buried pipe and rolled rice hay mixed with mud to act as a plug. If there was too much water after a heavy rain, we waited until the tide went out and the river was low to let the desired amount of water out by unplugging the pipe. If more water was needed in the field, we waited until the river was up.

Mom watched the field at night by herself and I was always afraid for her. I worried that some crazy man or drunk would try to hurt her and there would be nothing she could do. There were no houses around, only a few mini huts like the one Mom built, and none of those were very close. The huts were made so cheaply that it was almost impossible to lock the door. I continually begged Mom to let me stay overnight with her until she finally gave in to my wishes.

One night, a heavy rain settled in and continued way into the night. Mom was getting very concerned about the water level in the field and I could see her getting stressed out waiting for the river to go down.

With the cloudy skies making it pitch black outside, Mom kept a rain coat ready and would run out to the field every time there was lightning. That was the only time she could see if the river was low enough to remove the plug and drain the field.

I had a difficult time falling asleep that night. The rain and wind were so strong at times, I worried our hut might blow over. Water began running in from under the sides and completely covered the floor. The roof started to leak in several places, making me sit up and search for a place on the bed that wasn't wet.

After curling up and getting cozy in the driest spot I could find, I stared at the flickering light broadcasted from a small oil lamp sitting next to our fire pit. The thought went through my mind that the lamp was almost out of kerosene and soon would be dying. Before I could do anything about it, I fell asleep.

When I woke up in the morning, I could tell it was already daylight by the light shining under the door.

Mom already had the rice cooked, and it smelled so good. The small fire under the pot was almost out and Mom was already out working in the field. Before I could get up, I had to untangle my long hair that had gotten caught in between the bed's bamboo sticks. The bed's uneven, hard surface had given me the worst body ache I'd ever had.

After finally making it out of bed, I removed the lid covering the pot of rice to make sure it was done. Not only was it done, there were also a half dozen okra lying on top of the rice being steamed. It looked delicious! I placed the lid back on the pot and prepared to go outside.

The moment I stepped through the door was unforgettable! What a beautiful morning! What a view! Nature magically transformed itself overnight.

All the trees and vegetation were such a brilliant green, so much greener than the day before. The heavy rain cooled everything down and it felt so good to stand in a puddle of water in my bare feet.

The world around me looked more beautiful than ever. Combining this with the rich smell of damp vegetation, I was left with a feeling that would remain with me forever.

My attention wandered to the sound coming from a large number of frogs croaking nearby. I imagined they were as happy about the new day as I was. I didn't want to move.

Sitting beside me was a bucket filled with fresh rain water. I squatted down and dipped both hands in and splashed the cool water over my face, allowing it to run down my cheeks and neck. The feeling could only be described as heaven on earth.

Rushing back to me at that moment was a memory from the first time I came to our rice paddy:

There was water in a giant hole that looked like it was made just for me.

"Look at this hole; it's perfect!" I had said as I splashed around.

Mom laughed. "That's because it's a bomb crater."

I was small and panicked at the word "bomb." I began screaming and swimming as quickly as I could to get to the bank.

"No, no, no!" Mom explained. "The bomb isn't there anymore. It exploded a long time ago and that's what made the hole. You're safe!"

It took her a few tries to convince me, but finally I decided to stay and swim some more. I was really happy because the water felt so good on my skin.

With my eyes closed and deep in thought, I was startled by the sound of Mom's voice saying, "You shouldn't put your hands in the bucket; that's our drinking water."

I stood up in a hurry and wiped the water from my face. Mom walked over and tied my hair up in a bun while saying, "You really need a haircut."

"No Mom, I want my hair to be long and beautiful."

"Why?"

"Because my hair is the only secret weapon I have," I said with a sheepish smile. "It's going to attract a prince charming who will show up and rescue me from this paddy forever."

"Very funny!" Mom said with a chuckle.

CR∎SO

Two and a half months later, the rice had grown to a height of about one foot and was ready for transplanting. Since the sprouts were sown heavily at the beginning, the plants had grown densely together and needed to be pulled and separated.

As the plants were pulled, they were tied into bundles using dried stems from last year's rice plants. Each bundle was purposely made small so it could be held in one hand so the other hand would be free for transplanting.

All the required work was to be done in two days to ensure the entire field was ready to harvest at the same time. To get the extra help that was needed, Mom asked about ten family members with the promise that she would help them in their fields when the time came.

The worst job we had was the day we pulled all the plants out. The leaves of the rice plant were thin and sharp which made everyone's hands bleed.

There were also a hundred different kinds of bugs that were constantly biting my legs (at least it seemed like a hundred). I would get yelled at for stopping every five minutes to kill bugs and scratch my itchy legs, or for not pulling the plants out the right way.

To treat my bleeding hands, Mom rolled some warm, cooked rice into two balls. She then placed the balls in my hands and told me to make a fist and squeeze.

"I really don't see how that's going to do anything," I said.

"People have been using this trick for a hundred years. Trust me, it works."

We had all the rice plants pulled, bundled and ready to go by lunchtime. To be ready for planting the next day, Mom made arrangements with my brother to come after lunch and distribute the bundles evenly over the entire field. He was stronger than any one of us and could get the job done in half the time.

The following morning, Mom woke up around 3:00 AM to cook a big pot of sticky rice with coconut and yellow beans. It would be a treat at lunch time for everyone that helped.

Around 5:00 AM, she attempted to wake me up several times while running back and forth between the kitchen and our bed in the living room.

By the time I finally managed to wake up, Mom had everything loaded on the boat and was ready to go. Just as we were shoving off from shore, I mentioned how my hands were feeling so much better after being cut the day before.

"I told you so!" she replied.

I hated it when she said that.

We arrived at the field a little after 7:00 AM and none of our help was anywhere in sight. Mom was becoming worried, but, one by one, they all began to show up, each wearing traditional Vietnamese bamboo hats with black pants and long button down shirts.

Along with Mom and the other ladies, I rolled my pants up to the knees as we prepared to step into the flooded paddy and get started.

Mom said I wasn't ready to do any transplanting because I wasn't quick enough. That actually didn't hurt my feelings one bit. Once everyone got started, they'd be bent over and wouldn't have a chance to stand up until lunchtime.

Transplanting rice required a lot of practice and skill. While standing bent over in about six inches of water and holding a bundle of plants in one hand, you removed one plant at a time from the bundle and used your thumb to push the roots of the plant as deeply as possible into the mud. Using your fingers, you then packed mud around the plant to secure it in place. If not done properly, the plant would come loose and float to the surface before the roots had a chance to take hold.

Everyone would line up in a row and work side by side with each worker planting four plants about four inches apart, starting left to right and then right to left. When finished, the worker would step backwards and repeat the process. It was very important that everyone move at the same speed and then step backwards at the same time to prevent a slower worker from stepping on plants just put in by the person on either side of them. Nobody wanted to wait for someone working slowly which kept the pace of the whole process moving along.

My job was to stay with the women and hand out bundles of plants when needed. They all liked me because I made their job a lot easier and most commented to Mom that I was doing a great job.

They all wondered why I wasn't planting and Mom's only reply was that I was in training and should be ready in a couple of years.

It was a truly amazing sight to see all those women planting rice. Their moves were all performed in such a beautiful, quick and uniform manner.

After eating lunch, everyone wanted to lie down out of the sun and give their backs a break. Our little hut didn't have enough room for ten people, so half of the women, including myself, decided to take a ten minute walk over to my uncle's hut. He wasn't around but I knew he wouldn't care if we used his hut for a break.

The fire was almost out under his pot of rice and I couldn't resist lifting the lid to see what else he had cooked. It was full of large chunks of snake. *Yuck!* I quickly replaced the lid. I had eaten snake before but not in pieces that size. The one I had eaten was chopped up really fine.

Everyone lay on the dirt floor to rest.

The city girl side of me went on full display when I began complaining, "My legs itch, I hate my pants being wet, and I also hate those stupid bugs!"

"You're spoiled! You have nothing to really complain about!" my older sister snapped at me. "You should have been working in the rice paddy right after the war; you would have cried every day!"

"Why?" I asked. "How could it have been any worse than this?"

"I'll tell you how. There were leeches all through the rice paddies back then. They'd get on your legs, suck your blood and wouldn't let go. The only way I knew to get them off was by dumping salt on them."

Once everyone had rested their backs, we went right back into the field and continued planting.

Late in the afternoon as the sun was beginning to set, everyone's spirits improved from knowing we'd all be going home soon.

Mom made sure nobody quit until the entire field was planted. My aunt complained about having young children at home that were too young to build a fire for cooking and were probably hungry. She also worried about feeding her chickens and ducks before they went to bed.

Finally, just as the last plant was placed in the soil, Mom called it a day.

Almost everyone went home in boats, but my aunt and two others walked back in their bare feet. They would walk through or around many rice paddies on their way, plus wade across a couple of deep streams with chest-high water.

Watching them walk so fast, rushing to get home after a long day, made me scared to realize how that could be me someday. I doubled my attempts to avoid all country boys from that moment on.

The following morning, a few of the rice plants were floating on top of the water, so Mom and I went all through the field replanting them.

A month later, as the rice was beginning to really take off, the weeds had started growing extremely well also. It was a very uncomfortable job pulling out the weeds when you had to stand in water up to your knees and the rice plants poked you in the face every time you bent over. It was even worse early in the morning when the dew was still on the plants and it made your face all wet and itchy.

While the rice was growing, the paddy became Mom's life. Between pulling weeds, spraying for insects or regulating the water level, it consumed most of her time.

If there was a good amount of rain during the season, the rice always did well and that made everyone happy.

During the periods when there was a lack of rain or too many bugs were eating the plants, the entire field would begin turning brown.

Everyone would start to worry during those times, especially Mom.

I worried not only about a shortage of rice to eat, but also because we always harvested the rice right before the New Year. If the rice did poorly, we wouldn't have extra money to celebrate.

Mom was quite the rice farmer. She always knew when it was time to harvest. When ready, the plants took on a certain shade of golden brown. The rice grains formed in clusters at the top of each stem, similar to wheat plants.

To harvest, we used a special knife that was made in the shape of a "C" to cut all the plants off at about five to ten inches above the roots, depending on how tall the rice was. To keep the clusters of rice from getting wet, Mom showed me how to take the plants I just cut and lay them across the top of the stubs of previously cut plants.

To separate the grains of rice from the plants, we had a wood box built on top of a small sleigh that one person could pull around the field while keeping the box up and out of the water. The box had what looked like a miniature ladder that angled up from the bottom and rested on top of an end wall. The remaining three walls were extended upwards with a woven bamboo curtain to keep the rice grains from flying out.

Taking a handful of plants while holding them at the cut end, we'd swing the plants over our shoulder and slap the rice clusters over the ladder. You had to swing the rice plants several times, as hard as you could, before all the rice grains would fall off.

My brother would do most of this work because he was much stronger than the rest of us. Every so often, I had to stop cutting and go help him empty the rice from the wood box into bags. We threw the rice straw into a big pile off to the side and laid the filled rice bags on the straw pile to keep them dry. After several bags were filled, I'd help my brother place a bag over his shoulder, and one at a time, he carried them over to the boat and stacked them.

I attempted to carry a bag myself one time but kept falling down in the slippery field. It was too heavy.

By the end of the day, our little boat was stacked full. With my brother sitting in the back and me up front, we paddled while Mom and my younger sister sat in the middle, on top of the bags.

I always worried our boat would flip over every time the wind picked up or a large boat went by. With Mom not knowing how to swim, it only made things more stressful.

Soon after arriving home, my brother carried all the bags of rice into the house and emptied them onto the living room floor to let it air dry. When the weather was good and the ground was dry, we moved the rice outside to dry under the hot sun.

Sometimes the drying process took a little longer if a rain storm moved in quickly and we didn't have time to gather the rice into a pile and cover it.

Some of the wealthier neighbors made a cement pad in front of their homes just for drying rice.

We dried ours on the bare ground and some of the rice would always fall into the cracks that were formed when the dirt dried under the sun.

To avoid this, Mom would ask a neighbor for a bucket full of fresh buffalo feces. She added some water and stirred the mixture with one of her feet, going up and down inside the bucket.

"Yuck! Why don't you use a wood stick to mix that up?" I asked.

"This is how your grandfather always did it," was all she replied.

Mom poured the mixture onto the ground and used a broom made from a coconut branch to sweep it back and forth. After letting it dry, she repeated the process one more time, making it smell horribly around the house for a while. This process was repeated every single year.

Once the rice was completely dry, we stored it in the back room of our house in a large woven bamboo container. Mom knew exactly how much rice we needed to last all year and if there was any extra, we were sure to have a good year by selling the surplus.

Every two to three months, we'd take a few bags of rice to the local mill and have the outer husks and bran removed from the kernel.

The trip to the rice mill would usually turn into an all-day event. Most of the time, there was a line of people waiting, and it gave everyone a chance to socialize with members of the community they hadn't seen for a while.

The thing I remember most about being there was the loud noise of the milling machine and all the dust created inside the building.

As our rice was being processed, the kernels and bran were bagged separately right at the milling machine while the husks were blown into a pile located in a separate room. Since the mill owners wouldn't allow anyone to take more than three bags of husks for every five bags of rice brought in, Mom watched carefully to make sure each of our bags was fully stuffed.

Working slowly, I'd dump a small amount of husks into the bag and then stop to pack it down tightly with my hands.

After a few times of doing this, I'd fold the top of the bag over and step on the bag to pack the husks down even tighter by using my entire body weight. This process was repeated several times until the bag was full. Instead of stopping a little short to leave room for tying the bag off, Mom made me continue until the husks were close to the top.

At that point, she would reach into her pocket and pull out a needle with some strong thread to sew the bag partially shut. Even though the top wasn't sealed off tightly, nothing would fall out as long as the bag remained upright during the trip back home.

The husks by themselves could be used in a fire pit to burn for cooking or they could be mixed with ashes to clean the outside of pots and pans that turned black after sitting over an open fire. The husks mixed with the bran and a little water was used for duck feed and the bran by itself mixed with water was used for pig feed. The chickens would only eat the husks that had a kernel of rice inside or just the kernel itself.

If nothing else, I learned to never let anything, no matter how small or insignificant, go to waste.

Chapter Twenty-One

Months after quitting school and working in the rice paddy, Mom finally let me take a day off to go to town.

That morning, I walked out to the main path and saw several girls riding by on bicycles, wearing black pants and green shirts. They all looked so happy and I couldn't stop wondering what was going on.

After walking half way to town, I heard a voice call out from behind me, "Trang! Trang!"

I turned and smiled, pleased to see two old classmates of mine with a group of girls from school. They were all dressed in the same black pants and green shirts.

"Oh my goodness! What are all of you doing in those uniforms?" I asked. "Did you guys quit school, also?"

"Yeah. We had to quit for the same reason as you," one of my classmates answered. "We're all working in a large shrimp factory now."

"Where?" I asked. "Are they hiring?"

"Up in Saigon. The factory is called Tom Dong Lanh Hung Vuong. They just opened a few months ago and are still hiring, but today is the last day they're taking applications. You better hurry and get up there. Hundreds of girls have already applied."

For the next few minutes, we all mingled together, tapping each other on the shoulders and grabbing each other's arms as a way of showing we missed each other. (Most Vietnamese don't give hugs or use the words, "I miss you" or "I love you". We find it too embarrassing.)

Saying our goodbyes, I turned around and headed for home to pick up some items I needed for the job application. I was grateful my friends told me about the shrimp factory. I really wanted this job. It would be so nice to earn some money again to help Mom.

My uncle was working outside and saw me walking by. He stopped picking okra for a second and yelled, "You back from town already?" He seemed surprised.

"No, I never made it there," I answered while continuing down the path. "I ran into some friends and they told me about a job. I need to hurry home and get ready."

I felt bad running off like that; normally, I would stop and talk to him. But I knew he would understand.

I took my usual shortcut by walking through Grandma's house. She was sitting on her kitchen floor cooking rice and I hoped I could make it through without her seeing me. Just as I reached the back door I heard, "Is that you, Trang? "

"Yes, Grandma, it's me."

"Are you back from town already?"

"No Grandma, I never made it there. I hate to run off but I'm in a hurry and need to get some stuff from home. I'll tell you about everything later. OK?"

I rushed home and walked straight to the wood cabinet where I knew Mom kept all our important papers. I needed to have copies made of my birth certificate and family ID.

With everything in hand, I hurried over to my secret corner in the back room and removed some old rags covering my piggy bank. So many times, I wanted to take a little money out of that piggy but didn't want to break it trying. I knew they purposely designed the banks so it was only easy to put money in.

Being in a big hurry, I broke the bank without thinking twice and gathered all the money, leaving the broken pieces scattered on the floor.

As I started the long trip to town again, I became angry with myself for letting my sister borrow my bicycle earlier that day. I didn't have much time to waste and walking seemed to take forever.

After crossing the river by ferry and walking through the market, I went directly to the only place that would take and develop my pictures immediately. I had heard rumors that the guy owning the business liked to harass young girls, so I stood at the door for a few moments, being too scared to go in.

I touched the handle of the heavy wooden door several times while trying to build up my courage.

Suddenly, it opened toward me and I took two steps back to keep from being hit. Right in front of me stood a tall, middle aged man. He had a large camera hanging from his neck and it looked as if he was just leaving to go take pictures somewhere.

He simply stood in the doorway, staring at me and said nothing.

"Can I get my picture taken?" I quickly asked.

"Um, what kind do you need?"

"I need two small pictures, the kind for a job application."

"All right, come on in," he replied while holding the door open for me to enter. "I'll stay and do it just for you." He gave me an odd looking smile.

Oh gosh, what if he is a bad guy, I thought. I didn't like that strange smirk, but I needed my pictures.

My heart was beating rapidly in my chest as I stepped into the house. We walked down a hallway, past a couple of rooms filled with pictures hanging everywhere, before reaching a room set up to take pictures.

Breaking the silence, he said, "Sit there and I'll be with you in a second." He pointed at a chair sitting in front of a cloth background.

I was too paranoid to say anything.

"Why do you look so scared?" he asked with a puzzled tone.

"I'm not!" I said, shaking my head.

Once he had his camera ready, he took my picture and said, "It'll be ready in an hour."

"Ok, I'll be back." I left the room and headed for the front door as fast as possible while resisting the urge to run.

After going outside, I breathed a sigh of relief.

Suddenly, I felt guilty for treating the guy like a criminal. He didn't do anything to me.

After picking up my pictures and making copies of my birth certificate and family ID, my next step was to walk to the police station and have everything notarized. It would take me two hours to accomplish this and make it to a bus stop, and I began to worry about getting to the city before 5:00 PM.

While walking to the station, I decided to hurry things along by running. Any hopes of making good time came quickly to a halt when rain began pouring down and turned the dirt road into a muddy mess.

Finally, after getting everything completed and making it back to town, I went directly to the section where buses always parked.

Sitting on the bus, waiting to leave, I counted the money in my pocket to make sure there was enough for the bus fare. I was hungry and thirsty but wouldn't dare buy anything.

When the bus arrived at the factory, I was in awe of the size and beauty of the building. I couldn't wait to go inside. Getting off the bus, I ran straight to the factory door and reached to pull it open.

"Stop! Stop!" A security guard shouted at me. "You can't go in there!"

"Why? " I asked as panic set in.

"You need to be wearing dress clothes. Mainly black dress pants. Hurry up, you only have thirty minutes until we close."

"Oh no! I live far away in the country and will never make it back in time!"

I stood there hoping he would feel sorry for me and let me in, but he remained firm. I walked away from the guard but still wasn't ready to give up and go home.

There has to be a way, I thought. *Maybe I could walk to the market and buy a cheap pair of pants*, but quickly realized I didn't have enough money.

Closing my eyes, I tried to remember if Mom or Grandma had ever told me about a relative who lived in this area.

Unable to think of anyone, a wave of sadness swept over me and I began to think there was nothing more that could be done.

Suddenly, after opening my eyes, my hope was restored. Sitting just a few feet away from me was a girl selling cigarettes on the side walk. She was wearing black dress pants! Taking a deep breath, I walked towards the girl and she stood up to get ready to make a sale.

"Sorry, I don't need any cigarettes, but was wondering if you could help me?" I pointed toward the security guard and told her what had just happened. "Would you consider trading pants with me?"

She didn't say anything for almost a full minute; she just stared at me with a look of disbelief.

"Follow me," she finally said while motioning toward the house sitting directly behind her. "I know the people who live there."

The door was unlocked and I followed her into the kitchen area. There was a middle-aged woman and two guys who looked to be in their twenties sitting at a table, eating. They spoke Chinese to the girl I was with and I became nervous not knowing a word they were saying.

As soon as they finished talking, the woman got up, walked out of the room and returned with a pair of black dress pants in her hand. She handed them to me.

The girl selling cigarettes pointed to the bathroom and said I could change my pants in there and walked out of the house.

The woman and two guys kept on speaking Chinese to each other so I didn't say a word, not even "thank you".

I made sure to leave my pants in their bathroom so they would know I was coming back.

With the black dress pants on, I went back to the shrimp factory as quickly as I could.

At the door, the security guard stopped me again. Feeling completely confused, I just stared at him for a moment.

"Why am I not allowed to go in?" I finally asked. "I'm wearing black dress pants just like you said."

"Because you lied to me! You said you lived far away, and now you're back this quick?"

"No, no, no!" I tried to explain, but he wouldn't listen.

"I don't appreciate you lying to me," he said among other things I didn't hear as I desperately tried to explain.

I wouldn't give up. "But I—"

The guard wouldn't back down either. "No buts about it. You said you lived far away and couldn't get back in time. Then you return just a few minutes later. That kind of dishonesty isn't welcomed here. You need to leave."

I was very upset that he would not let me explain, but I had no choice. As I hung my head and turned to go, I heard a young woman's voice say, "Excuse me."

I looked up to see the girl who had been selling cigarettes that had helped me. "I think I can clear things up."

The guard listened as she told him the story and reassured him I was not a liar.

He hesitated a minute, then looked down at me and said, "You got lucky. Go ahead and go inside."

I graciously thanked the girl for coming to my defense and stepped through the door with a great sense of relief.

After a short interview, I was hired on the spot along with several other girls. It was so exciting to have a real job for the first time ever. Not only did I get a chance to get away from working in the rice paddies, I also gained some freedom to visit my boyfriend without Mom ever knowing.

ୠ▪ஐ

Every day, I pedaled my bicycle two hours each way to get to and from work. I'd leave the house at 5:00 AM, sometimes earlier if it was raining, and come home at 9:00 PM. Once in a while, I wouldn't get home until midnight after working over and there was no way I could let Mom know about being late.

This worried her a lot, so most nights, she'd walk to the ferry landing and wait for me. The ferry only operated until midnight but if you needed to cross the river later than that, you could yell for the owners who lived along the river and they'd come and pick you up.

After a couple of weeks, I began to work late all the time. Mom wasn't pleased at all about that and came up with an idea to help me out. She took a bus into the city to talk with the monks at the Buddhist temple, the same one that kept my brother during the war. As soon as Mom explained my situation, the monks permitted me to stay overnight at the temple whenever I needed.

After a long day working with shrimp, I smelled terribly, especially my hair and clothes. One day before going to the temple, I wanted to stop at an open market to buy a bar of soap that could make the smell go away. Back home, Mom always bought the cheapest soap she could find, sometimes we even had to do without.

Everyone always told me that anything from America or France was the best and the bar soap that was especially good was a name brand called "Zest". One of my cousins used to tell me how Zest was used only on special occasions and was considered to be one of the best gifts you could give because of its wonderful fragrance.

Stopping at the first soap vendor at the market, I was amazed at how many different kinds of bar soap there were and how great they all smelled. I found myself looking at them for the longest time while trying to make the big decision of which one to buy, until I found out the price. Each bar cost almost one dollar, which would take me two days of work to earn.

I shopped around at several different vendors until I finally bought a bar of Zest.

I was so grateful for the monks at the Buddhist temple; they always treated me like family, especially the head monk who stayed there full time. He was a very kind and gentle person but I was always too afraid to talk to him. All I could do was stare at his bald head and the strange orange outfit he wore.

Spending the first night at the temple was a little scary and I had a hard time falling asleep. The room given to me was an old unlit storage room all the way in the back and was cleaned out by the monks just before my arrival.

Lying wide awake on a hard wooden bed having no mattress, the sounds from moments earlier of monks chanting while tapping on a small bell were fresh in my mind. It reminded me of the stories my brother used to tell us about his stay at the temple during the war. The story that stood out the most was about people bringing ashes of a deceased family member to the temple for keeping.

Just thinking about those ashes created an overwhelming fear in me, and I tried focusing my attention on anything else. I strained to hear the familiar sounds of the street outside or anything I could grab ahold of to find comfort. There was nothing but complete silence.

Convinced the temple was haunted with spirits, I got up and went to the front to burn incense and pray. Noticing small vases sitting around everywhere, I couldn't help but wonder if that was where everyone's ashes were stored.

After finishing my prayers, I wandered around, looking at the statues of Buddha, all looking so peaceful. It wasn't long before it was almost impossible to keep my eyes open and I returned to my room. Within seconds after lying down, I fell asleep.

From that day on, each time I stayed at the temple, it became less and less frightening until it actually became a peaceful place to be in.

I earned about fifteen dollars a month, depending on the shrimp season. Sometimes I made a little more, and sometimes less. I was very happy to have such a large amount of money coming in every month. Working in the rice paddies, I received nothing except for what Mom would give me from time to time.

When I received my first pay check, I was overcome with joy. The first thing I did with the money was stop at the market on my way home and buy Grandma a large bag of sugar. I was so excited, I couldn't peddle my bike fast enough.

Grandma was sitting on her living room floor, smashing Trau Cau in a small metal tube. (Also known as betel nuts. It's an areca nut wrapped in betel leaves and is used like chewing tobacco.) After losing most of her teeth over the years, she couldn't chew anything hard and needed to soften the nuts up. Along with not having teeth, her eyes were getting worse every day and she could no longer see very well.

Grandma was in tears when I handed her the bag of sugar. "Oh thank you! Thank you!" She said. "But wait! Don't leave yet. I'll only keep some of it and you can take the rest home."

"No, Grandma, I bought that just for you."

"But, Trang, this is a lot of sugar. It must have cost you a lot of money."

That's the way Grandma always was. She made a habit of sharing everything.

Mom came home from the rice paddy a short time later and I was so happy to give her some money. "This is all yours!" I said with an excited voice while placing half of my pay in her hand.

"Are you sure? You might not have enough for yourself. You're going to need money for the ferry and food every day."

As I handed her the money, I noticed Mom was really happy, even though she did her best to hide her emotions. I always felt that the way Mom dealt with carrying all the responsibility for our family was to present herself as being hard and strong.

"Don't worry, Mom, I'll be fine," I said.

It turned out that Mom was right. I was short of money before my next payday. After paying for the ferry twice a day when I came home and buying an extra meal on the nights I stayed in the city, it all started to add up. I did everything to keep from asking Mom for some of the money back.

Many nights when I stayed at the Buddhist temple, I rode my bike around the city trying to find the cheapest food for dinner. One night I stopped at a vendor along the street to buy a "banh mi thit" (sub sandwich). (The twelve inch sub is made with French bread, specially prepared pork meat, a special sauce and vegetables.)

I saw the vendor had many loaves of French bread stacked in a large bamboo basket sitting beside a cart with a glass cabinet sitting on top. All the meat and vegetables were stored inside the cabinet. The subs were all priced differently, depending on how much meat people wanted in them.

"How many sandwiches do you need?" The lady asked as soon as I jumped off my bike.

"Um...can I buy just one fourth of a sub?" I asked.

Shaking her head, the lady said, "No, we don't sell any that small. How about half of a sub?"

"No, thanks anyhow," I said and rode my bike away.

After stopping at the third vendor, I got lucky. The lady sold me one fourth of a sub and she cut it in a sharp angle so it looked a lot longer.

I was starving! I parked between two street vendors to eat while sitting on my bike. After taking the last bite, I so wished I could have afforded to buy a whole one. That was the best sub I ever remember eating.

One thing I realized early was, if I ever wanted the whole sub—or anything else in life, I was going to have to learn to budget my money a little better.

Chapter Twenty-Two

In 1990, Mom received good news. Lien, her younger sister living in America, was coming home to visit. Mom hadn't seen her since 1973, the year Lien left for America to marry her fiancé. She met him while he was serving in the US Air Force at Tan Son Nhut Air Base in Saigon.

For the first two years after leaving for America, Lien and her family stayed in touch on a regular basis by mail. In 1975, Lien began making arrangements to fly back home for a visit when the war came to an end and everything changed. All flights and communication with Viet Nam were immediately cut off.

For fourteen years, Lien continued writing to family and friends but never received a single reply. Finally, in 1989, one of her letters made it through and reached one of her cousins.

Lien could barely contain her excitement when she opened her mailbox door and saw the letter from Viet Nam lying inside. Overwhelmed by the good news that everyone in the family was doing well, she read her cousin's reply again and again.

After quickly sending out a letter addressed to her mother, Lien began wondering if it was possible to return to Viet Nam for a visit. She kept watching the news, hoping to learn if it was safe for her to return.

One day, a customer came into her place of employment and talked about a Vietnamese friend who made the trip with no trouble. Lien began making telephone calls to several different travel agents. She was informed by many that relations between the US and Vietnamese governments had improved greatly and it was now safe to return.

⚬▪⚬

When Lien left Viet Nam, my grandma never stopped thinking about her. When the letters stopped coming in 1975, she kept waiting year after year to hear from her daughter. Just to know she was OK, would have been enough. Grandma continually prayed for Lien's wellbeing and dreamed that somehow, someway, my aunt would find a way to come home. Grandma knew all her dreams were coming true the moment she received word of my aunt's letter.

On a very exciting day in August 1990, Mom and several family members went to the airport to pick up Aunt Lien. Being able to go to the airport was a really big deal for everyone, but Grandma rented only one small bus and there wasn't enough room for me. Mom spent the entire day with my aunt at Grandma's house while my younger sister and I waited for our older sisters to come home so we could all go visit together.

"You take too long to get ready!" Quyen yelled at me.

"I just want to look nice for Aunt Lien. I bet she looks beautiful!"

"I know. I bet her skin is really light since being in America."

"What do you think her clothes will look like?" I wondered out loud. "And will she still be nice, or will she think she's better than us because she's an American now?"

When my older sisters finally arrived, we continued talking as we walked to Grandma's house. The hard rains had come the night before and muddied our path, so the normal thirty minute walk took about an hour.

"Do you remember her at all?" Quyen asked.

I shook my head. "No. I was only two years old when she left and you weren't born yet. Mom always said you look like her."

When my sisters and I arrived at Grandma's house, we didn't even get a chance to wash our muddy feet off before Aunt Lien came running out the door and gave each of us a hug. It was the first hug we had ever had.

She was very nice and funny. Since she couldn't speak Vietnamese very well, my Aunt laughed a lot and sometimes mixed English and Vietnamese together in the same sentence.

Everyone found it a little difficult to understand her but we still enjoyed listening to her stories about America.

"What kind of job do you have there?" I asked.

She told us she *was* working at a store in a shopping mall that made cookies, but when she asked for time off to visit her family in Viet Nam, her boss refused to give it to her. Aunt Lien said she was forced to quit.

"You mean you don't have a job anymore? What will you do? Will you have to work in the rice paddies like we do?"

Aunt Lien laughed and, in her broken Vietnamese, explained, "Don't worry, Trang. There aren't any rice paddies where I live in America. There's corn, soy beans, oats and wheat fields. And some of the farms are huge! They go on and on for miles!"

"How does a family take care of that?" Quyen asked.

"They have big machines," Aunt Lien explained. "The machines pick the corn and such and throw it into a big box on wheels and carry it to the barns."

We tried our hardest to imagine what she was talking about but couldn't. We just sat there with our mouths gaped open, waiting to hear more.

"No, I won't be working on a farm," she went on. "I have a job that's waiting for me when I go back. It's a place called McDonald's."

"Oh!" everyone said together.

I spoke up and asked what we were all thinking. "What is a McDonald's?"

"It's a restaurant where they serve hamburgers and French fries."

She could tell by the look on our faces we were still lost.

She tried to explain better. "You get beef from cows. . ."

Quyen interrupted, "Are there many cows in America?"

"Yes, lots of them. Some farmers raise them for their milk and others for their meat."

"You mean they have *two* or *three*?" I asked.

"Hundreds," Aunt Lien explained.

We all gasped. None of us could imagine owning hundreds of cows. In Viet Nam, only the richest people owned cattle, and then they usually only owned one.

The more Aunt Lien tried to explain what things were like where she lived, the more confused we became. Between her poor Vietnamese and our lack of knowledge, we ended up with some pretty funny ideas about America. The entire family eventually broke into uncontrollable laughter trying to figure things out.

When we were done laughing, Aunt Lien stood up and said "Hey! Let's go outside. I want to take everyone's picture."

We all followed her to the front of the house. There were about thirty of us, including several small kids.

Before Aunt Lien started, I asked, "Could you take a picture of just my sisters and me together?"

"Sure!" she replied. "I'll take as many pictures as you like."

All four of us lined up in order. No one in our family ever owned a camera before, so it was the first time we would have our picture taken together. To hear we could take more than one picture was a dream come true.

Left to right – Chi Ba, Chi Tu, Myself, and Quyen

I remembered one time during the New Year, there was a photographer walking around our neighborhood and he stopped at my uncle's house while Mom and I were there. I wanted to have a picture taken of me so badly that I started begging Mom to let me have just one.

Mom said, "No!" after finding out how much each picture cost.

I continued asking Mom at least a dozen more times, but she kept refusing.

I didn't give up but the camera man did. He walked away after he figured out Mom wasn't going to give in. My heart broke as I watched him go. I kept hoping she would change her mind, but she never did.

In almost twenty years of my life, I had never seen as much food at Grandma's house as there was since my aunt had come home. Because she hadn't eaten any true Vietnamese food for such a long time, Aunt Lien would buy all the different kinds of food she liked by the dozen.

One day, I went shopping in the city with her along with some of my cousins. Aunt Lien rented a three wheel bus with a driver. After much shopping, the bus was full of food but my aunt insisted on making one more stop. While everyone else went shopping with her, I stayed behind to keep an eye on everything loaded on the bus. My aunt told me I could eat anything I liked, so I began sampling a little of each food I had been so hungry for. For some reason, I still looked over my shoulder every so often thinking someone was going to yell at me.

Growing up, I always heard that America was the richest country in the world, and now I believed it. Whenever Aunt Lien would start running low on money, she would exchange $100 USD's for almost two million Vietnamese Dong. It was a large stack of money. Most people in Viet Nam at that time made no more than fifty cents (US) a day. That made my aunt the richest woman in our area.

Chapter Twenty-Three

There always seemed to be some excitement in my family. A few months after Lien had returned to America, the focus turned to my younger sister. Quyen had turned eighteen and was preparing to marry a man Mom had chosen for her.

Quyen's engagement party at our old home

Ewww! I said to myself. *I want to pick out my own husband.*

Mom was very unhappy with me because I was older and should have been married first. She was constantly giving me a hard time because she knew I was still seeing my boyfriend, even after she told me I wasn't allowed.

The biggest problem was with my boyfriend's mother. She didn't accept me and wouldn't allow us to be married. (No one in Viet Nam at that time was able to get married without the parents' approval.)

While I kept waiting for her to change her mind, many people had been coming to our house trying to fix me up with someone who they thought would be a good husband for me.

During one of those visits, a woman I didn't know wanted to arrange a marriage with the son of one of her friends. The boy's parents asked this woman to talk with Mom because they were aware she knew Mom and thought they would have a better chance if she did the asking.

When the woman came into the house, I bowed my head to say "Hello" to her. I immediately walked to the kitchen to make some hot tea, because that was a common courtesy given to anyone who stopped at the house to visit.

The woman had a loud voice and I could hear almost everything they were talking about. "My friend's son would make a wonderful husband for Trang," she told Mom. She went on to describe the good qualities of the young man and his family.

I was sick to my stomach, worrying Mom would agree to this.

I breathed a sigh of relief when she replied, "I need to think about it and will get back with you later."

That's when the woman commented, "It's not a good thing to let your child pick their own husband or wife; they're too young to know better." She continued, "Many of the girls I helped arrange marriages for all have better lives. That is why I wanted to help.''

After listening to all this, I just wanted this woman to leave! With proper respect, I served them the hot tea and quickly sneaked out of the house. I ran over to the neighbor's to hide and avoid talking to Mom after that woman was done with her visit.

A little while later, Mom started yelling my name, wanting me to come home. The neighbor's house was far enough away that I couldn't hear her. My cousin heard Mom from her house, so she ran over to where I was to tell me. I thanked her and ran home as fast as I could.

"Why did you run off like that?" Mom said with a scolding voice. "I need to go to the market to buy some bug spray for the rice field. Make sure you stay home!"

I felt so relieved. "OK, Mom," I said, still breathing hard from running so fast.

Mom headed for the door and then suddenly turned around. "That woman who came to visit a little while ago. . ." Mom started to say.

Oh no! I thought, while giving Mom a "please don't" look while rolling my eyes.

Mom continued, "She wants to fix you up. So don't give me that look! You're twenty years old and not a kid any more. You need to start thinking about a husband or you'll end up being an old maid."

I just listened and said nothing.

After Mom left, I didn't move. I just stood, looking out at the river, feeling so depressed.

Mom was right. Most girls my age were already married. I was getting older and my clock was ticking.

I started getting angry again at Tung's mother for not letting me marry her son. He'd been my boyfriend for the last four years and I was madly in love.

He kept telling me, "Just hang in there. I'll keep bugging my mother until she lets me marry you. I *promise*, we will be together. I just need more time."

And so I waited and waited, and every day I prayed for good news. Little did I know, my whole world was about to change again.

CR■SO

When the mailman came to our house and handed me a letter, I was thrilled beyond belief. We rarely received any mail, maybe once every three years if we were lucky.

I thought, *Our envelopes are so thin and cheap looking, but this one was nice and thick!* I started running to the house screaming, "Mom! Mom! We got a letter from Aunt Lien!"

"Sign this paper please!" the mailman yelled while running after me.

As soon as the mailman left, I opened the letter as fast as I could and began reading it to Mom. (Never attending school when she was growing up, Mom never learned how to read.)

Aunt Lien's written words were as chaotic as her speech. I had a hard time figuring out the letter. One part, however, was very clear: she wanted to know if I would be willing to leave my home and come to America to marry a guy there.

I started thinking how cool it would be to go to America, but at the same time it felt so scary. Just to learn how to speak English would be so amazing.

Plus, I had a boyfriend, and I wouldn't leave him for anything.

Mom knew how I felt. It was easy to tell she really liked what my aunt was asking, just by the way she was smiling.

I gave her the look again. "Oh, no. Don't even think about it!" I handed Mom the letter and walked away.

A week later, the mailman delivered another letter, but this time I wasn't home. Mom had my younger sister read it to her.

As soon as I came home and walked through the door, I heard, "Trang! Trang!"

I turned and saw Mom walking toward me really fast while holding a letter. I'd never seen my Mother looking that excited before.

She handed me the letter and made sure I knew there was a picture inside.

"Wow! A picture of an American guy," I said.

"He's good looking and seems to be the kind of guy that's down to earth, you know," Mom said.

"Mother, that's real funny! Did you see his hair?" I asked.

Mom didn't say a word.

"His hair is long! Don't you remember? You never liked guys with long hair!"

"But he's an **American!**" Mom answered.

"I can't believe you just said that," I said while rolling my eyes. "Look at the picture, he isn't even smiling. But I do love his light hair and skin."

"Ok! Hurry up and read the letter," Mom said.

In the letter, my aunt was serious about wanting me to come to America. She wrote that after returning to Ohio, she and her husband went to visit some good friends and showed them all the pictures she had taken in Viet Nam.

After listening to Aunt Lien's stories about her family and what life was like in Viet Nam, her friend asked if he could keep the picture of my sisters and me. He said he wanted to show it to his youngest brother, Jay, the next time he came back to visit from his home in western New York State.

Two weeks later, Jay returned to Ohio to visit his parents and stopped to see his oldest brother.

His sister in-law met him at the door with a huge smile and said, "Jay, guess what? We found you a wife." She then handed him the photograph she was holding.

"Oh great! That's *just* what I need," Jay sarcastically replied.

His brother and sister in-law told him all about Lien's trip to Viet Nam and explained that the four girls in the picture were Lien's nieces. They said he could pick out the one he liked and that maybe he could at least correspond with her.

Jay slipped the picture into his pocket and took it with him when he left. A few days later, he phoned his brother and said that he was interested in the girl "second from the right" in the picture, the one with long hair and holding a comb. He said he would return to Ohio in a week and asked to meet with Lien to learn more about her niece.

After Aunt Lien and her husband, Raymond, met with Jay, my aunt explained the name of the girl he was interested in was Trang.

After a long conversation about me, my family, and the country of Viet Nam, Jay became even more interested in knowing about me.

He asked Lien to write to me and make sure I was interested in meeting him before letting things go any further.

Lien said she would write a letter and get it in the mail as soon as possible. She then asked Jay to sit on the steps inside her house and took a Polaroid photograph of him to send along with it.

After reading my aunt's letter, I was shocked and didn't know whether I should be happy or cry. I would love to go to America, but I already had a boyfriend whom I'd been in love with for over four years.

While I was not sure what to think, Mom's eyes were lighting up. She clapped her hands and said, "You are so lucky!"

She was right, and I knew it. Yet I walked away and said nothing.

While growing up, I watched my brother and two of my sisters have their marriages arranged. They had to listen to Mom. I just wanted to be different, and it scared me to think I wouldn't be able to change that.

Mom was a very strong woman. She always had a way to make us listen. It scared me just thinking about her not giving up, and just like my brother and sisters, I would also give in. One by one, each listened to her about the person they would marry.

During the next few days, Mom wouldn't leave me alone. She kept following me around and constantly nagging me. "I can't believe you don't want to go to America!" she'd say. "There are a million girls out there that would love to go but can't. I want you to go so you can have a better life."

"Mother, I can't do that!" I'd always say.

Mom knew the reason why, but kept asking anyway.

"Why won't you go?"

I didn't answer because I knew what she'd say. I tried to walk away, but Mom ran after me, preaching.

"I know you're waiting for your boyfriend, Tung. Don't you remember? His mother doesn't want you marrying him! If Tung's mother never changes her mind, does that mean you have to give up your life? She's the kind of person that would always look down on you and be disrespectful to our family. You need to think hard about this, and don't wait until it's too late. An opportunity like this often comes only once!"

Mom was right. I became really angry again at Tung's mother for not coming to the house and talking to Mom about marriage. If she had, he and I would have been married already.

Nobody I knew ever got married without their parents' approval. That stupid tradition had killed so many hopes and dreams of many couples in love. It made no sense to me. I'd already asked myself a hundred times, "Why can't my boyfriend and I just get married without his parents' approval?"

A couple of weeks later, Mom demanded I reply to my aunt's letter. Since Mom couldn't read or write, I could write whatever I wanted, and not what she wanted.

I wrote the letter to my aunt, telling her, "I liked Jay's picture, he seems like a good guy, but I can't come to America." I didn't tell her why I couldn't come because I didn't want to say anything about having a boyfriend. Mom would kill me if Aunt Lien found out.

"Did you send a letter to your aunt yet?" Mom asked. "And what did you tell her?"

"Yeah, I sent it. I didn't say much."

I could tell Mom wasn't happy with my answer by the look on her face. I felt horrible. We didn't talk for the rest of the evening.

Mom was very quiet for a few days. *Maybe she gave up on the idea*, I thought.

Just as I was starting to feel better, Mom suddenly began preaching again when I came home from work. This time, she teamed up with both of my older sisters. I should have known better; Mom never gave up that easily.

My sisters were trying their hardest to explain about the hard lives they had. They were both complaining, "Look at us, we're broke, poor, and trapped. We don't have much freedom because we live in the same houses with our mother in-laws. We'll be their slaves for a very long time. We were very unlucky, marrying into a family that only had one son, so we'll never have a chance to move out. That's just the way it is, and you can't get out of it. Unless, you go to America!"

They both stood there looking at me as I gave them an ugly look.

My sister, Chi Tu, continued, "If I were you, I'd go to America. I hear they are the richest country and the people have a lot of freedom. Women don't have to remain in the kitchen and eat with other women only!"

"Whatever! My boyfriend has brothers younger and older than he, so none of that applies to me! Nice try, anyhow." I turned around and ran off to Grandma's house.

When I returned home, Mom met me at the door. "You have to write another letter to your aunt! This time, you better do it right!" she demanded.

I began to panic. I didn't know what to write. I wanted to tell Aunt Lien about me having a boyfriend, but that might not work.

What if she asks me to breakup with my boyfriend just as Mom did? I asked myself.

Maybe I should lie, I thought. *I could tell her I'm sick with some kind of disease, but what kind? I heard that America was very strict about not letting anyone with certain diseases come into their country. How about tuberculosis?*

That sounded good, so that's what I wrote.

Lying is something I grew up with. Most people I knew lied all the time. I guess it was one of the ways everyone survived in the tough world we lived in. Before trusting anyone, we always made them swear to never repeat what was said or done. Sometimes I got yelled at by family members and friends for being honest.

I became scared as I made up the story in the letter. I never made one up this big before. I worried Mom would kill me if she knew what I did, but that didn't stop me. I felt sick after sending the letter. I hoped that when my aunt received the bad news, it would be the end of it.

Instead of solving my problem, it became worse. My aunt wrote back telling me that she had talked to Jay, and he learned from a reliable source that my disease was treatable and not a problem.

Oh no! My letter wasn't working. What am I going to do? I thought. *They're so nice. How could I lie to them like that?* I felt so foolish and unkind.

It wasn't long before Mom found out everything I wrote in the letter. Her younger brother had also been in regular contact with my aunt. I was in big trouble for daring to lie and be disrespectful to Aunt Lien.

"How dare you!" Mom screamed at me with a sad look on her face. "Can't you see we only want what's best for you?"

Because of my respect for her, I didn't talk back. She knew, however, I still wasn't going along with her wishes. After trying for a month to get me to change my mind, Mom didn't get anywhere.

Then, one day, my brother approached me.

"Trang, come into the house. I need to talk to you," Anh Hai said as he walked toward the living room.

I had no clue what he wanted. He had never done that before.

As I followed him into the house, I became nervous when he pointed his finger at the table and said, "Sit down." (Something had to be very important. That table was only used when elderly people got together. I had been told many times by Mom and other family members, "**Never** sit at the living room table at anybody's house.")

I didn't feel comfortable sitting there across from him.

I still had no idea what he wanted until he asked, "So, what's going on? Mom tells me that you won't go to America."

I was shocked. I would have never guessed he would talk to me about this subject. I looked down to the floor and didn't answer.

He went on, "Take a look around us! There's nothing of any value in this entire house! We've all had a rough life so far, especially Mom."

Again, I said nothing.

My brother realized he was the only one talking. He turned his head as he looked up at the ceiling, and with an emotional voice, said, "This house, it's worth almost nothing, but it's all we have. Remember the last time Mom was sick? Thank God, it was nothing too serious. We barely had enough money. The next time, if something really bad happens, we could sell our house and still not have enough, and there's nothing we can do except bring her home to watch her die."

He continued, "Haven't you seen how hard Mom has worked? She has never been able to go anywhere, do anything, or eat anything good. All because she had to take care of us."

Anh Hai paused for a couple of seconds to look at me before saying, "You're very lucky. If you won't do this for yourself, then I ask you to do it for the family."

I took a deep breath but remained quiet.

He stared at the floor to hide his tears, but I saw them anyway. With a sad tone in his voice, he said, "I wish I could trade places with you. If it were me, I would do this for our family in a second. Just give some thought to what I've said." He stood up and walked away.

The second my brother left the room, tears began rolling down my cheeks. Every word he said hit me deeply. I knew I could no longer keep fighting this.

That night, I cried myself to sleep. *How can I betray Tung like that? After all we've been through? After all the years he has waited for me?*

During the days that followed, I felt like he was dying, except he was still living.

My chest hurt and I gasped for air every time I thought about breaking up with him. I began to wonder if maybe it was me that was dying.

CR∎SO

Aunt Lien was happy when it was made clear I wanted to come to America. Soon after, I started receiving letters from Jay. We wrote back and forth often, with my aunt helping Jay translate my letters, while an English teacher helped me translate Jay's.

Six months later, I received word that Jay was coming to Viet Nam to meet me and my aunt was coming with him.

Several times, I planned to tell Tung what was going on, but it never happened. Each time I saw him, I couldn't say anything.

One day, when Mom was not home, I sneaked out of the house and rode my bike to town. This time, I was determined to find Tung and explain everything. Jay was coming in two weeks.

Since I would never dare go to the house where Tung and his parents lived, I went to the coffee shop nearby to sit and wait. It was the same shop where he and I would meet almost every day after school.

A couple of the girls working there knew me and sent someone to his house to bring him to me.

I ordered a glass of lemonade but couldn't drink any. This used to be my happiest place, but now, with my heart beating so fast, I was just trying to make myself act normal.

How can I tell him the bad news and break his heart? I asked myself. My arms and legs started to shake.

Five minutes later, I saw my boyfriend's older brother, Hung, trying to cross the street. The traffic was heavy and people were everywhere. I stood up and walked over to the sidewalk to meet him.

"Where's Anh Tung?" I asked.

"He went up into the city and hasn't returned yet," Hung said.

We walked back inside the café and the waitress came over to the table as soon as we sat down. She looked at Hung and asked, "Unsweetened ice tea for you?"

My drink was still full.

"Yes, beautiful," he said with a smile.

"Please don't make her your next conquest. I know you!" I jokingly said as the waitress walked away.

"Too late, I've already gone out with her a couple of times".

"You're so evil. You mean to tell me you've broken up with the other girl already?" I raised my hand up like I was going to hit him, but he knew I wouldn't.

Hung was a fun guy. Sitting there with him made me forget all about my stress and sadness. When I finished my lemonade and there was no sign of Tung, I stood up to get ready to leave.

"No, don't leave. My brother has some big news for you!" Hung said.

"What's the big news? You better not lie to me!" I said.

Hung said nothing. I could tell he was just dying to tell me, but felt like he couldn't.

"Come on, you're allowed to tell me. Come on, come on!" I kept bugging him and didn't give up.

"Ok," he finally agreed. "My brother will kill me for telling you, but I can't keep it a secret any longer."

"Tell me!" I pleaded again.

"Ok, I said I will! It's big. Really big. The biggest news ever!"

"Tell me before I die of excitement!"

"Think about it," he said, still not giving me any details. "What could be the biggest, best news you could ever hear?"

"Hung, I don't know. Please! Just tell me."

"OK! Mom finally said you and Tung can get married!" he said with a huge smile while waiting for my reaction.

I know he expected me to be happy, but instead, I sat there in shock.

"She did what?" I finally asked. I pasted a fake smile on my face.

"It's true. I overheard Mom talking to Tung about finding someone to talk to your Mom about the wedding," Hung added.

I didn't want to hear any more. It was too painful.

He continued, "Tung was so happy. He can't wait to see you."

I still pretended to be happy, but felt like I was dying inside.

I screamed to myself, *Why? Why now? Why not sooner?*

I didn't have the guts to tell Hung I couldn't marry his brother. I just wanted to get on my bicycle and go home.

Suddenly, Tung's little sister came running up to me with a big smile. "Mom wants you to come to the house so Dad can meet you," she said. She was almost out of breath from running as she pointed her finger towards their house. "Look!" she said. "They're standing in front of the house waiting for you." She grabbed my hand and started swinging it back and forth while saying, "Come on! Come on!"

I should have said no but didn't. I followed Hung and his little sister to the house. The open market was packed with people, but I could still see Tung's parents as they watched me walk toward them. I was so scared. I had never met his father before, but his mother, I'll never forget.

One day, Tung had asked me to go to his cousin's house for a party. While we were there, I met his mother for the first time. I walked up to her with both of my arms crossed and my head bowed. When I said, "Hello", she turned her back to me and walked away. She wanted nothing to do with me. I felt horrible and embarrassed. So many people were standing around watching. I wanted her to like me so badly, but didn't know what to do.

For the past four years, Tung and I always met at the café. At that time, having a boyfriend or girlfriend was considered a bad thing, so we avoided going to each other's houses. One day, while we were sitting in the café, Tung remembered that he had to watch his aunt's baby and wanted me to go with him. I really didn't want to go, but he assured me that everything was OK. He said his aunt was a sweet and very cool person.

"Are you sure she won't yell at me?" I asked.

"I told her all about you. Come on, let's go."

When we reached his aunt's house, Tung went inside first while I took my time standing at the door, waiting for his aunt's reaction.

A minute later I heard, "Trang! Welcome! Come on in!" His aunt was walking toward me with a smile. Even though they were sisters, she looked nothing like Tung's mother. She became even friendlier when I was inside the house. "Would you like something to drink?" she asked.

"No thanks. Tung and I just had something at the café before we came," I said.

While his aunt was getting ready in the back, Tung motioned for me to come into another room to see the baby. She was lying inside a mosquito net, sleeping. I saw her front lip was missing but I didn't want to say anything.

Tung whispered, "Look at her lip. My aunt was very upset when the baby was born, but she felt better after learning it could *be fixed when she gets a little older. She's on the waiting list of a doctor from America. They have the best doctors in the world. They come here doing missionary work, so it'll cost my aunt almost nothing."*

"That's great!" I whispered back.

We returned to the front room and sat down. Tung pulled his chair really close to mine and grabbed my arm.

"Don't do that while your Aunt is still here!" I said while giving him a dirty look.

"You worry too much," he said with a laugh.

I stood up and pulled my chair away, but then leaned over to whisper, "I am so happy your aunt likes me."

A few minutes later, we were both shocked when Tung's mother unexpectedly showed up and the front door opened.

As she stormed toward me, she began yelling, "What the hell are you doing here? How dare you! Just what kind of girl are you?" The look on her face as she was screaming made me wonder if she might kill me.

I began to freak out and stood up against the wall behind Tung.

His aunt heard the noise and came running, but even she looked scared.

Every time Tung started to talk, she would cut him off. She stopped directly in front of me and pointed her finger at my face. "Get out!" she yelled. "A girl doesn't go looking for a boy, the boy looks for the girl! You don't belong here! Don't you have any respect for yourself?"

I was taught to never talk back to an older person, so I kept my mouth shut. I didn't want to cry, but tears started running down my cheeks anyway.

CR∎SO

I could never forget Tung's mother! Seeing her again brought back that memory like it was yesterday. However, his dad looked like he could be a nice man.

I stopped in front of them with my arms crossed and my head bowed. I said, "Hello" and they both seemed very happy to see me.

"I like your long hair, it's very beautiful," his dad said with a smile.

"Thank you."

"Come on in the house," Tung's Mom said.

I was surprised how differently she was treating me. When we got inside, I was even more surprised when she pointed at the living room table and said, "You can sit at the table with me, dear."

I waited until she told me twice before I sat down. She knew without her permission, I would never sit at that table.

After sitting down, she immediately got back up and said, "Let me go get you a bowl of sweetened sticky rice."

She was so nice that I couldn't say "no". She came back from the kitchen and set the bowl of rice in front of me. "You go ahead and eat. We just finished eating a few minutes ago."

I didn't want to stay very long, but now I couldn't eat and run.

About ten minutes later, I noticed Tung's mother and I were the only two remaining in the living room. She waited until I finished taking my last bite before saying, "I just wanted to let you know, my husband and I have agreed to let you and our son get married."

I smiled and pretended to be grateful.

She went on, "You need to go home and tell your mom what's going on and get back with me. OK?"

I already knew what Mom's answer would be, but I went ahead and told her, "OK. I'll tell Mom as soon as I get home, and then I'll let you know." I wished I had the strength to tell her the truth, but I didn't.

I felt like a horrible person after leaving the house. A million things went through my head while I was on my bike. Everything looked sad that day; the road, the trees, everything!

At that very moment, I turned my head and saw Tung behind me. I slowed down and waited for him. As soon as I saw his smile, all my problems went away.

We rode our bikes side by side as slowly as we could, but we both knew the road would be ending soon. To spend more time together, we got off our bikes and pushed them with a slow walk. Tung kept talking about how wonderful our future was going to be together.

I kept pretending to be happy while being eaten up inside with guilt.

He stopped walking and pointed at a place along the road. "Do you remember this spot?" he asked.

"Yes," I answered. "We had one of our first dates here."

"It *was* our first date. That drink at the coffee shop doesn't count; I don't care what Ha says."

I laughed and then said, "I remember it had been raining all day, and the road was very slick."

"It was my fault we fell off the bike," Tung said. "I felt really bad your notebook got all muddy."

"I was already upset you showed up on a bicycle instead of your motorcycle. That was one of the things I liked about you."

He rolled his eyes. "My stupid brother's fault. So I show up on a bicycle, you get on, and I dump you in a mud puddle. I'm so glad you didn't break up with me. If you would have, we wouldn't be here now. We wouldn't be getting married."

I wanted to have more time together, but when I looked up, I could see the end of the road. This was where Tung normally turned around and went back home.

We were so wrapped up in each other, we hadn't noticed the wind blowing in dark clouds overhead. We both looked up at the sky and at the same time said, "Rain is coming."

The first few drops fell onto our faces.

We stopped walking again and I said, "I think you should go home now. I don't have as far to go as you."

"I guess I'd better," Tung said. He turned his bike around and parked it next to me.

I looked around to make sure nobody knew me before I got closer to him. At that moment, the rain really started to pour.

I looked at Tung. "You better go," I said again.

"You go first, and then I'll go," he demanded with an ornery smile.

He expected me to stay and joke back and forth with him in the playful way we always did. Instead, I said once more, "You better go."

"We'll go at the same time."

We each went our own way. Several times, I looked over my shoulder to see him smiling back at me. I waited until he wasn't paying any more attention and then I stopped. I stood still in the downpour and watched him until he was completely out of sight.

I was thankful for the storm that cast a dark shadow on my face and dropped water on my cheeks. No one could see me cry.

CR∎SO

Every day, I got a little angrier at myself for not having the guts to break up with Tung.

One morning, when I was doing laundry by the river, my oldest sister, Chi Ba, and her husband, Anh Ba, came home for a visit. After greeting me, my sister walked over to the house.

Anh Ba remained standing beside me, looking at the river.

The tide was coming in and the water was moving swiftly upriver.

As Anh Ba looked at the water, he tried talking to me. He talked and talked but I wouldn't answer him. "Trang, what's wrong?" he asked after noticing I wasn't myself.

"Oh, nothing," I said as I kept my head down while cleaning the laundry.

"Ok, but let me know if you need anything?" he replied while beginning to walk away.

"Anh Ba, please come here," I blurted out.

Anh Ba was good friends with Tung and he was always easy to talk to. I thought I should tell him what was going on. "I want to tell you something, but you can't tell anybody, OK? Mom would kill me if she knew," I said in almost a whisper.

"I swear," he answered softly.

"Jay is going to be here in one week and Tung needs to know what's going on. I've tried to tell him, but I could never find the courage. I don't know what to do."

Anh Ba scratched his head for a second. "Man, this is horrible," he said. "If you want, I'll go find Tung and explain everything for you".

"Would you really do that for me?" I asked.

"Yeah, I'll do it, although it's not going to be any fun," he replied.

While feeling horrible and weak for putting all this on Anh Ba's shoulders, I added, "When you talk to him, will you please say how sorry I am for not telling him myself? It's hard enough to find the words to say, and Mom has been watching me like a hawk, so I can't even find the time to think, let alone get away to see him. Thanks for helping me. Tung has to be told what's going on!"

"Sure. I'll do it today and let you know later how it went."

I began to worry and get nervous just thinking about Tung getting the bad news. It was making me sick to my stomach.

A little while later, Anh Ba got on his bike and went to town looking for Tung. He spent hours riding around and sitting at the café. Finally, he found him.

Tung was so happy to see Anh Ba and they both went over to the café to talk. Rather than drink coffee, Anh Ba made sure they both had a few shots of rice whisky before he broke the news to him.

Maybe it was the whisky, or Anh Ba just did a good job of explaining, because when he received the bad news, Tung wasn't angry at me.

After supper that evening, I walked up the road to pick up a blouse that was being made for me. I hoped a new blouse would make me a little less sad, but it didn't. All I could think about was Tung. *How could I betray him?* I asked myself. I felt like such a horrible person.

On the way back home, I could feel rain drops falling on my arm. It was the rainy season, so it wasn't a surprise.

When I glanced down the road ahead of me, I was shocked to see Tung and Anh Ba coming my way on their bikes. Anh Ba turned off the main path and headed for my house while Tung continued coming toward me.

I couldn't believe my eyes and started to panic. I couldn't get enough air to breathe. I stopped walking and stood frozen in place.

Tung got off his bike and said, "Hi."

I kept looking down at the ground and didn't say a word.

Tung bent his head down to look at me. "I talked to Anh Ba earlier."

I still didn't move.

I didn't remember how we got there, but we ended up in a little café that was two minutes down the road from where I was standing. The hut was made of bamboo sticks, covered with branches and leaves from the nipa palm.

Like always, Tung ordered me a fresh lemonade and an iced tea for himself.

I was quiet and didn't even want to touch my drink.

There was a long skinny spoon in the glass of lemonade and the sugar was still sitting on the bottom. Tung reached over and stirred it for me.

The second I looked at him, tears uncontrollably rolled down my cheeks onto the floor. After a few seconds, I was a complete mess and had to leave the café.

Tung didn't cry out loud as I did, but he looked very sad and his eyes were all red. He followed me out to the main path and then we walked out on one of the rice paddy dikes.

Tears were flowing so hard, I had a hard time seeing. Sitting on the edge of the rice paddy, I continued to cry a long time before I could stop. At times, I thought I was going to be blind from crying so hard.

Neither one of us could talk for a long time. Finally, he said, "I couldn't let you go without seeing you at least one more time to say goodbye and wish you good luck."

"But I don't want to go!" I cried. "I want to stay here with you!"

He lifted my chin with his finger. "Trang, I care about you. America is a dream place. We all want to go there. You are the lucky one, and I'm happy for you. I'd be selfish if I tried to make you stay."

I knew he meant to comfort me, but instead, his words angered me. *How could he not fight to keep what we had?*

Every muscle in my body ached from sobbing. I wanted him to change his mind, to fight for me, to stop me from going.

Instead, he stood up. "Goodbye, Trang," he said. And then he was gone.

Chapter Twenty-Four

October 15, 1991: my life was about to change forever. I couldn't keep my mind or my hands still, so I started cleaning the house. That's when I heard two of my nephews screaming at the same time with the most enthusiasm I had ever heard, "My! My!" (Pronounced me, me, meaning American, American).

I knew it had to be Jay.

More screaming came from outside, "Trang, where are you?" my sister, Chi Tu, hollered as she came rushing into the house.

Once inside, she tried catching her breath with her mouth wide open before saying, "I saw Ong My (Jay, "Ong" meaning someone older than themselves, and "My" meaning American) and Di Sau (Aunt Lien) in town. They're waiting for the boat to bring them upriver. Hurry! You need to go change clothes and brush your hair; they'll stop and pick you up soon."

While I was changing clothes, I overheard my sister and nephews talking.

"Did you see how tall he is?"

"He's an American; what did you expect?"

"His skin is really white! Look at me; I wish I could be white like him."

I ran from the back room and asked Chi Tu, "Was he nice or did he look mean?"

"There must have been a hundred people surrounding him, most of them children. I couldn't get too close, but I saw he smiled a lot. We heard a commotion while shopping in the market and the minute I saw Di Sau (Aunt Lien), I knew right away what was going on. Mom was with them and she told me to hurry home to tell you to be ready. Just so you know, we didn't walk, we ran all the way here!"

Chi Tu was talking a hundred miles an hour and there was so much excitement going on around me that I started to get nervous.

"Why were so many people following Jay?" I asked.

Chi Tu replied, "Because he's the first American man to ever come to the village since the war was over. It brings back a lot of memories for the grownups, and the kids have never seen an American in person before. He looks and speaks totally different than we do you know! Let me tell you, there's a lot of excitement going on in town right now."

Suddenly, we heard our nephews yelling from over by the river, "They're coming! We can see them!"

"OK!" my sister hollered back and ran over to the river to look.

I was the only one left in the house and soon afterwards, I could hear the sound of the boat getting closer and closer. I got nervous, worried and excited all at the same time.

I was unable to go to the airport to meet Jay because I was still sick from the day before. Between my aunt and my family, we had misinterpreted their arrival date and had all gone to pick them up a day early. We waited for hours, only to have them not show up.

We figured the mistake had to do with the twelve hour difference in time between Viet Nam and Ohio and assumed they'd be there the next day. But the motion sickness got the best of me and I had to stay behind.

"They're here! They're here, now!" I could hear them yelling from the river.

"OK, I am coming," I said.

The boat pulled up to the river bank and Anh Tu tied it to a tree.

I could see Jay from the house; I knew it was him because he was the tallest one. I was scared but kept walking out toward the boat.

As soon as he saw me, he smiled. I got even more nervous. After I got into the boat, (there was an empty spot reserved for me, next to Jay) I looked at him, smiled, and said, "Hello."

"Hello," Jay said back. Right away I knew he liked my long hair because he kept on touching it with his hand.

Jay tried to talk to me, but I couldn't understand anything. He didn't understand a word I said either.

I listened to my Aunt and Jay speak English back and forth and it was amazing to me.

"I so wish I could speak English," I said while looking at my Aunt.

"Oh you will, and it won't take long for you," Aunt Lien said.

"Thanks, but I think it's going to take me five years to learn how to speak. It sounds like it's really hard to learn."

Aunt Lien and Myself

The whole time I was on the boat, I heard my aunts and uncles talk about nothing but the war. My sister, Chi Tu, was right. Seeing Jay brought back a lot of memories for them.

They all took turns telling American war stories; one of my uncles said, "Jay reminds me of the American soldiers. With his light hair, his height, and other similar features, he reminds me of them a lot."

Another uncle pointed his finger to the side of the river and said, "There, right there, that whole area was an American station. There was a time when you could hear the sound of guns day and night, especially at night when the VC were out."

Everyone pointed to another one of my uncles and said, "He was a VC!" The whole boat laughed, thinking it was funny.

That got Jay's attention, and he laughed when Aunt Lien translated.

As they were going on and on, I remembered that when I was a little girl, I heard war stories almost every day for about ten years. After that, I heard very little until today when Jay showed up and it started again.

It only took fifteen to twenty minutes to get to Grandma's house when using a boat with a motor. That was where I would spend all my time getting to know Jay with the help of Aunt Lien's translation.

When we arrived at the house, there were thirty or more family members waiting to meet him. Everyone was amazed by how tall he was. They stared at him from head to toe, making comments about his hair color and his features. They also kept looking at his backpack and tennis shoes, things we didn't see every day.

Word traveled fast throughout the area and by evening, Grandma's house was filled with people. More and more people from up and down the road came to see the American. Many sat on the floor, others on small chairs, some on the windowsills, and even a few on each other's laps. All were smiling and seemed really excited to see Jay. Kids weren't afraid to get close to him, and the first thing they liked to do was rub and lightly pull at the hair on his arms.

Jay felt badly that he didn't bring any candy with him. When he saw some of the kids playing in the dirt with a couple of old, worn out marbles, he went into the house and pulled out a box that was packed away in his suitcase. When he walked over to the kids and opened the box, their eyes almost popped out. The box was full of marbles with different styles and colors. Each one of the kids got several marbles and they all started running around the house screaming. Playing with marbles was something they did all day long, even during breaks at school.

CR∎SO

Everything was going well for Jay until he asked to go the bathroom. We all laughed as we pointed towards the back of the house.

"Why are they laughing?" Jay asked.

"Just follow me and you'll know why," Lien said, also laughing.

Lien pointed at the outhouse and laughed again. "You think you can use it without falling in the pond? Just watch your step, because there's a hundred catfish in the water waiting for you. You just have to learn how to squat like the Vietnamese do and you'll be all right."

"Oh, that's what everyone thought was funny," Jay said laughing.

CR∎SO

Grandma's house didn't have a shower or a bath tub, but instead, she had a little bathing hut. The hut was big enough for just one person and a bucket of water, and had a small cement pad on the floor to stand on. When I saw Jay getting ready to take a bath, I knew he would be in trouble. He had his hands full with clothes, a towel, shaving cream, and a razor.

Oh, no, I thought to myself, *There's nowhere to hang all that stuff, especially the bath towel that's so big it looks like a blanket.* Our towels were five times smaller and thinner, just like our clothes. We normally would stuff our clothes and towel in between the bamboo sticks. I knew Jay couldn't do that with his jeans and big towel, and there was no mirror for him to use to shave.

To help him out, I hurried and placed a small stool inside the hut so he would have something to set his stuff on. I also hung a small mirror in there for him. It was so small that he couldn't see his whole face at once, but at least he could see to shave. I also carried a bucket of water for him while following behind.

"I can carry my own water," Jay said. Since I couldn't understand him and wasn't able to answer back, I just kept carrying the bucket. I had heard that American people used machines to do everything, so I assumed Jay couldn't do anything by hand.

An hour later, when Jay came walking into the house, I noticed his jean bottoms were all wet. He didn't know that he had to hold his pants off the floor while putting them on. I tried not to laugh, but it was too funny.

Jay just smiled and didn't complain. After putting all his dirty clothes away, he used his towel to dry his hair some more.

He then used a Q-tip to clean his ears. I had seen the box earlier, but didn't know what they were, just like the mouth-wash and Kleenex. I never had stuff like that before; you couldn't even find them in the market. Growing up, I had always heard that Americans were rich, and that was when I knew it was true.

CR■80

Jay went from not eating any rice to eating it for three meals a day. Aunt Lien always made sure he got a piece of pork or steak with his rice, because our food was so different. He wouldn't eat duck or chicken feet and he also refused to eat a little fish that was cooked with its head still on. He did try the fish sauce and used chop sticks to eat with.

Learning to use chop sticks is one thing, but learning how to speak Vietnamese is another. Jay tried hard, but his accent was so heavy, I couldn't understand a word he tried to say.

Most of the evenings, Jay and I would walk out to the main path, sit underneath a coconut tree and watch the moon for a long time without saying a word.

Every day I was getting a little less scared of him. He was so kind that I started to like him a little more. The thing I liked most about him was that he always smiled every single time I looked at him.

Jay and I at my grandma's house

I always learned something new whenever I was around him. One time after he had finished eating some sticky rice on a banana leaf, he wouldn't throw the leaf on the floor like we always did. He walked around looking for a garbage can, but there weren't any. Nobody's house had one.

"Just go outside and throw it anywhere on the ground," Grandma told Jay. As she talked, Grandma used hand gestures to make sure he understood.

Jay just smiled but still wouldn't let the banana leaf out of his hand.

When Aunt Lien walked by and overheard us talking, she went over to the table, picked up an empty plastic bag, handed it to Jay and said, "Here you go."

"Thanks, Lien," Jay said.

Aunt Lien looked at us and said, "Now you all know why I yell at you guys when you throw trash everywhere. In America you could get a fine if you're caught doing that."

"Get a fine? Are you serious? That's crazy!" we all exclaimed.

"I'm telling you the truth. Ask Jay," she said.

"It's true," Jay said as he nodded his head.

Grandma said jokingly, "Trang, make sure when you go to America you don't throw trash on the ground. OK?"

"What if I don't remember?" I asked.

"Then you'll have to pay," my uncle said while laughing.

As time went by, I noticed how Jay put every little thing that was trash in his pocket, especially when we traveled. When we came back home, he would empty his pockets out into a plastic bag. I was so impressed! Who does that in Viet Nam? Nobody. We had big piles of trash everywhere we went.

Jay had little knowledge about Viet Nam; most of what he knew, he learned from coworkers who were veterans, and from war movies on TV.

Coming to Viet Nam took Jay twenty-two hours in the air, four different flights and about ten hours of layovers. That didn't bother him, but as the airplane was getting ready to land and he looked out the window and saw all the rice paddies below him, the full weight of what he was doing hit him. Jay started to get very nervous and said to Aunt Lien, "Let's go back home."

"Everything is going to be OK," Aunt Lien replied. "Besides, it's too late to turn back now."

It didn't take long for Jay to fall in love with Viet Nam. He liked being in the country, where everything was so green and had a pleasant, rich aroma. He loved lying in a hammock while listening to the sound of the boats going up and down the river. He loved the chickens making noises every morning, the little kids following him everywhere he went, and mostly, he liked me a lot.

He was having the time of his life! Until one late afternoon, when five policemen in full uniform showed up at the house and demanded Jay's passport.

For a few minutes, I could see fear in Jay's eyes when he handed them his passport. He was very worried because there was no American Embassy in Viet Nam at that time. If something bad were to happen, he'd have a difficult time getting help. Since Jay couldn't understand anything they were saying, they started questioning Aunt Lien.

"What is this man, this American, doing in our country?" the policeman demanded. "Is he related to you?"

"No, he's not," she explained.

"Do you know that it is against the law for him to be staying in your mother's home? All foreign visitors must stay at a hotel."

"I'm so sorry," Aunt Lien apologized again and again. "I didn't know that. I notified the police he was coming, but no one mentioned where he could or could not stay. I'm sorry!"

It was a very tense moment. But everyone sighed with relief when the police decided to let Jay go with a warning. They left but they took his passport with them.

I knew Jay was relieved when I saw him wipe the sweat off his forehead.

I could tell Aunt Lien felt bad for him because she kept saying, "It's OK now, it's OK."

The next day, Jay had to go to the police station in Ho Chi Minh City. After paying a fine, the police returned Jay's passport and gave him permission to remain where he was for the duration of his visit.

Jay got over that bad incident quickly and he started having fun again. He preferred spending his time out in the country where there weren't as many people taking notice of him.

People treated him like a celebrity; everywhere he went, someone was waiting to see him. Women would stare out their windows until they couldn't see him anymore; kids ran after him on the street and kept saying, "Hello, hello," because that was the only English they knew.

When we went shopping in the local village or Ho Chi Minh City, we were always with Aunt Lien. Since she always bought lots of stuff, many family members would come along to help carry everything back home. For that reason, Jay and I were never alone in public, but that didn't stop people from figuring out what was going on between us.

It wasn't long before I became the talk of the town, because I was going to be the first girl in the village to marry an American since the war had ended.

Two weeks went by so fast; I remember the day before they had to go back to America, Aunt Lien said to Jay, "We have to pack."

"I don't want to leave; you can go without me," Jay said jokingly. He knew there was no way for him to stay.

All day long, Aunt Lien reminded Jay to pack, but he kept putting it off until the very last minute.

There were a lot of family members wanting to go to the airport, but the bus could only take thirty passengers. Some of them were really sad they weren't able to go. Going to the airport was a big deal to everyone. Aunt Lien apologized to all of them and promised it would be their turn the next time.

We arrived at the airport a little early and Jay stayed beside me the whole time. We couldn't talk but I could tell he didn't want to leave without me. We both were sad.

Just like everyone, I liked Jay a lot. We didn't need words to feel his kindness.

Aunt Lien came over and asked me, "Is there anything you want to tell Jay?"

"Sorry, but you know I can't speak English," I said to her.

"I meant, you can tell me what you want to say and I'll tell Jay for you," Aunt Lien said while laughing.

I smiled and didn't say anything.

We don't do hugs, but Aunt Lien didn't care. Before she and Jay walked inside the airport, one by one, she gave the entire family a hug anyway.

Since Jay saw we weren't comfortable with it, he just waved his hand and said, "Bye, everybody."

He smiled sadly as he said goodbye to me, touching my shoulder one more time right before turning to go. As he was walking toward the airport entrance, I could see him looking back at me.

I kept waving my hand and watching him walk as long as I could.

Just before he disappeared, he stopped and whispered something to Aunt Lien.

She took a step back in our direction.

We all listened anxiously.

I felt a warmth in my heart as she relayed his message. "He said, 'Tell Trang I'm coming back for her.'"

Chapter Twenty-Five

As soon as Jay was back in America, he immediately started on the paperwork required to bring me to America. Since there were no diplomatic ties between the US and Vietnamese governments at that time, everything was a little more complicated.

Aunt Lien and Uncle Raymond were watching a satellite wild feed station when an advertisement from a lawyer came on. The ad stated their office specialized in helping Vietnamese citizens immigrate to America. Aunt Lien quickly wrote down his name and number and gave it to Jay.

After the war, many Vietnamese died trying to make it to America in boats. A system was set up between our two governments (Orderly Departure Program, ODP) to help anyone with a legitimate reason to safely immigrate to America.

The way the system was supposed to work for me was: after Jay filed a Fiancée Petition with US Immigrations and received approval, the Immigration Office would forward the approval to the ODP office at the American Embassy in Bangkok, Thailand.

After I received a passport from the Vietnamese government and was issued an interview number, an interview would be scheduled with American officials in Viet Nam. The whole process would take two to three years to complete.

The lawyer helping Jay said there was a faster way, but there was a chance it wouldn't work. He explained that once the Fiancée

Petition was forwarded to the American Embassy in Bangkok and after I received my Vietnamese passport and a Visa into Thailand, Jay and I would fly to Bangkok and then walk into the American embassy and apply for my Visa into the United States.

Without giving it a second thought, Jay decided to use the faster way.

While waiting for the process to work through the system, Jay said good bye to New York and moved back home in Ohio where he would be closer to Aunt Lien and his family.

Not having any luck finding work in the oil fields, Jay worked a short time as a maintenance man at a nursing home and then later as a carpenter for a housing contractor. He made a lot less money compared with his old job in the oil fields, but he received a lot of help from his family and Aunt Lien.

His oldest brother let him live rent free in one of his mobile homes while Aunt Lien gave Jay a piece of their land with the hope that he would clear the land and someday build a house. After clearing a section of the land, Jay's parents loaned him the money to buy a used mobile home.

ରେ ▪ ⁊ର

Two weeks after Jay left Viet Nam, I received a letter from the police station requesting me to come in for questioning. I was scared to death, and wondered if they thought I was a spy for America or something, especially since the station that sent out the request wasn't local.

Mom made sure she went with me to the station.

When we arrived, a police officer stopped Mom at the door and commanded, "You wait right here. You're not permitted to go in." The same officer signaled me to follow him with a motion of his head.

After walking through the door, I could see at least a dozen policemen sitting at desks on both sides of the room. We walked halfway through the room and stopped in front of a desk, at which time the escorting officer signaled for me to sit down. I was so scared and quickly sat as instructed.

The police officer sitting behind the desk had been waiting for me.

I sat silently, waiting for him to speak.

He had a piece of paper in his hand and suddenly began firing questions at me, giving me only a split second to answer before asking another:

"How did you meet this American, Mr. Donald Jay Moreland?"

"What kind of relationship do you have with him?"

"Where did you go when he was here?"

"What does he do in America?"

"Was this the first time he has been in Viet Nam?"

"Is he coming back? If so, when?"

I responded honestly to all of them.

After about twenty minutes, I was told I could leave. I felt relieved. Just as I was getting up from the chair, the officer spoke again.

"Just a second. You can go home now, but we may need you to come back in a couple of months. OK?"

For what? I thought. I didn't dare say that out loud. I answered, "Yes sir."

As I was walking toward Mom, I could see the worry all over her face. "Let's get out of here." I quietly said, and swiftly walked away from the police station as fast as we could. That was the last time I ever heard from them.

Jay and I sent letters back and forth constantly. Each letter required twelve to fourteen days to make a one way trip. Jay wanted to make a phone call to speed up the exchange of information between us regarding requirements of the Vietnamese government. That was almost impossible because a telephone was something you couldn't find anywhere in our neighborhood or even in our local village. I knew they had telephones in the city, but you had to be super rich to own one.

Jay wouldn't give up on the idea and discussed the problem with Aunt Lien. My aunt contacted a Vietnamese friend living in America, who in turn, put her in touch with a wealthy lady living in Ho Chi Minh City. The lady had a telephone installed in her home and Aunt Lien was able to make arrangements for me to use it. My aunt then sent me a letter with the lady's address, along with the exact time and date Jay would be calling.

Since the lady's house was far up in the city, Aunt Lien made sure her youngest brother, Cau Muoi, went along with me. We couldn't find the house at first and I began to panic, thinking Jay would call and I wouldn't be there. We were ten minutes late when we finally arrived.

When the lady came to the door, I couldn't get over how beautiful and friendly she was.

We followed her up to the second floor to a room with a front wall made entirely of glass, including the door. The room was unbelievably clean and had two round wood tables, one big and one small. The larger table was positioned in front of a beautiful couch while the smaller one with the telephone sitting on it, was placed between two chairs. I was so excited; that was the first time I ever saw a telephone in real life.

"You can sit anywhere you like; I'll be right back," the lady said.

After she left the room, Cau Muoi asked, "Do you know how to use a telephone?"

"No," I answered. "But I've seen people use them in the movies. When the phone rings, you pick it up, hold one end to your ear and say hello in the other end."

Cau Muoi laughed.

We walked over to the window facing the street and looked down. People were everywhere and the traffic was really heavy.

"Now you know why this room is all closed in," Cau Muoi said. "It keeps all the noise out so you're able to talk on the phone." He had an answer for everything.

We knew the lady went to the kitchen to make us something to drink. She never asked if we wanted anything because she knew we would have said "no". (People in Viet Nam judge each other by how quickly the person accepts the offer of food or drink, and the manner in which they eat or drink.) A few minutes later, the lady returned and set two glasses of fresh lemonade on the table in front of us.

"Thank you," we both said. (To show respect, you always drink what is given to you and it doesn't matter if you like the drink or not. You must always be sure to drink more than half of the glass or else you will be considered "a snob". Also, never try to finish the drink to the last drop, because they'll think you're dirt poor and will look down on you.)

"I'm surprised the phone hasn't rung yet," the lady said.

After waiting fifteen more minutes, the phone started to ring. We all jumped.

But it wasn't Jay; it was the lady's husband. We were all disappointed, but I was glad to have a chance to see how the lady used the phone.

Another ten minutes went by and the phone still didn't ring.

"I think they forgot about us; maybe we should leave," Cau Muoi said, as he paced back and forth.

"No!" I instantly snapped back. "I don't care if we need to wait half a day; this is important!"

"I'm sure they'll call," the lady said. "Maybe there's some confusion with the time difference. Trang, when the phone rings again, you pick it up. OK?"

"OK, thank you."

A few minutes later, the phone rang and I picked it up, as scared as I could be. "Hello," I said.

"Hi, Trang! How are you?" I heard Jay say.

It was amazing. I didn't know how the phone worked, but I did see a wire running from the phone which connected to the wall. I thought, *How can I hear Jay all the way from America with that skinny wire?*

Jay talked and talked, but the only words I could completely understand were, "I miss you; I hope to see you soon."

The only words I knew how to say to Jay were, "I love you; I miss you; and I see you again soon." I kept repeating the words over and over.

Jay could tell I didn't understand him very well so he handed the phone to Aunt Lien to translate for us. With her help, we talked for almost an hour.

I found out later, they made the call from Aunt Lien's house and the phone bill was almost $200. Jay offered to pay for it but Aunt Lien refused to let him.

"I'll pay for it this time," she said jokingly and then added, "but let's use your phone when we call again."

ℭℛ ■ ℭ℘

Jay and I continued writing back and forth while waiting to hear from the US Immigration office. Finally, the day came when a letter arrived stating the Fiancée Petition had been approved and that it was forwarded to the American Embassy in Bangkok.

Jay sold his motorcycle and sent me the money so I could buy a Thailand Visa and a round-trip airline ticket to Bangkok. (The Vietnamese government required the round-trip ticket so I would be ensured a way back home if things didn't work out.)

Jay made a copy of the petition and sent it to me along with other forms and documents required by the Vietnamese government. Once he knew I had received the paperwork, he made reservations with the airlines to come to Viet Nam in two weeks. The only problem was, Jay didn't understand the Thai Embassy was in Hanoi, not Ho Chi Minh City. I had to somehow get in contact with the Thai Embassy to get my Visa. I didn't know what to do and began to panic.

The following morning, I went into Ho Chi Minh City with the idea of spending the day looking for help. I thought, *Surely, there must be some way to avoid making the long trip to Hanoi.*

First, I went back to the office where I got my passport, but nobody there could tell me what to do.

As soon as I was back out on the street, I saw several guys with "xich lo's" (three wheel bicycle taxi's). Some of the guys were riding around looking for customers, but many of them were just sitting on the sidewalk, waiting.

I got scared when they started fighting amongst themselves over who would talk with me first. They all asked if I wanted to go somewhere and I just kept shaking my head "no".

I remembered being told many times, "Anytime you need to know about something in the city, or where to go, always ask a xich lo driver." But there was so many of them. I walked away from the group as fast as I could, wondering how I would be able to talk with one of them without all the commotion.

After walking for a few minutes, I saw a xich lo driver sitting by himself, parked on the sidewalk. I explained to the driver what I was wanting to do, and asked if he knew of any place that could help me.

Taking his hat off to wipe the sweat from his forehead, the driver thought for a minute. "I think I might know a couple of places. Get in," he said.

"Wait a minute. How much will this cost me?" I asked. After hearing his price I quickly replied, "I can't afford that!"

"You're going to America soon. If you don't have money, then I don't know who does!" the driver said while laughing.

People always assumed that if you had any connection with America, you were rich and had a lot of US dollars. Even though his price was a little high, I finally took the deal. If Mom were with me, she would have never agreed and walked away.

The xich lo driver took me around the city, going up one street and down another, until I was totally lost. A short while later, he stopped in front of a building with a sign that read, "We help with documents in and out of country".

I had to pay the driver as soon as I got off, even though he was going to wait for me. Inside the office, they didn't know what I was talking about, so I walked back out and got into the xich lo.

This time, while riding around, I kept looking at the signs in front of the buildings and told the driver when to stop.

Inside the second office, the girl at the front desk also told me she didn't know what I was talking about. I felt hopeless but didn't want to leave.

When I looked around the lobby, I noticed a man wearing a black suit with a blue tie and carrying a briefcase. He had just walked out from one of the offices. I ran up to him and asked, "Do you know anybody in this building going to Ha Noi?"

"Why?" he asked.

When I explained what I needed, he knew exactly what I was talking about. "You're very lucky," the man said. "I was just on my way to the airport right now to fly to Ha Noi. It'll cost you $50 US dollars."

"OK. Are you sure you can do it?" I asked.

"Don't worry, I've done this several times for other people. I'll be back here tomorrow around 5:00 PM with your Visa," he said.

After handing over my paperwork, including my passport, I went home and prayed hard that I could trust this stranger and he would pull through for me.

The next day, I went back to the office a couple of hours early because I couldn't sit still at home. While sitting in the lobby, I kept thinking, *I can't believe all my paperwork is in the hands of a man who I don't even know. Not even his name!*

When 5:00 PM came and went, the man in the suit was nowhere in sight. I started to panic but then began making excuses for him.

Maybe his flight was late, or maybe the traffic was holding him up.

After waiting for another thirty minutes, which felt like an eternity, the man in the suit came walking through the door. I jumped to my feet, feeling so relieved.

"Sorry, my flight was late, but I have all your paperwork," the man said.

"Thank you! Thank you so much!" I said with a big smile.

"You're very welcome," the guy said as he handed me my passport and papers. I paid him the $50 US dollars and ran out the door feeling like a thousand bricks had just been lifted off my shoulders.

❦

When Jay returned to Viet Nam, he was able to stay and visit for only two days. We needed to spend at least two weeks in Thailand getting my paperwork processed and Jay didn't want to miss a lot of work back in America.

The only things I owned in Viet Nam were my clothes and a bicycle. When I gave the bicycle to my nephew, Khang, he was so thrilled and had the biggest smile I'd ever seen. That made me happy.

Jay made sure to bring along an empty suitcase for me because he knew I didn't have one.

Putting my clothes in that suitcase was one of the hardest things I have ever done. It made me realize I was about to leave behind all the people I loved and everything I knew my entire life.

The night before I left, all my sisters and their families came home to spend time with me and stay the night. We all stayed up late, cooking and eating most of my favorite foods. (Mom knew I wouldn't have a chance to eat any of them for a very long time.) While my sisters and I sat on the kitchen floor cooking, they started moving closer and closer to me and didn't want to leave my side.

We were all talking, eating and having a good time, until my oldest sister started to cry. We all looked at her and stopped talking.

As she was crying, she managed to get out, "The next time I come home to see Mom, and you're not here, do you know how sad that'll be? I'll miss you and won't know what to do!" She continued to sob.

Hearing that, my other sisters began to cry.

When we heard someone walking toward the kitchen, my youngest sister whispered, "Shhh! Mom is coming."

My sisters quickly wiped the tears from their eyes and rushed out the back door.

Mom was surprised when she walked into the kitchen. "Where did your sisters go?" She asked.

"I don't know," I said while stirring the chicken and rice soup with a bamboo stick. I tried my hardest to not let Mom see the tears rolling down my face. (In our house, crying was only allowed when someone died.)

A couple minutes later, my younger sister walked back into the kitchen but avoided looking at Mom. I could see her eyes were still red.

I suddenly heard the voice of my older sister, Chi Tu, call out, "Here comes Grandma!"

Because Grandma couldn't see very well, Chi Tu let her hold onto her arm as they walked toward our house.

Since she lived next door to us, we would see Grandma many times a day, but we still got excited when she came to our house to visit. My younger sister and I dropped what we were doing and ran outside.

"Where's Trang?" I heard Grandma ask.

"I'm right here, Grandma. You can hold onto my arm with your other hand," I said while standing at her side.

Looking very happy, Grandma said, "I need you and your Mom to come into the living room with me."

Grandma asked Mom to sit at the table and face the altar which had a picture of my father and a vase filled with sand for burning incense. Grandma instructed me to stand beside Mom and face her. She then asked everyone else to leave the room.

Right away, I knew what was going on because I remembered her doing the same thing when each one of my sisters got married.

"Trang, before you go on and get married, you need to thank your mother for carrying you, giving you birth and raising you." Grandma requested. "After that, I ask that you get down on the floor and bow to your mom, then while holding three burning incense, bow to your father's picture and ask his spirit to help in protecting you."

As soon as I got down to bow at Mom's feet, she reached down, tapped me on the shoulders and pulled me up with her hands. She looked at Grandma and said, "I would be happy if she just bowed to her father and skipped me."

Grandma didn't say anything. She reached on top of the altar, retrieved three incense and held them over the kerosene lamp before handing them to me.

While facing my father's picture, I held the three burning incense and bowed three times while asking for his protection. I then placed the incense in the sand filled vase so they would continue burning.

While the incense was burning, Mom and Grandma took turns talking to me. "When you get to America, remember to be kind and always help people," Grandma said.

I nodded.

Mom looked at me and said, "When you get there, don't be afraid. Remember, you know how to work hard, so money is always at the tip of your fingers. Also, everything that you need to know is on the tip of your tongue, just ask.

"Take care of yourself and write home often.

"And don't be shy. When you meet someone, just *smile* and say *hello*."

CR■SO

The next day when Jay and I were ready to leave, the house was full with family members, friends, and neighbors. They all came to see us one last time. Most of them wanted to go to the airport with us, but some would need to stay behind. I made sure there was room for my best friend, Ha. Mom only rented one bus because they were very expensive. It was waiting for us in the local village of Cho Dem.

Five minutes before we left, I took one last good look at the house, river, boat, the coconut trees, and the bamboos. I was going to miss seeing them every day, but nothing could compare with how much I'd be missing my family.

We walked down the main path to Cho Dem and stood at the ferry landing. While waiting for the ferry to take us across, a large group of people, young and old, began to gather on both sides of the river and watch us. Many of the people spoke up and said, "Good luck, Trang!" while others didn't say anything and just stared.

Jay was surprised at the number of people who knew my name.

I overheard a group of women talking, "She's so lucky! She's going to be a rich American and is going to have beautiful kids because they'll be half and half."

Someone else said, "I just hope she doesn't act like a rich snob when she comes back."

Jay was completely surrounded by the kids again. They were all saying, "Hello! Goodbye!" They didn't know which one was proper, so they figured they'd say both.

Jay just smiled and said, "Goodbye." Some of the kids came close and lightly pulled at the hair on his arms.

The bus only had thirty seats, but we were able to squeeze in forty. Some sat on another person's lap, while others stood in the aisle, but they were all happy.

One and a half hours later, we arrived at Tan Son Nhut airport.

As soon as we got off the bus, my sisters ran over to me and grabbed my hands. They all had tears in their eyes.

My brother and Mom kept walking around us, trying to hold back the tears. I hugged my brother and each one of my sisters.

Mom was the last person I hugged at the door. She was like a dead person, no smile, no crying, and she couldn't speak.

After looking at her sad eyes, I turned to ask my brother and sisters to take good care of her while I was gone, but suddenly became choked up and couldn't say anything.

As soon as I let go of Mom, Jay and I stepped through the door and I kept walking, never looking back. It was the longest and hardest walk I ever made.

Chapter Twenty-Six

While I was sitting in the airplane, waiting for it to take off, I thought about my cousin, Be Lon. When we were little, she told me that airplanes were as big as a house or bigger, but I didn't believe her. If she were with me now, she'd be saying, "I told you so."

Unfortunately, I have very few memories of my first ride in an airplane. Shortly after taking off, I developed a severe case of motion sickness and spent the entire time with my head in a barf bag.

After arriving in Bangkok and getting settled into our hotel room, I was starting to feel much better.

I instantly fell in love with the city but felt completely lost. Neither Jay nor I understood any of the Thai language and we also struggled to speak to each other.

We soon learned to communicate by finding words in an English-Vietnamese/ Vietnamese-English dictionary and then writing them down on paper. We also drew a lot of pictures.

Traveling to Thailand was a big deal for me. Sitting in an airplane that's flying above the clouds, riding in an automobile taxi, and staying in a large hotel that looked so fancy and clean, were all things I never dared to dream about. Now, it was all happening in one day.

During the first day in our hotel room, I remember standing in the bathroom, staring at the toilet for a long while. I didn't know for sure what it was.

I walked over, pushed down on a small handle on the front of it and was surprised when water started going down. I instantly understood what it was really for and felt proud I figured it out myself.

The following morning after eating breakfast, we had a taxi take us to the American Embassy to apply for my visa. After filling out my application, the Embassy informed us they needed thirty days to schedule an interpreter for my interview. I was also required to have blood tests and x-rays performed by an Embassy approved physician and have the results available at the time of my interview.

Jay hadn't planned on us staying in Thailand that long and began worrying about his job and having enough money to last for thirty days.

I wasn't worried at all; I assumed all Americans had lots of money, including Jay.

Every day, we wandered around the city, looking at many beautiful buildings, going to the mall, and eating good food. I enjoyed everything so much because it was the first time I didn't have to worry about money. I thought it was so cool how every time we needed cash, all Jay had to do was go to the bank and hand them his credit card. I had no idea how credit cards worked, but I liked it.

In Viet Nam, no one I knew ever went to a bank. We had no checkbooks, no credit cards, nor savings accounts. There were some banks in the city that were used by businesses and rich people, but there weren't any close to our area.

Bangkok was not that different from Vietnam, except that it was more modern. I loved when we walked around the city where vendors sold clothes and food on both sides of the street.

The one thing I didn't like, was that there were too many pimps. Many times as we were walking along the street, the pimps would pull Jay over to the side and say, "I have girls for you."

I was shocked. What really made me mad, was that it was in the daytime, and we were holding hands.

A few days before my interview date, we learned that because of some formalities, Jay's Thailand visa was about to expire and he was required to leave the country. We weren't sure what we were going to do, but after talking with an immigration officer, Jay discovered that if he crossed the border into Malaysia, and immediately turned around and re-entered Thailand, his visa would be good for another fourteen days.

Jay's credit card was almost maxed out, and to save money, he decided to take a bus into Malaysia instead of flying.

I made sure to stockpile enough food and then locked myself in our hotel room until Jay got back. I worried that pimps might try to kidnap me.

The following day, Jay returned with his new visa, and with only two days remaining until my interview, we thought our troubles were behind us.

When my interview date finally arrived, we made sure to be at the American Embassy with time to spare before my appointment. My interview went very well and everything seemed to be in order, until the immigration officer pointed out that my birth certificate needed to have a certified translation attached to it.

After returning to the waiting area, I was able to explain to Jay what was needed.

As we were discussing what to do next, I noticed a Vietnamese couple whom we had met days earlier at our hotel also sitting in the waiting area. The Vietnamese man, who was from America and understood English well, agreed to translate my birth certificate and also knew the location of a notary within the embassy.

After successfully completing my interview, the immigration officer handed me a sealed envelope while giving explicit instructions: "This envelope is to be handed to an immigration officer upon your arrival in the United States. If for any reason the envelope seal is broken, your visa will be revoked and you will be required to return to Viet Nam."

A short while later, I was issued a US visa.

After leaving the embassy, Jay and I wasted no time getting over to the airlines office to purchase my ticket and schedule our flight.

It wouldn't be much longer now!

Chapter Twenty-Seven

September 23, 1992. Finally, I was going to America! With all my paperwork in hand, Jay and I were so happy to board the airplane and take our seats.

Compared to the airplane that flew us from Viet Nam, this one was much larger and I wondered how it could possibly fly with so many people in it.

Another thing different about this flight was, I took medicine for motion sickness before boarding and was going to be able to actually pay attention to everything. I couldn't wait to see America, but it would be almost fourteen hours before we arrived at the Los Angeles airport.

Soon after taking off, I was surprised to learn we would be getting food and drink while on the airplane. I was impressed when the flight attendants periodically asked if we needed anything to drink and would serve me a *whole* can of soda pop with a clean cup of ice.

Thinking of my family still living the life I had just left behind made me feel guilty. I ate three meals during the flight and each time was given a choice of what I wanted! Even though we were sitting in economy class, I felt like I was being treated as royalty and never knew the difference.

When we arrived at Los Angeles, my eyes couldn't stop wandering around. So many people with blond hair, blue eyes and beautiful light skin like the Vietnamese women always wanted.

Almost everyone here was taller than I and, for the first time in my life, I felt like the shortest one in the crowd.

They all talked fast, reminding me of sounds made by birds.

The airport was so large and clean. It was modern and rich looking, just like I expected America would be.

When it was our turn to approach the immigration counter, the officer took the sealed envelope from the US Embassy, along with my passport and visa. We were then directed to a row of seats off to one side to wait until my papers were processed. After a brief interview by another immigration officer, I was granted permission to continue to my final destination in Ohio.

Once we arrived at the Akron-Canton airport in Ohio and picked up our luggage, we found Aunt Lien and her husband, Raymond, waiting for us. I was surprised and disappointed at the same time when I saw only the two of them. I had expected to see at least a dozen of Jay's family members. I felt so unwelcomed, but didn't say anything. Among the many things I had yet to learn, going to the airport was no big deal for people in America.

Aunt Lien rushed over to give me a big hug and introduced me to her husband.

"Welcome to America!" Raymond said as we hugged.

"Thank you," I said with a smile.

Aunt Lien placed a heavy jacket around my shoulders. (September might still feel warm for the people living in Ohio, but it felt extremely cold to me.) When Aunt Lien noticed I still looked chilled even with the jacket on, she laughed. "Wait until the snow comes and it really gets cold."

During the one hour drive from the airport to Aunt Lien's house, I kept looking out the window in amazement at how many cars there were on the road. I had always heard America was rich, and now that I'd seen it with my own eyes, I knew it to be true.

Before reaching their house, Aunt Lien and Uncle Raymond wanted to buy us dinner and stopped the car at a place called KFC.

As I was sitting at a table and listening to Jay and Raymond talk, Aunt Lien came walking over with a large bucket in her hands.

When I saw what was inside the bucket, my eyes must have grown to the size of silver dollars. There was so much chicken, and each piece was huge!

When Aunt Lien said, "Eat all you want," I felt like I had just won the lottery.

It was more evidence that America really was a rich country. I kept looking at the bucket of chicken while eating and thought about my family in Viet Nam. My sisters and I used to fight over who would get the largest portion of one small piece of chicken.

A short while after leaving the restaurant, we arrived at Aunt Lien's farm. When I stepped through the door into the kitchen area, I was overwhelmed at the sight of a refrigerator, stove, washer and dryer, and a large TV sitting in the next room. I immediately realized my dreams had always been too small. When I was younger, I thought I'd be lucky to own a refrigerator one day!

Just as I was thinking nothing could get better, I noticed the floor was covered with carpet. I couldn't believe my eyes! I thought only kings and queens lived this way.

Later that night, Jay's oldest brother and his wife (the brother who gave Jay the picture of me), came to see me. I couldn't speak much to them, but I felt better that someone actually wanted to see me.

After they left, I asked Jay, "Why did you call your older brother by his first name?"

"Because that's what his name is. We always call him that."

"In Viet Nam, I would never *dare* call any of my older family members by their name. It shocked me when I heard you do that! It's so disrespectful!"

"Honey, it's OK! In America, we call people we know by their first name."

Even after being assured it was proper, I avoided calling any of Jay's older brothers by their first name. I also noticed no one bowed to their elders either.

Later that evening, I went to take a shower and was astonished to see how many large bath towels Aunt Lien had.

The hot and cold controls in the shower were unfamiliar to me, and when I turned the water on, only the hot came out. I immediately jumped back and let out a scream.

Aunt Lien came rushing in and couldn't help but laugh as she showed me how to adjust the water temperature.

Sensing how silly I felt, she reassured me, "Don't worry; you'll learn all the tricks soon enough."

CR∎SO

The next day, Jay asked me to go visit the rest of his family.

The thought went through my mind, *Are you kidding me? Your family didn't even come to the airport to see me, and now you ask me to go see them?*

Thank God I didn't know how to speak English yet and never voiced my thoughts.

I didn't realize people in America had such different social customs than the people of Viet Nam. When no one came to the airport to see me, I just assumed they didn't care for me.

After getting in Jay's truck to go to his parents' house, I realized that I no longer had to walk, paddle a boat, or ride a bicycle. It was a great feeling.

As we were driving down a country road after leaving Aunt Lien's, my attention was drawn to a large herd of cattle grazing in a beautiful green pasture. I began asking myself, *How could America have so much, while at the same time, so many people in Viet Nam struggled just to put food on the table?*

Many times while I was growing up, I saw people who hungered so much for meat that whenever they saw a dead duck, chicken, or dog floating down the river, they would pull it to shore and cook it for their next meal, provided it wasn't decayed too badly.

When we arrived at Jay's parents' house and were getting out of the truck, I noticed a small, curly, white haired dog running toward us. Jay reached down, picked him up and began petting it.

Jay's Mom and Dad were standing at the door, waiting to meet me.

I could see where Jay got his height from. His dad was a big man whose head was close to the top of the doorway.

Jay's mom was much shorter and petite. She was wearing white pants with a pretty flowered blouse and had the most beautiful short, light colored hair. It was nice to see her look so modern.

At that time in Viet Nam, older women never cut their hair short and always wrapped it in a bun. They also only wore black pants with a traditional Vietnamese long sleeve blouse.

I quietly asked Jay, "What do I call them?"

"You can call them Mom and Dad."

I was happy with that. After being introduced, I smiled and said, "Hello."

"Hello! It's so nice to meet you," they replied. They seemed really nice.

Just as it was at Aunt Lien's place, Jay's parents appeared to have everything. My eyes kept wandering around the house looking at the decorations and pictures hanging on the walls.

When we walked into the living room and sat on the couch, we were joined by the dog I saw outside a few minutes earlier. Mom commented that the dog's name was *Fred*, and I noted how her face would light up whenever we talked about it.

"American people love dogs," was what I used to hear in Viet Nam. Now I knew that story was also true. Still, I found it difficult to believe that a dog could be that important to someone. I didn't know what to think.

Just as we were about to leave, Jay said he wanted to show me a clubhouse he had built for his nieces and nephews located in the back yard. "Do you like it?" he asked as I stared up at it.

I nodded my head yes, but all the while I really thought it was a waste of money. I grew up extremely poor while living in a house with a dirt floor and a roof that leaked horribly. Whenever it rained, we constantly needed to go throughout the house and place bowls under the leaks to prevent the floor from becoming muddy. Just the thought of spending money to build such a nice place, just for kids to play in, was difficult for me to understand.

"Oh, one more thing before we go," Jay said. "I want to show you Mom's pig."

I followed him over to a pen located in a corner of the back yard. In it was the largest pig I'd ever seen. "Wow, it's so big! How old is it?"

"It's about a year and a half old, and his name is Arnold."

"What? The pig has a name? I never heard of such a thing! Why would you name something you're going to eat?"

Jay laughed. "It's not for eating; he's Mom's pet!"

"That's crazy! I don't believe you."

"It's true! Mom has had him since he was a baby. I remember her feeding him with a bottle!"

That was the silliest thing I had ever heard. I didn't know what else to say. I just stood motionless, staring at the pig.

After leaving Mom and Dad's house, we stopped at a home belonging to one of Jay's brothers. The whole family was very nice to me.

I was surprised to see Jay's sister-in-law smoking a cigarette in front of everyone at the kitchen table. Seeing a woman with that kind of freedom was shocking to me. If any of my sisters or I ever did that, Mom would have punished us. Women in Viet Nam were never permitted to smoke.

We continued on to visit another one of Jay's brothers and also his sister. Everyone had beautiful homes and I loved how most things were so different than in Viet Nam. They all had inside bathrooms with hand soap, toilet paper, and plenty of towels. Each person had their own bedroom with nice, thick mattresses. I was completely amazed when I saw a water bed in one of the rooms. I never knew there was such a thing.

After seeing everyone's food pantry and how much they stored, I thought to myself, There's *more food in one home here than in an entire convenient store back home! Nobody here needs to go out and catch fish or search around the rice paddies for a vegetable every day just to have something to eat with their rice. How wonderful!*

In one of the pantries, there was a whole case of soda pop. It wasn't unusual to see someone walking around with a can in their hand whenever they wanted, like it wasn't a big deal.

Where I grew up, nobody would even think about having a can of pop. With the average wage being fifty cents a day, a drink like that was a luxury no one could afford.

A couple of the homes had a swimming pool outside. I noticed there was a car for each person old enough to drive, sitting in their driveways. In Viet Nam, none of my family, neighbors or friends had a car.

It's true what people have always said: "America is rich." I still couldn't get over that most of the floors were covered with carpet.

On the way back to Aunt Lien's, I kept wondering, *What is America's secret? How did they get to be so blessed to have all these things? They must be a genius people.*

My brother once told me, "American people are very smart. The kids are even smart, just like the boy in the movie 'Home Alone.'"

I began to worry, *Would I ever be smart enough to fit in? Where would I start?*

As soon as I saw Aunt Lien, I told her I wanted to get a job and start earning some money.

"No, you can't just yet," she replied. "First, you must get married, and then you need to apply for a green card. You'll be able to get a job after that."

Aunt Lien wanted me to remain at her house for a few days before moving into a temporary place provided by Jay's oldest brother.

Jay was setting up a house trailer on the property given to us by my aunt, but it wasn't ready yet.

One day, she took me to a supermarket. I was amazed at how peaceful it was with not having to negotiate the price for every single item. Everything in the store was so clean and organized, and the shelves were full of many different products.

Aunt Lien bought so much food that our shopping cart was nearly full. When she picked up a five pound bag of sugar and put it in the cart, it immediately sparked a memory of shopping in Viet Nam.

During that time, my family and I could afford to buy only a few spoonfuls of sugar at once. Once or twice a week, Mom would go to the local market for supplies with no more than 6,000 Dong (fifty cents) in her pocket.

After dividing that money up between other basic needs, such as kerosene for our lamp and cooking oil, there wasn't much left for sugar.

I never knew anyone who could negotiate the price of products down and make their money go farther than my mother could. Still, we had to buy small quantities of most things.

On the way home, Aunt Lien stopped at a McDonald's restaurant and pulled her car up beside a box that had a speaker in the middle of it. She talked into the speaker, and a voice talked back to her.

I thought, *Wow! This is some of the high-tech stuff people in Viet Nam always talked about.*

At first, I didn't understand what was going on, but when Aunt Lien pulled up beside a window and I looked inside, everything became clear. I thought that ordering your food and then picking it up without leaving your car was the coolest thing.

"This is the restaurant where I work," Aunt Lien said.

I didn't understand what Aunt Lien was saying to the workers inside, but soon after, many of the employees took turns sticking their heads out the window to say, "Hi," to me.

I just smiled and said, "Hello." People were very friendly, and that made me happy.

When a girl at the window handed each of us an ice cream cone, I couldn't believe my eyes. I was holding in my hand the biggest ice cream cone I had ever had, and it was soooooooooooooooo good!

Vietnamese ice cream was not as rich and creamy as *this* and it also had a completely different taste. If I was ever so lucky to get a cone in Viet Nam, it had no more than one spoonful of ice cream on top with nothing down inside. You could choose between three different colors, but regardless which one you picked, they all tasted the same.

CR ■ ℘

Two weeks after my arrival in America, Jay said the house trailer he had been preparing was ready. We moved mostly Jay's stuff, because the only things I owned were a few outfits. All my clothes were very thin and wouldn't be good enough for cold weather. The only exception was the two sweaters I received as a gift.

On October 17, 1992, almost two years after starting this adventure, we were married by a pastor from the Methodist Church Jay attended. The traditional American ceremony was held at Aunt Lien's house with a few of Jay's family present.

It was nothing like I had always imagined my wedding would be.

I had to borrow a wedding dress from one of Aunt Lien's friends who worked at McDonald's and Jay borrowed a suit from Uncle Raymond.

Even though I understood very few words in the ceremony and my dress was nothing like I would have worn in Viet Nam, it turned out being a happy day for Jay and me.

Our house trailer was situated on a large flat area that was cut out on the side of a hill. The yard area around the trailer didn't have any grass, only dirt and a lot of rocks. There was *so* much work that needed to be done before we could even think about planting grass.

Every day before going to work, Jay would hand me a bucket and insist I work on picking up rocks.

I thought, *I worked in the rice paddies almost every day in Viet Nam! What makes you think I came all the way to America just to pick up rocks?*

Thank God again I didn't know how to speak English very well. I would just give Jay an ugly look.

In Viet Nam, the only thing about America I thought I knew for sure was what I had seen in the movie "Home Alone". I assumed everybody in America lived that way. I was expecting that type of lifestyle to be waiting for me when I came. I *hated* picking up rocks.

Thank God my mother-in-law would come and help me. It looked like she enjoyed it a lot more than I did. We spent hours picking up rocks and the only thing we would say to each other was, "Hello" and "Goodbye." That didn't stop Mom from helping me every day.

Mom helped me with so much more than just picking up rocks. She would take me to a local teacher who taught me English at her house.

The teacher didn't know what she was getting herself into. I didn't know English, and she didn't know any Vietnamese. She would point at objects in her house and make me pronounce the word that corresponded with each object. Sometimes she would take me to the grocery store and we'd walk up and down the aisles pointing at items.

A couple of months later, Jay heard about a program at a local vocational school that taught English to foreigners. I stopped going to the teacher's house and went to the school instead. There were Chinese and Russian students in the class, but I was the only Vietnamese. The teacher was super nice, but just like the first one I had, she didn't speak any Vietnamese either.

I couldn't believe how big, nice, and clean the school was. It had so many great things about it such as indoor bathrooms, water fountains, and a cafeteria, just to name a few. I was very impressed.

At break time, I loved to go to the cafeteria and get a cup of cappuccino. While I always paid for my drink with loose change, a young Chinese woman who sat next to me paid with paper money only. She had just came to America also, but she always had several hundred dollar bills in her wallet. I found out later, her husband owned a well-known Chinese restaurant in town.

At that very moment, I promised myself, *One day, I'm going to own a restaurant.* I didn't know how or when I was going to make it happen, I just knew I would find a way. More than anything, I wanted to make a lot of money to help my family, especially Mom.

രു∎ഇ

Six months after I arrived in America, Aunt Lien was able to get me hired at McDonalds. When I first learned I got the job, I became so excited, I couldn't sleep that night.

On my first day at work, I had to go in for orientation. The supervisor took me around the building for a tour. When we walked into the kitchen, I couldn't get over seeing so many hamburgers and cheeseburgers. I'd never seen that much meat in my life. It was fascinating to watch how the burgers and Big-Macs were prepared. This was what Aunt Lien was trying to describe to us in Viet Nam, and now I was seeing it for myself.

The next day, with my uniform on, I was ready to work. Since my English was poor, the managers made sure I worked only in the kitchen. That was fine with me; I was happy just to have the job.

Everyone was nice to me; they all thought it was cool that I had an accent when I talked.

There were a lot of times they said things to me that I wasn't sure what they meant, but I always nodded my head like I understood. I worried they wouldn't like to talk to me anymore if I didn't understand everything they were saying.

By the end of my first day, I was able to make all the sandwiches without messing up. For that, I must thank the restaurant for having a system which helps people like me learn quickly. I was really impressed when I saw pictures posted on the wall describing how to make a sandwich, in case anyone ever forgot. To this very day, I still remember, "It's always mustard, ketchup, onion and pickle, in that order, to be placed on a burger."

Working at the fast food restaurant helped me a lot with my English, but I still messed up quite often. I kept calling everybody by the wrong name, and one time when I was making pizza and ran out of pepperoni, I couldn't ask for more because I was unable to pronounce "pepperoni". Words with that many syllables were always hard to remember. Fortunately, they took pizza off the menu after one year.

It wasn't long before most of my co-workers, including the managers, liked working with me. I worked hard. Really, really hard. I would come in when someone called off, and I worked every weekend. I always showed up to work on time, most of the time early.

I didn't understand why the other employees hated to work on the weekend? Weekdays or weekends were all the same for me. I didn't know the weekends were a big deal until most people kept asking for them off.

Working at McDonald's was better than any job I had in Viet Nam. I vividly remembered working in the rice field with muddy feet, bug bites, bending over all day, and drinking warm rain water with mosquito larva floating on top.

Now, I couldn't be happier. Having a value meal for my lunch and keeping my feet dry all day were just a couple of the many blessings I received.

Because I worked really hard, I was able to get full time employment and even some overtime. After six months, I received a fifteen cents raise, which was the maximum amount you could get at one time. Once I learned everything I needed to know in the kitchen, I asked the manager if I could work at the cash registers in the front.

"No, not yet," she replied. "Wait until your English gets a little better. Until then, I'll let you work at the drive through window part-time."

"Thank you so much," I replied. I was just so happy to be earning my own money.

Every other week, I deposited my entire paycheck into the bank. I thought I was doing the right thing, saving all my money, until it started fueling arguments between my husband and me.

"Why are you putting everything into savings and not helping pay any bills?" Jay asked me one time.

Not understanding, I replied, "Well, you can save money too. I've seen your paychecks."

"Yes," he answered, sounding a little testy, "but I have expenses."

He then had to explain to me something about America I had never considered: *bills*. Electric, trash, gas, truck payment, insurance, taxes. . . *credit card bills*. . . And so many other things that I had never heard of in Viet Nam.

Plus, Jay had gotten behind on some payments due to staying in Thailand so long, spending so much of his money, and not working his job.

Once I understood how things worked, I was a bit more willing to help out.

CR∎SO

On one of my days off during the spring, my husband and I went over to his parents' house after his dad requested help with a project he was working on. While Jay stayed outside helping Dad, I went inside the house and greeted Mom as she was standing in front of the stove.

My attention was drawn to dozens of eggs sitting on a counter next to a large pot of water. I walked over and began touching the eggs with excitement.

I asked, "Mom, what are you going to do with all these eggs?"

"Oh, I'm just boiling them for Easter," she replied.

Mom could tell by the look on my face that I didn't understand. She explained that after boiling the eggs, each one would be decorated using food coloring. On Easter Sunday, Dad would hide them in different places all over the yard and the grandkids would come with baskets and hunt for them. "Would you like to help color the eggs?" she asked.

"I would love to, but are you going to cook all of them?" I asked.

"Yes," she said with a puzzled look on her face.

"But...but Mom, there's ten dozen of them. That's 120 eggs!"

"I know, I do this every year."

Looking at all those eggs made my head spin. It brought back a memory in Viet Nam when I stole an egg from our family chicken...............

There was always a need for more chickens to sell, so my mom would allow the mother hen to sit on her eggs until the chicks were hatched. Occasionally Mom would let us take a fresh-ly laid egg from the hen to eat with our rice.

Once the egg was boiled, we broke it in small pieces and placed it in a bowl of fish sauce that was mixed with garlic, hot peppers, lemon and some seasoning.

I always tried to pick out the biggest piece. While eating it, I imagined what it would be like to be able to have a whole egg just for myself.

One day, just after Mom left to go to the market, I saw the hen jump into the bamboo basket that was used as her nest. The basket, filled with straw, sat on a ledge on the kitchen wall that was built for that purpose. I waited for a long time until I heard the hen make its usual loud clucking noise, which told me she had just laid an egg.

I rushed over to the basket and carefully slid my hand under the hen in search of my valued prize. Protecting her property the only way she could, the hen pecked me. That didn't stop me from stealing the very warm, fresh brown egg.

I placed it in a small pan of water and started a fire. I was scared of being caught and getting into trouble, but somehow I couldn't stop myself from boiling that egg.

As soon as it was done cooking, I took it out of the pan of water and passed it from hand to hand to help cool it off. I ran outside and hid on the backside of the kitchen where no one could see me.

Breaking the egg into small pieces, I ate very slowly, trying to make it last as long as possible and savor every bite. I loved the egg white as much as the yolk and had a hard time deciding which one I should save for the last bite. I finally decided on the yolk, and it was the best egg ever.

I made sure to clean up well, so no one would find out.

When Mom returned from the market, she went straight to the basket as usual to count the eggs. I tried to keep a distance from her to avoid showing the guilt that was all over my face. I can still hear her words, "Why hasn't the hen laid her egg yet?" I felt so horrible, but said nothing……….

CR∎SO

My father-in-law was tall and always wore a hat. Every day after picking me up from work, we would stop at the VFW (a club for Veterans of Foreign Wars). While Dad drank a couple of beers and talked with some friends, he would give me a candy bar and a can of soda. He always told me, "Don't tell Mom we stopped here. OK?"

"OK, Dad," I would always say. I found out sometime later that he had diabetes and shouldn't have been drinking alcohol.

One day while we were sitting at the VFW, I said, "Dad, I wish I knew how to drive."

He got up from his chair, tilted his head back to finish his can of beer and said, "Let's go." He took me directly to the drivers' examination station to pick up a permit handbook.

Two weeks later, I went to the examination station to take my test. I informed the lady at the counter my English was very poor and asked if I was permitted to use an English – Vietnamese dictionary.

Not only did she let me use my dictionary, she ended up helping me throughout the test. She would ask a question, I would answer, and then she would mark it on the test for me.

I was doing really well until she asked about beeping the horn when passing another vehicle. Panic overtook me because I didn't know where the horn was located in the car, and I was certain she was going to ask. She never asked the question, and I passed the test.

When my husband came home from work that evening, I asked him to teach me how to drive.

He took me over to a side road that saw very little traffic and let me get into the driver's seat. It ended up being a lot less fun than I always thought it would be. Jay yelled at me the whole time.

"Watch where you're going!" he shouted. "You can't drive on someone's yard like that!"

"I didn't mean to!" I yelled back. "I'm only off the road a little bit!"

"There, you did it again! People aren't going to be very happy with us!"

I became *so* mad and shouted, "All you do is yell, I **never** want you to teach me again!"

On the way home from Walmart a few days later, Mom pulled over to let me drive the rest of the way.

A few miles down the road, she said, "Trang, you can't keep moving the wheel back and forth like you're driving a bicycle."

"I know, I'm trying not to," I said.

When my driving continued to get worse, Mom became scared and told me to pull over.

"I don't think you're ready to drive on the main roads yet."

I was glad to pull over; I had no idea what I was doing.

When we arrived back at their house, Mom told Dad how scared she was after letting me drive.

"Oh, it couldn't have been that bad," Dad quickly replied. "Let me take her out for a drive."

As soon as I finished helping Mom unload her car, Dad said, "Come on, let's go."

We jumped into Mom's car and Dad let me drive. After a few minutes, I looked over at him and he didn't seem very scared, so I thought I was doing really well.

On the way back home, I asked, "Am I doing good, Dad?"

He thought for a minute and slowly replied, "Let's just say, if you keep driving like this, it's going to take you at least a year to get your license."

A few days later, I enrolled in a driving school. It was so much better. The instructor taught me all the tricks to navigate around cones in a parking lot before venturing out into traffic. She was really nice, and she never yelled at me.

Three weeks later, the instructor said she didn't think I was ready to take a driver's test yet, but thought it would be a good idea to go ahead and take it anyway. "That way you'll know what needs to be worked on," was her reasoning.

I used Mom's car to take the test and was shocked more than anybody when I passed.

When Dad picked me up at work a few days later, I was in for a surprise. Instead of turning into the VFW as he usually did, he went in a different direction.

"Dad, where are we going?" I asked.

"You'll find out soon enough," he said with a smile.

I was completely confused minutes later when he pulled into the parking lot of an insurance company. Everything became clear when I noticed a beautiful, clean car, sitting in the corner of the lot with a "For Sale" sign on it.

"I can't afford to buy that car," I said while looking at Dad.

"Yes, you can! I already talked with the lady who owns it, and she's asking $400."

"Only $400? Really? I want it! I want it! Can we buy it today?" I asked.

"Yes, yes, you can buy it today. I will pay the lady now so no one else will get it, and you can pay me back when we get home. We'll come back and pick the car up later after Jay calls his insurance company and picks up temporary tags," Dad said.

I didn't know used cars were that cheap in America. In Viet Nam, you had to be very rich to think about buying a used car. For the average person, it was considered unrealistic to even dream about it.

I was so excited when I picked up my car. On the way home, Dad made me stop at a gas station to make sure I knew how to put gas in it. At the station, I paid close attention to how everything worked. It was easy.

A week later after work, I called Mom on the phone and asked, "Could you or Dad bring me some money for gas? I'll pay you back tonight."

"Ok. I'll have Dad bring it to you now," Mom said. Dad showed up ten minutes later at McDonalds and saw me standing by my car.

"What's the matter, did you forget your money?" Dad asked with a big smile. He reached into his pocket and handed me a $20 bill.

"I don't need twenty; I only need five" I said.

"Why only five? You might as well take the twenty and fill your tank up," Dad said.

"I only need five because I already have $8.00 in my purse," I said.

"You have $8.00? If you have $8.00, why in the world did you ask me to bring money?" Dad asked with a confused look on his face.

"Because, I need thirteen! Remember when you showed me how to get gas after I picked up my car? When the thing on the pump went 'click', that's how much it cost!" I said.

"Oh boy!" Dad said while scratching his head with a smile. "I assumed you *knew* the pump could be stopped at any time!"

"No! How would I know that? You never told me."

We both started laughing. Another lesson learned about life in America.

CR ∎ ΩO

In the spring of 1993, I found out we were expecting our first child. I was so happy! Since I had an older brother, I hoped it would be a boy. I always wanted one boy and one girl, and hoped to have the son first.

Everyone was excited for us, especially my Aunt Lien, since she never had children of her own.

As we prepared for the arrival of the baby, I started to wonder about working after I gave birth. *Who would babysit? Would I be able to keep the hours I had before?*

I wanted to be a good mother but I also wanted to continue to make money to help my husband and my family in Viet Nam.

In November 1993, our son was born. For my husband and me, it was the best day of our lives. We named him Rick Minh Moreland.

All my family in Viet Nam had black hair and they were hoping Rick would be born with blonde. We knew there was little chance of that happening; he looked cute with his black hair anyhow.

I was so lucky, my mother-in-law fell in love with Rick the minute he was born. When I went back to work, I didn't have to ask her twice to take care him.

Chapter Twenty-Eight

In 1995, I returned to Viet Nam for the first time after coming to America. During the time leading up to the trip, I became so excited, I couldn't sleep or sit still for days. It had been three years since I left my family, friends, and neighbors. I couldn't wait to see them again. I also couldn't wait for everyone to meet our sweet son, Ricky.

After boarding four different airplanes, enduring ten hours of layovers and twenty-three hours flying, all with an infant nursing on a baby bottle, we finally arrived at the Tan Son Nhut airport in Viet Nam.

One of the first things I couldn't help but notice after stepping off the airplane, was Viet Nam's unique smell. I assume the smell is a combination of high heat, humidity, vegetation, and air pollution.

It took almost two hours to go through Immigration, wait for our luggage, and then be screened by Customs. Those two hours felt like twenty. The anticipation of seeing my family again was almost unbearable.

Unlike the airports in America, anyone who wasn't a passenger, government worker, or an employee of the airport, was required to remain behind a fence outside the terminal building.

As we were standing in line waiting for our luggage to be screened, I could see through large panes of glass a large crowd of people packed together and pushing their way up to the fence. Everyone was smiling and waving their arms, trying to get the attention of someone inside the terminal. The sound of all those people laughing and shouting created an overwhelming excitement in the air.

Not having been around many Asian people for the past three years, I found myself staring at them in a way I'd never done before. A part of me couldn't believe this was where I came from. Their black hair, dark skin and the way they dressed were pleasant reminders.

As we made our way toward the exit after clearing customs, I caught the first glimpse of my family standing among the crowd. Just the sight of them created such an emotional feeling that my eyes began tearing up.

I could see their faces light up the moment they saw us come through the door. Some were standing on their tiptoes trying to look over the top of the person in front of them while they all shouted and waved. I wanted to run straight out and hug them all, but instead, I was forced to wait for the slow moving line to inch its way forward.

Moving toward the gate that opened into the crowd, our path took us along the security fence that held everyone back. A lot of people were staring at us, but mostly at our son Rick.

I overheard one lady say, "Look! Look! That boy is *so* cute!"

Another woman replied, "Of course he is! He's half American and half Vietnamese!"

My family was worried we wouldn't be able to see them, so they repeatedly waved their hands while shouting out our names. (Because of the way Vietnamese people pronounce the letters of the alphabet, nobody could pronounce Rick's name correctly. They always called him *Yit*. It sounded so cute.)

When we finally reached the section where my family was standing, Mom was the first to reach over and touch Ricky. The proud and loving look on her face at that moment remains forever in my memory.

Everyone followed us to the exit gate, and each began insisting they should be next in line to hold Ricky. As much as everyone was happy to see us, they all looked so embarrassed when I hugged each one of them. (I wondered if hugging would ever become commonplace in Viet Nam.)

Mom was so overjoyed when she held Ricky for the first time. It was surprising to see how little he resisted her show of affection. Ricky even allowed the rest of my family to take turns touching and holding him.

The excited atmosphere continued on the bus ride home. The bus was full of laughter as we talked non-stop, trying to bring each other up to date about our lives during the past three years. While we were talking, I couldn't keep my eyes from staring out the window as we slowly worked our way through the city traffic.

All those motorcycles packed together on the narrow streets, the sound of honking horns, music playing, people shopping and eating on both sides of the street, all combined to unleash a flood of thoughts and feelings. The contrast between the two worlds I'd lived in was amazing.

The bus could only move at a very slow pace with the driver constantly putting his feet on the brakes and beeping his horn every few seconds as he inched his way through the city. There were no red lights and most of the traffic was motorcycles and Xich lo's, with just a few cars and buses mixed in.

There didn't appear to be any set directions for people to follow and everybody passed each other *whenever* and *wherever* they wanted. Making things worse, people were walking across the street between intersections at any place they felt like. Instead of paying attention and making an attempt to avoid the traffic, they let the traffic worry about them. When I was growing up and living here, none of this seemed the least bit unusual.

While gazing at all the buildings, people, and crazy traffic, my eyes lit up when I noticed a food vendor selling a type of Vietnamese food I hadn't eaten for a very long time. Pointing my finger at the vendor, I shouted, "Look! Look over there! That's one of my favorite foods! I want to eat some of that so badly!"

My brother immediately asked the driver to pull over in front of the food vendor where we could buy through the open window. I bought everything by the dozen, which was more than enough to feed everyone in the bus, including the driver.

It was easy to understand how Aunt Lien felt when she first returned to Viet Nam. Now it was my turn to be treated with true Vietnamese food again, and everything tasted so amazing.

The back of the bus had become much quieter while my nieces and nephews were all enjoying the food. It was a special treat for them as well.

As we were all eating, Mom turned to face the back of the bus and reminded everyone, "Do you know how lucky you all are? You got to go to the airport to pick up Ricky," she paused for the laughter, "and now you're treated with some really good food while some of the family had to stay home. Next time, when it's their turn to go, make sure you don't whine and cry about it."

"I don't want to stay home next time!" shouted one of my nephews.

"Me neither!" another yelled out.

It took almost one hour and thirty minutes for the bus to work its way out of the city and arrive in the village of Cho Dem. The driver took us as far as he was able to go and then let us off in front of the market.

It was late in the morning, which put us right at the end of the busiest part of the day. The best way of describing all the activity in the market at that time of day would be to call it *organized chaos.*

Bicycles, motorcycles, trucks, and miniature buses were continuously traveling up and down the road in front of the market. They constantly beeped their horns at each other and at people crossing the road. Women wearing Vietnamese hats with traditional clothing had temporary stands set up along both sides of the road, each one usually selling one particular product.

As we walked along the edge of the road, our ears were flooded with the sound of traffic and music in the background as people negotiated the price of a product. Experiencing all those sights, sounds, and smells of the busy market made me feel as if I had never left.

To get to Mom's house, we needed to walk through the market, cross the river on a ferry and then walk another twenty minutes on a dirt path surrounded by rice fields. The male members of my family unloaded our suit cases from the bus and carried them away on the back of hired motorcycles.

As we began walking though the market, I quickly realized it was going to take a long time to make it to the ferry. Everyone who knew me from before wanted us to stop and talk for a while. They all wanted to know about my life in America, and while asking, made a big fuss over Ricky.

One woman laughed at me and said, "You sound so *American!*"

She was right; just like Aunt Lien, I had lost a lot of my Vietnamese vocabulary. I could understand everyone but had a difficult time answering them with the proper words.

"When are you coming back to town?" another woman asked. "I would love to see your son again!"

"Soon, I promise," I always replied.

One lady replied, "Good! Please let me know *when* so I can tell my sister! I know she'll be thrilled to see you and your son!"

Word traveled fast. By the time we made it to the ferry, there were small groups of people gathered on both sides of the river waiting to see us.

Stepping onto the ferry and looking at the river lined with coconut trees and buildings brought back so many good memories.

So many times, when I was living here, I stood in line waiting for the ferry with many of the people who were treating me like a celebrity now. I felt proud yet unworthy of all that attention.

Once we stepped off the ferry on the other side of the river, we made sure to stick around and give the people waiting a chance to see Ricky. Some of the people stood quietly and just stared at him while others took turns talking to me.

One middle-age lady patted me on the shoulder and said, "You're so lucky to marry an American and have such a cute baby.

A lot of people have always wished to be just like you, but they'll never have the chance."

"Thanks, I know how lucky I am," I said with a smile.

A moment later, a lady from the back of the group squeezed her way to the front and said, "Hi, Trang, I have a sister who is smart and very pretty. Could you try to fix her up with an American man?"

"Sure, give me a picture and I'll do what I can."

"Thank you! Thank you so much! I'll get a good picture of her and give it to you the next time you come to the market!" The lady did a little happy dance while she laughed and clapped her hands.

People started laughing and I heard someone say to her, "I can't believe you just did that! You're so funny!"

As we were leaving the ferry landing, all my family took turns holding our hands while walking. It was like they hadn't seen us in a hundred years.

As soon as Jay caught sight of the rice paddies on both sides of the path ahead, he looked at me and said, "Welcome home, honey!"

After walking for almost twenty minutes, we finally reached the small path that led off to the right and went back to my family's houses. This particular spot was where my best friend Ha would wait for me every morning before going to school. It's also the place where Mom waited with a big stick in her hand when I came home late after dark!

Just as we were making the turn, I stepped in front of everyone and began running down the narrow path. I really missed my Grandma and couldn't wait to see her.

The path was made on top of a dike separating two rice paddies and I ran to the far end (approx. 100 yds.) before reaching everyone's houses near the river. As I was running, I remembered slipping and falling into the water many times while growing up, especially when it rained and was dark out.

The first house I came to belonged to my uncle. It was the same old traditional Vietnamese hut with a dirt floor that I remembered, with the exception that it looked like it needed a new roof.

All around the outside was like walking into paradise. There were many different types of flowers planted all around, especially in front of the house. I couldn't keep myself from stopping, taking a deep breath, and enjoying the wonderful smell of one particular purple flower. It brought back so many good memories.

My uncle also had many fruit trees, such as starfruit, mangos, bananas, and my husband's favorite, dragon fruit. The tree I missed the most was the tamarind tree. It had been growing there since before I was born.

I was also happy to see the fish ponds beside his house. We were always allowed to use those ponds as swimming pools and take water from them for laundry.

When I reached Grandma's house, the doors were hanging wide open as usual. I ran through the back door and found Grandma sitting on a short stool in the kitchen, boiling water. With her back facing me, I could see her long gray hair wrapped up in a bun and held together with a stick shoved through it. She appeared to be wearing the same old and extremely faded Vietnamese blouse.

"Ba Noi!" I shouted while moving toward her as fast as I could. I kneeled down on the floor and put my arms around her.

Grandma grabbed my arms with her hands and for a few seconds, neither one of us could say anything. I got all choked up and Grandma started to cry.

"Trang! You're home!" Grandma's eyes had gotten really bad and she couldn't see any more. Using her hands, she began touching my face, squeezing my shoulders, and then my arms again. She didn't want to let go of me.

After drying our eyes, I led Grandma by the hand over to Mom's house where we could continue catching up on everything.

As we were approaching the house, I could see the head of a pot belly pig sticking out through a hole in the wall where the kitchen was. Mom hadn't changed anything.

The pigs and chickens continued to share half of the kitchen. (Mom kept them in the kitchen because she worried they would get stolen.)

I noticed our family boat was tied to a tree in the same spot as before. It was an instant reminder of all the days I paddled up and down the river with my family.

I stopped for a second after stepping into the house. *Everything* was the same as the day I left. The old tea pot with little cups was still sitting on the table in the middle of the house. They'd been sitting there for as long as I can remember.

Standing in a corner against the back wall was the old and worn out armoire that I used to love so much. It had a large mirror in horrible condition mounted on one of the doors, but I always managed to find a small area where my reflection was clear. Standing in front of that cabinet was my favorite place to get ready for school. Mom would have to break up fights between my younger sister and me in that corner. I can still hear my sister's voice as she was crying, "Mom! She won't let me have my turn looking in the mirror!"

I promptly walked over to another cabinet that was standing directly behind the table with the old tea pot. On top of that cabinet was the altar with my Dad's picture sitting in the center. I lit three incense sticks, bowed to my Dad's picture and then ran outside to wash my face with rain water dipped from a large ceramic pot. The feeling from the cool water splashing over my face felt like heaven on earth.

After spending time with Grandma, I walked out to the river where I found Jay and Rick standing with some of my nephews. As we stood there looking at the river, my sisters came walking out and asked me to sit with them under a tree. With our backs against each other, we began reminiscing about some of the good times we had while growing up.

A short while later, my sister, Chi Tu, turned to look at me and said, "You know, after you left for America, this was the saddest place ever. It was so sad that we didn't want to come back here."

My younger sister added, "That's so true! We didn't want to come home because it felt like someone had died. It was horrible! The whole neighborhood was sad. So sad, we couldn't discuss it."

She continued, "After you left, Mom couldn't eat or sleep for months. She was getting skinny and we were getting really concerned about her. As time went by, and after receiving more of your letters, she began to improve."

"When Mom received the good news you guys were coming home, she was so happy and became herself again," Chi Tu quickly added.

As busy as my husband and I were while visiting with my family, Ricky was always our number one priority. I wanted to give him a bath before everyone became busy preparing supper, but I was sure Ricky would object to bathing the Vietnamese way.

Instead of standing on a flat rock or a cement pad and dumping water over him, I filled a three gallon plastic bucket with warm water and had him squat down inside. He loved every minute of it! Even with Ricky jumping up and down inside the bucket and splashing water everywhere, I somehow managed to finish his bath.

After drying him off and getting him dressed, Jay led him over to a small open area in front of Mom's house to play. It only took a few minutes before Ricky discovered one of the most exciting toys I think he ever played with: a stick and an old coconut. He spent the next hour hitting the coconut and watching it roll. Once in a while, he would try to hit one of Mom's chickens that happened to walk nearby, but the chicken was always a little too fast and he would give up and go back to the coconut.

My sisters and I walked into the house to help Mom with dinner. There were large pots of rice and vegetables, and a smaller pot of meat cooking with fish sauce. That was the biggest pot of meat I'd ever seen in Mom's house.

Mom made sure to cook one of Jay's favorite vegetables, bitter melon.

Ricky with his favorite toy

When it was time to eat, my brother was the only one who sat at the living room table with Jay and me. Everyone else remained in the kitchen.

Before starting, Jay asked, "Why doesn't everyone eat in here with us?"

"My mother has her way of doing things," I said. "She's worried everybody will eat most of the meat and not leave enough for us. She thinks we couldn't do without it since we're American."

"But they're the ones that need more meat in their diet, not us. Besides, there's enough here for everyone!"

"Good luck trying to tell that to my mother. You think she'd listen to me about that? No way. I know her too well."

Once we finished eating, Jay walked into the kitchen to see how everyone was doing. He stepped back into the living room and asked, "How come nobody else has any pop to drink?"

"Because Mom said pop costs too much and instructed my brother to buy only enough for us when he went to the market. I'm going shopping with my sisters in the morning and will pick up more."

"But I don't understand. I thought we gave your Mom enough money to cover all expenses. When you buy *anything* to eat or drink, make sure you get enough for everyone in your family. Ok?"

"Honey, I know you don't understand how they think any more than they understand how you think. This is one of the reasons why it was difficult for me when I first came to America. All your life, drinking a can of pop was not that big of a deal. At times you might have needed to buy a cheaper brand, but you always were able to have some. In Viet Nam, most people earn only fifty cents a day and a can of pop costs more than that."

I continued, "The only way you can live cheap in Viet Nam is to live like the locals. You eat rice with vegetables, drink water, and walk or ride a bicycle. But if you want to live good, like drinking pop, eating lots of meat, and driving a car, then it's going to cost you even more than it does in America. Most of the good stuff you're used to is shipped in from other countries."

Later that evening, nobody wanted to go home but there wasn't enough room for everyone to sleep. The house was already full with my brother, his wife and four kids living there with Mom. Two of my sisters lived close by and went home with their kids. My oldest sister and her family lived a three hour bike ride away and were given permission from Mom to stay the night.

Family members in living room at Mom's house

Again, we were given better treatment by being directed to sleep on the bed normally used by my brother's kids. My sister, her family and my brother's kids slept on woven mats spread out on the dirt floor.

I had forgotten about the need for mosquito nets until I noticed my nephews hanging them up over the mats right before bedtime.

Everyone, except my sisters and me, fell asleep right away. We got up and went into the kitchen where we could stay up late and talk. Mom walked in a couple of times and yelled, "You girls can talk all day tomorrow. Go to bed!"

"OK, Mother," we said while rolling our eyes. As soon as she walked away, I whispered, "Mom hasn't changed a bit!"

"Heck no!" my sisters replied.

I smiled, happy to know things were just how I left them.

ᴄᴿ■ℰᴏ

Early the following morning, all my sisters and I got up and headed out to the market. It was early enough in the morning that the roosters were still crowing and the government radio station was blaring from speakers placed on top of poles scattered throughout the area.

I felt so weird not being dressed like my sisters. They were wearing traditional Vietnamese clothes while I wore shorts and a t-shirt. The one thing I had on that was the same was a cone shaped bamboo hat.

While we were walking, my sisters took turns holding my hands and squeezing my arms. They repeated how much they had missed me and how things were not the same with me gone. My oldest sister, Chi Ba, was the worst. She didn't want to let go of my hand.

When we reached the market, the vendors were all happy to see us because they assumed I had a lot of money to spend.

My sister, Chi Tu, kept warning me, "Tell us what you want, and let us negotiate the price!"

While living in America, I'd grown accustomed to going into any store and seeing the price of each item labeled. Returning to Viet Nam and having to negotiate the price of everything was a stark reminder of our differences.

My youngest sister, Quyen, added, "They're going to jack the price up because you just came back from America."

There were so many different kinds of food I loved for sale, I got carried away and bought way too much. I quickly realized I shouldn't have done that, because there was no car to load everything into. Just as I was beginning to worry how we were going to carry everything back home, three of my nephews showed up with their bicycles. They took everything we bought back to Mom's and continued checking back with us.

To make my sisters' day, I said, "Let's go over to the clothes section!"

Their faces lit up instantly.

As we were walking by the first clothes vendor, someone tapped me on the shoulder and called out my name. When I turned around to see who it was, a woman asked, "Do you remember me?"

Immediately recognizing who she was, I responded, "Of course I do! How are you, Chi Chin?"

She was so happy I remembered her name.

"Are you guys looking for clothes?" she asked. "If so, you don't need to go any farther. I have everything you need right here, including name brands."

Before I could finish nodding my head, Chi Chin had a chair brought out for me to sit down on while her daughter offered assistance to my sisters. After making sure we were sincere in wanting to buy from her, Chi Chin quickly ran over to a nearby coffee shop and ordered an iced coffee for me to drink.

Even though Chi Chin was sincere in her friendship and kindness toward me, I understood that being treated like a rich and important person was just one of the tactics vendors used to get you to stay and spend money.

With an entire outfit costing less than a dollar, I told my sisters to get as many outfits as they wanted and I would pay for them all. Vietnamese clothes at that time looked colorful and very pretty, but one of the reasons they cost so little was because they were cheaply made and would never last very long.

None of my sisters were talking any more, they were too busy looking through the stacks and stacks of clothes. Rather than picking out clothes for themselves, they were selecting shirts and pants for their husbands and school clothes for their kids.

Trying to sell as many clothes as she could, Chi Chin said with a smile "Don't worry about money, Sisters, Trang's treat! Right, Trang?"

"Sure! You guys can get as many as you would like, but no more than a hundred dollars' worth," I said while smiling back.

My youngest sister quickly replied, "No! We don't need to spend so much of your money. Fifty dollars is *more* than enough. You know that's fifty outfits! We're so lucky!"

While drinking my iced coffee and enjoying everyone's excitement about picking out clothes, I noticed the market was getting more crowded by the minute and people were constantly bumping into me. In the middle of the crowd, I noticed a middle age woman wearing a traditional Vietnamese outfit, walking straight toward me. Her head was covered with a large bamboo hat held on with a cloth strap running under her chin. I could tell she didn't like dark skin because she was wearing a long pair of gloves that covered her arms and her face was covered with a scarf, leaving only her eyes and nose exposed.

"Please buy some lottery tickets from me," the woman said while uncovering her face and exposing a beautiful smile.

I set my drink on the ground and took the stack of tickets from her hand. While flipping through the stack, I noted the most expensive one was almost fifty cents and the cheapest was less than ten cents.

"Please, please help me!" the woman begged. "Buy as many tickets as you can! I've been having terrible luck and sold only a couple of tickets so far today."

I continued to slowly look through the stack but didn't select any. Not being sure which numbers I wanted, I handed the entire stack back to her.

With a very sad face, the women took the tickets from my hand, turned, and slowly began walking away.

"Just a minute," I said before letting her get too far away. "Tell me how much it will cost if I buy them all."

Rushing back to me with a huge smile, the woman quickly counted the tickets and looked towards the sky with her eyes closed while doing the math in her head. "Hai tram ngan dong," (just a little under ten dollars) she answered.

When I handed the woman enough money for all of the tickets, she looked at me with tears in her eyes. "You don't know how much this means to me! *Thank you* for being so kind," she said with a grateful tone in her voice.

There was no way I could have let that woman walk away without buying her tickets. If I hadn't been so blessed with the opportunity to go to America, that could be me standing there instead of her.

While browsing through the clothes, Chi Tu happened to look up and see I was buying tickets. She quickly came running over and demanded, "How many tickets did you buy?"

When I told her how many, she began yelling at me for getting carried away. Grabbing the tickets from my hand, she grumbled, "Let me count them and make sure this woman didn't rip you off!"

I thought the woman had been completely sincere and gracious, and now my sister ruined the moment. As the woman turned to walk away, I wished her well and apologized for my sister's overprotective remark.

"Do you know how many people sell lottery tickets in this town?" Chi Tu asked in a scolding tone. "They talk to each other, and *now* they're *all* going to try selling tickets to you! Let's pay for our clothes and leave here now!"

Chi Chin inventoried all the items my sisters had chosen and after a little haggling, we settled on a price.

Just as we had everything bagged up and were ready to leave, Chi Tu approached Chi Chin and forcefully said, "I want to tell you right now! You better not have overcharged us, because if I find out you did, I *will* bring everything back!"

I gave my sister a look that said, *I can't believe you just said that!*

Chi Chin placed her hand on my shoulder and said with a smile, "Its OK, Trang. This *is* Viet Nam, you know. Your sister is just making sure I'm not taking advantage of you."

Just as we turned to walk away, a large group of children and middle-aged women surrounded me, all holding lottery tickets in their hands. They were all talking simultaneously and trying to hand me their tickets. I didn't know what to do and my only response was to say, "Sorry, I bought way too many tickets already."

The entire group wouldn't leave and each one had a sad story as to why I should buy from them instead of the others. Looking at desperate faces, the old clothes they were wearing, how skinny and worn out they all looked, made me feel sympathetic to their condition. I couldn't afford to buy all of their tickets, but trying to be fair, I decided to buy two tickets from each one of them. Some continued begging me to buy more, but I wouldn't budge from my decision.

When my sisters and I returned home from the market, Ricky was waiting for me to pick him up. Mom thought it was funny how she could spend time with Jay and Ricky without understanding a single word they were saying. The only thing she knew was that Ricky wanted me, because he ran around the house saying "ma-mi, ma-mi." I didn't understand at first what Mom was talking about, but then it dawned on me that Ricky was saying "Mommy, Mommy."

Jay walked up to me after Mom finished talking and said, "Trang, I've got to tell you something funny that happened today! I kind of feel badly for Ricky, but it was so funny, I had to laugh.

"Earlier today, while Ricky was taking his nap, your mom and a few other women were standing around his bed looking at him. I wish you could have seen the look on Ricky's face when he first opened his eyes. All those women hovering over him, excited after seeing him wake up and then talking Vietnamese 100 miles an hour.

"Poor little guy got so scared, he started screaming!

"It was priceless!"

CR∎SO

Once I looked around the house and saw how much food I'd bought earlier, I quickly realized Mom needed a refrigerator. I bought too much at one time and some of the food would go bad before anyone had a chance to eat it. Besides, it would be a nice gift for her since she had recently gotten electricity.

Jay and I talked it over with my brother and he wasted no time getting over to the local market to get information about one. As it turned out, the only place that sold refrigerators was in the section of Ho Chi Minh City called Saigon. Early the following morning, we gave my brother enough money to buy one and he left to go into the city.

When my brother returned with the refrigerator, all the members of my family and a lot of the neighbors were all waiting for him like he was the president. What they really wanted to see, was the refrigerator. Mom was the first in our neighborhood to have one.

For the next few days, more relatives and neighbors came over to check out the refrigerator while wishing they could have one. My uncle's wife suggested that Mom could make a lot of money by selling small bags of ice. Mom just smiled and didn't say anything.

Some of my family, mainly the kids, couldn't leave the refrigerator alone, especially the top part where the ice was. The kids would eat the ice cubes like candy.

My sisters started making treats for the kids by using different combinations of coconut juice, coconut meat, cooked yellow beans, and different fruits. They would put their mixtures in small plastic bags and place them in the freezer.

Every five minutes, the kids would ask, "Are they ready to eat yet?"

"Leave the door alone! Come back tomorrow and they'll be ready then!" Mom would yell at them.

"But there won't be any left when we come back! We'll just stay here and wait!" the kids protested.

"Ok! But you better leave the door alone or I'm going to chop your hands off!" Mom jokingly replied. The bags of treats were gone before they had any chance of freezing.

ՀՋ∎Ֆշ

I enjoyed visiting my family, friends, and neighbors, but I couldn't get over how poor most of them were. Before, when I was one of them, I didn't know the difference and couldn't see just how bad it was. Most of them lived in very old huts that appeared to be ready to fall down.

I also hadn't realized how skinny we all were. When I first saw them at the airport, they looked sickly to me. I wondered what could be wrong with them. Then I realized that this was normal in Viet Nam. I wondered if I looked "fat" to them.

Sitting along both sides of the path leading to the market, there were a few huts belonging to some extremely poor people. Most of these huts sat fifty to one hundred feet from the path and were surrounded by rice paddies on three sides.

Whenever we walked to the market, we would see four or five little girls standing in front of one particular hut, watching every move we made. From the path, I could see they all had long black hair that almost took over their skinny little bodies. Their clothes were very old and poorly fit.

Every time we walked by, Jay would casually wave at them. The girls didn't know what to think and just stared at us. One little girl would always get scared and run into the house.

"Jay! You're scaring them!" I yelled after about the fourth time he did that.

"I don't mean to. I thought they would be accustomed to seeing us by now. I know I look different, but judging by the way they act, you would think I came from another planet."

While trying not to laugh, I couldn't resist saying, "I know. I thought the same when we first met, and I still do sometimes."

Jay just gave me a funny look. "Do you think we should get the girls some candy and give it to them on our way back?"

"Candy? Why candy?"

"Why not?"

While not having a good answer, I took the opportunity to clear up a question of my own. "I was just wondering. When you mentioned candy, it reminded me of something Mom told me when I was younger. She said when the war was going on, American soldiers would pass out candy whenever they would see any kids. Why do Americans like to do that?"

"Because we know most kids like candy. Kids here *do* like candy, don't they?"

"They do, but that's not the most important thing to them. When I was young like them, I loved candy, but I would have much preferred if someone gave me a new outfit or a notebook I could write in."

"Ok, I see your point. Let's buy them whatever you think they need the most, but make sure we also buy them some candy."

While continuing our walk toward the market, I heard a lady's voice call out from behind me. "Trang! Trang!"

Turning around, I saw a woman with two little kids coming toward us on a bicycle. The woman acted so excited to see us, but I didn't recognize her. Once she was a little closer and I finally realized who she was, I began to scream, "Thuy! Thuy! Oh, my goodness, I'm so happy to see you!"

"You remember me!" Thuy said with a smile. She turned to face Jay and bowed her head a couple of times to acknowledge him.

"Of course I remember you! We were neighbors for many years until you and your family moved away. What are you doing here?"

Continuing to smile, she pointed to a tiny brick house we were standing in front of and said, "I live here."

"How long have you lived here?" I asked.

"We've been here for about a year now. My husband is working up in the city and only comes home late at night. Please, come in and visit for a little while."

Thuy's house had to be at least three times smaller than any other home in the area. The walls were constructed with hollow bricks and the roof was made of corrugated metal. (The Vietnamese Government has a social program designed to construct this type of home for veterans and the very poor.)

Thuy cautioned us to watch our step as we followed her inside. Scattered across the dirt floor were hundreds of grass reeds that she used for weaving bags of various sizes. Sitting on the table was a large stack of completed bags, ready to be delivered to a buyer. It reminded me so much of the old days.

I sat down on the floor and began using my feet and hands in concert to work on a bag that was only half completed.

Thuy was impressed I still remembered how it was done.

After watching me weave for a few minutes, Jay asked "How much money does she earn in one day making these bags?"

"I'm sure she doesn't make very much. I'll ask her."

I translated her answer, "She said about twenty to thirty cents a day, depending on how quick you are."

Shaking his head in disbelief, Jay commented, "Just by looking at their house, it's plain to see they have nothing. Spending so much of her time and energy making these bags and earning so little makes me wonder how they could possibly get ahead? I know we can't help everyone, but do you think we should help her family out a little bit?"

"I really want to, but it just isn't that easy. Many of the poor people around here are very proud and won't accept any help if they think you're looking down on them."

Thuy was taken by surprise when I tried to hand her some money as we were leaving. As expected, she reacted by saying, "No! Oh no! I can't accept that!"

I quickly explained, "Jay and I understand just how lucky we are to live in a country that has so many opportunities. I know that if the circumstances were reversed and it was us that needed help, you would be more than willing to do the same."

When Thuy realized my sincerity, she took the money. In a very low voice and with her eyes turning red while trying not to cry, she said, "Thank you, thank you so much."

CR ∎ SO

Before reaching the market, I wanted to stop at my old school for a few minutes to point out where my classroom used to be and where I used to sit.

Standing motionlessly while looking through the doorway, I thought of all the good and bad times I experienced there. The feeling of wanting a notebook so badly suddenly returned to me like it was yesterday. Just as I was stepping away from the door, an idea suddenly came to me. I immediately stopped to tell Jay.

"I was just thinking, the little girls we always see standing in front of their house, I'm sure *they* go to this school. Instead of us buying notebooks for only those girls, why don't we get enough for all the kids in this school? You don't know how much that would mean to the kids, and to me!"

Giving me a strange look, Jay responded, "I suppose, if you really feel that strongly about it. First, I think we should find out how many children are in this school and then see how many notebooks we can afford."

Later that day, after returning home from the market, I asked my brother to sit and talk with me about the elementary school I used to attend.

At first, he looked surprised and unsure about buying notebooks for all the students, but as our conversation continued, he warmed up to the idea. Anh Hai agreed to gather as much information as possible the next day, and then we could decide if we wanted to continue.

After coming home from work the following day, my brother sat across from me at the table and said, "I talked to the school principal today. He said there are about three hundred kids attending that school. Also, notebooks will cost you ten cents apiece, or one dollar for a package of ten with a small box of crayons. Let me know what you decide as soon as possible, because with that many notebooks, I'll need to go up into the city to place the order."

Pleasantly surprised the notebook prices were well within the range of what we could afford, I instantly told my brother to go ahead and order the "package of ten notebooks with crayons" for each kid, and to also order a few extra, just in case.

It only took a few days for the notebooks to be packaged and ready for pickup. Anh Hai hired a small bus and had them delivered at our local market. Worrying they would be stolen if he took them directly to the school, my brother paid a man with a motorized cart to bring the packages to our house for safekeeping.

Looking at the large stack of notebooks sitting in the corner of our living room, I imagined how exciting it would have been to receive one of those packages as a kid.

That evening, just as every evening before, most of my family gathered at Mom's to visit with us. My sister, Chi Tu, came rushing in and sat down beside me with a huge smile. Speaking with a dramatic tone, she said, "I don't know how the word traveled so fast, but everywhere I went today, people were asking about the notebooks, including my neighbors. They're all excited in a way I've never seen before."

"Really?" I asked while being pleasantly surprised.

"Yes, really! What you're doing is going to mean a lot to everyone. People around here have never seen anyone try to help so many of the kids at one time."

My oldest sister, Chi Ba, asked, "Do you already have a plan for how you're going to handle all of this?"

"Sure, it'll be easy! All we have to do is make the kids line up and hand each one a package of notebooks. Done!"

Sitting over in the corner, Anh Hai was giving me the strangest look before finally saying, "Are you kidding me? If you just hand out the notebooks like that, there'll be kids from all over showing up to get in line. I can guarantee you we won't have enough for the kids attending our school."

"But we could tell everyone it's for the *Ap Bon School* only."

Looking frustrated, my brother commented, "This girl has lived in America too long. Don't you remember how things are in Viet Nam?

"**This** is how it's going to work: the teachers will give each student a ticket with their name on it, and I will have a list with all of their names. When I call their name, that student must come up and show me the ticket before receiving their notebooks. It's the only sure way it can be done."

CR∎SO

The following Sunday was the big day. Anh Hai woke up extra early that morning to get dressed up for the occasion. Wanting to have everything ready by 8:00 AM, he enlisted the help of every-one in my family and started moving the notebooks over to the school. Most of my family carried large bundles tied on the back of their bicycles while some just carried a few in their hands.

Jay offered to help, but everyone refused to let him, saying, "You're visiting, and we don't want to make you work."

Feeling helpless, Jay gave me one of those looks that de-manded an explanation.

"You're from America, and they think you can't do anything by hand, just like I used to think. Remember when you first came to Viet Nam and I carried your water every time you took a bath? They still think that way and it's going to take some time to change their minds."

When the last of the notebooks were loaded on the back of a bicycle, Jay, Rick, and I began to follow on foot.

As we approached the school a few minutes before 8:00, we could see hundreds of kids running around the playground. All the parents and many who were just interested in watching, were lined up inside and outside the fence in front of the building. It was like they were waiting to attend a concert. We were all excited.

While picking Ricky up so he wouldn't be scared, I said to Jay, "Look at how many people there are! Can you believe it? The crowd is even blocking the people wanting to go to and from the market!"

Amazed by the whole scene, Jay said, "You know, if you told me this many people would be excited about notebooks, I wouldn't have believed you. Just look at all those women with woven bags and baskets in their hands, looking through the fence. I think they forgot all about going to the market. There was never a time in my life I was in need of a notebook. That was one of those things everyone always had and took for granted."

As we approached the open gate which led into the school yard, all the people (mostly women) turned around and looked at us with big smiles. The majority of them knew me and were saying, "Trang! Thank you so much for what you're doing!"

"You are all welcome!" I replied. The next thing I knew, we were surrounded by a large group of women, all staring at Ricky and Jay while squeezing my shoulders or holding my hands. It was their way of being friendly.

A woman with a woven bamboo hat hanging on her left arm and a shopping bag on her right, stepped up to face me. While grabbing hold of my hand, she said, "I just wanted you to know, we are all *so* grateful for what you are doing."

The other women nodded their heads in agreement.

The first lady added, "Not only are you making the kids happy, you're also helping us parents. *Thank you* a million times over!"

"You're very welcome. Are your kids here with you?"

With a huge smile, she pointed to the classroom with a movement of her head. "They're in there, my son *and* daughter," she said. "They were so excited to come here today, especially my daughter. She woke up extra early to get dressed up and to make sure her brother was ready. We've been waiting here for almost two hours!"

"Two hours? Why'd you come so early?"

"My daughter! She was *so* worried there wouldn't be enough notebooks for all the students in the school, and she'd be left out. The only way to calm her down was to get over here as fast as we could."

A tall woman standing in the back of the group spoke up with a worried look on her face. "Trang, we live here, but my two kids are teenagers and go to a different school. Is there any way for them to get some notebooks?"

While waiting for my response, another woman standing in the group blurted out, "No, you can't! I already asked Trang's brother earlier. They will only give to the kids attending *this* school, from first to fifth grade."

Feeling badly about the tall woman's situation, I tried to ease her despair. "Let me talk to my brother and see what I can do," I said. "Maybe we'll have some extras that I can give you, but you'll need to wait until the end before I'll know for sure."

"Oh, thank you! And please, please don't forget me. My kids really need them."

Another lady listening to our conversation grabbed my hand and said, "Trang! Trang! She isn't the only one that has kids going to a different school. There's a lot of people here with the same problem."

With her finger, she pointed to an old woman standing away from the crowd. She looked to be eighty-five years old, wearing a head wrap, and holding onto a cane. "That woman wants some notebooks for her grandkids, but she's afraid to ask."

At that moment, my brother hollered, "Trang! I need you!"

As soon as I excused myself from the group of women and turned to walk toward Anh Hai, I caught sight of Jay and Ricky standing in one corner of the school yard. They were surrounded by women and a group of school kids. Some of the kids were taking turns walking up and saying, "hello," and then running away.

Just as I was about to reach my brother, I ran into another group of women who were squatting in a circle, busily talking. I was surprised after noticing several of them were old classmates of mine.

"Trang! Trang!" They shouted after noticing me and then standing up. Everyone's faces expressed excitement as we tapped each other on the shoulders.

"Trang!" Anh Hai hollered again. "It's time! Are you ready?"

"I'm ready. Let's get started."

"OK, kids! I need you to line up starting right *here* while holding your ticket in your hand!" My brother shouted as he pointed to an area in front of the classroom where all the notebooks were located.

Students lining up for notebooks

He didn't have to say it twice. All the kids lined up almost instantly in an atmosphere of excitement. It was so gratifying to see all those smiling faces, and at the same time, it broke my heart to see the kids in the back of the line worrying there weren't going to be enough.

A few minutes later, I saw one of my nephews remove some kids from the line who were not holding tickets.

I didn't give the situation any thought and immediately protested, "Let them be! They need help too!"

The kids looked relieved, until my brother shouted, "Trang, you can't do that! What if we don't have enough for the ones we promised?"

I wasn't happy with what he said, but I knew he was right. Trying to console the kids, I slowly worked my way over to them and whispered, "I'll make sure all of you get notebooks later, I promise."

With the list of names and pen in hand, my brother scratched off each student's name, one by one, as they stepped forward to receive their notebooks and crayons.

After watching the agonizingly slow process for about five minutes, I complained to him, "Hey, this is taking way too long! Why don't we just let the kids come up and get their notebooks on their own? That sure would be quicker."

My brother quickly disagreed by making an ugly face at me and said, "You can't do that! Have you forgotten that this is Viet Nam?"

"Why *can't* we do it that way?"

"Because, what's going to stop the kids from coming back again and again? Plus, you can't keep track of the ones that don't have a ticket. I told you about this earlier, didn't I?"

He looked very unhappy with me, so I just walked away.

Ricky had no idea what was going on but looked content as he stood beside one of my sisters.

Jay was running around with our camera, trying to capture all the special moments of the kids with their notebooks.

Happy to receive notebooks

With their package in hand, some of the kids rushed out through the gate to go home while others couldn't wait and wanted to open it immediately. Those kids would squat down in the schoolyard, counting, touching and smelling the notebooks.

A couple of hours later, the crowd started to thin out. Several of the women finally went to the market to do their shopping while many remained waiting. As the last of the students were getting their names scratched off my brother's list, I could hear the people without a ticket starting to cheer. There were a few packages of notebooks still remaining.

Anh Hai cross-checking his list

Without saying a word to my brother, I ran over and grabbed an armful of the remaining notebooks.

By this time, the sun was beginning to get really hot and the poor old lady with the cane was still standing in the same place. I made sure she was first to get one of the packages.

There weren't enough extras for everyone who was waiting, so after doing a quick head count, I sent two of my nephews over to the market to buy the required amount. No one went home empty handed.

Tired from our busy morning and the scorching hot sun, we started our walk back to Mom's house. As we were exiting through the gate, I commented to my husband, "Wouldn't it be great if we could do this for the school kids every time we came to Viet Nam!"

Looking at me with a smile, he replied, "You know, that really would be great. Especially after seeing how much it meant to them."

CR ■ ℘

The remaining days we spent with family and friends went by so quickly. The next thing I knew, we had our bags packed and were saying goodbye at the airport. Those final moments spent with my family, right before we walked through the entrance, were heart wrenching for everyone.

Receiving our boarding passes, checking in our luggage, and clearing customs all helped to take my mind away from saying goodbye to my family. While sitting at the gate and watching our boarding time inch its way closer, I felt a wave of excitement begin to come over me. In twenty-four hours, I'd be back in America with all my creature comforts.

Chapter Twenty-Nine

July 1996 brought the birth of our second child. I was thrilled when the doctor announced, "It's a girl!" Now I had the family I had always wanted! We named our beautiful, dark haired daughter Melissa Tran Moreland.

My mother-in-law fell in love with her as well and was more than willing to baby sit her and Ricky when I went back to work.

Rick and Melissa with their grandma

I had left McDonald's the year before, shortly after returning from our first trip to Viet Nam.

Aunt Lien had announced she and her husband were opening a family style restaurant and asked if I would like to work for her.

The opportunity gave me a chance to earn more money, and I said, "Yes!" without giving it a second thought.

Being a waitress was more challenging than I had expected. I started by studying the menu for an entire day, trying to memorize how to spell basic words like "hamburger" and "French fries".

I thought I was prepared, but my mind went blank when I tried to write on that little notepad. At one point, I handed my pen and paper over to the customers and had them write their own orders!

During the following three years, I became a very good waitress and an excellent cook. Having conversations with the customers daily greatly improved my English and forced me to learn how to spell correctly, and eventually, take my own orders.

When my aunt needed help in the kitchen or wanted some time off, I was happy to fill in and quickly learned how to prepare all the American dishes on the menu. The entire experience gave me a new found confidence.

At the end of the third year, Aunt Lien decided to sell the restaurant and I agreed to stay on and work for the new owners. I was enjoying the money that I was making and I was learning a lot about how to run a business.

The new owners operated the restaurant for nearly two years before deciding the business demanded more of their time than they were able to give. When they closed the doors and put the restaurant up for sale, I found myself without a job.

After my last day of work, I drove home and sat around wondering what my next move should be. Going back to the fast food restaurant was something I preferred not to do, but I had no experience or training to work anywhere else.

I had promised Mom a new home; thinking of that only added to my frustration.

Suddenly, an amazing thought occurred to me:

Why don't I buy the restaurant?

Keeping the idea to myself for the time being, I began writing down everything I wanted to do and what might be needed if I actually owned the business.

Later that week, after my husband came home from work and finished eating his supper, I sprang my idea on him and was met with an "are you crazy" look. Before giving him a chance to say anything, I quickly laid out my plan.

"I know I can do this!" I said. "During the past two years, I've paid close attention to how the business was operated and what changes should be made to make it successful. I know what kind of food I want on the menu, how many employees I'll need, and how many hours I am going to work."

After absorbing what I was saying and seeing how determined I really was, Jay cautiously responded, "If you're *sure* this is what you want to do, and you're ready to take on the responsibility, then I'm OK with it. Before you do anything though, we need to talk with the bank and see if they're willing to loan us the money."

I was *so* excited, I couldn't sit still or go to bed that night.

The following day, I became a little upset after the first bank we talked to wouldn't give us a loan. The bank felt the restaurant was in a poor location ("too rural"), and because of it, a poor investment.

Determined not to let this stop me, we continued checking around until we found a local bank that was willing to work with us.

After signing the loan papers, for what I thought at the time was an unbelievable amount of money, we drove home feeling the full weight of the responsibility we were taking on. With the thought of paying back all that money running over and over in my head, my nervousness and fear reached a point where I became sick to my stomach and threw up.

ଓଃ∎ଌ

With the restaurant key in hand and excited determination, we went to work making preparations for opening day.

Jay took care of the remodeling while I prepared the kitchen, lined up food suppliers, and hired employees.

We underestimated our startup costs, which forced me to spend all the tip money I had saved over the last five years—the money I intended on sending back home to build my mother's house. Even with the tip money, there was only enough cash to keep the doors open for a month.

Jay and I stood to lose everything if the business failed. I could possibly end up with nothing, which is what I started with. I was definitely getting an education in American economics.

But I knew I was a hard worker and a determined person, just like my mom.

So, with a little luck and a lot of prayer, we opened on a cold Tuesday in February 1999.

By Friday, we had people lined up outside, waiting to get in. I wanted to work even harder after seeing so many happy customers and hearing how everyone loved our food.

My restaurant at rush hour

Within one year after opening the business, I had enough money set aside to have a new home built for Mom. A three bedroom home with electric, running water, and tile floors throughout. The refrigerator would be moved in from the old hut.

To actually see my dream finally come true gave me a feeling of enormous pride and a great appreciation for the opportunities I'd had.

ᘓ∎ᘔ

Operating the restaurant required a lot of time and effort. One of my waitresses, Tina, noticed the amount of hours I worked without taking any days off. She would constantly say I needed to take a little time off for fun.

One day, Tina asked if I would like to join her and one of her friends for a *girl's night out*.

Thinking it would be nice to have an evening away from everything and just relax, I accepted her invitation. It also made me happy just knowing they wanted to hang out with me since I was at least ten years older than they were.

I was so excited when Tina and her friend, Beth, picked me up at my house. They both looked stunning, wearing make-up, cute outfits, and fancy hairstyles. After making several complimentary remarks about how attractive they looked, I complained about not having the same gorgeous figure.

Both girls laughed and Tina said, "Trang, you look really good in those shorts. Besides, you're a cute Asian and you'll get all the attention anyway!"

I felt like I was seventeen again!

"Where are we going?" I asked after leaving the house.

Tina said, "To a strip club. We're going to have some drinks and watch a male revue."

"What's a male revue?"

"Have you ever seen a stripper before, Trang?" Beth asked.

"I've heard about it but never seen one," I said.

"A male revue is a group of hot looking guys who dance for women while taking their clothes off," Tina explained with a giddy voice.

"Really?" I asked while feeling myself blush a little. "I can't believe I'm doing this!"

"Just wait until we get there. I promise you're going to have fun!" Beth said.

The club looked very busy. Standing outside, waiting for the doors to open, was a long line of women with huge smiles, all dressed up and looking gorgeous. When the doors finally opened, the line slowly moved its way forward as everyone stopped and had their ID checked.

From the moment we stepped inside, my eyes couldn't stop wandering around the room. The sight of multi-colored dancing lights, loud music, and women sitting at the bar and around tables, all created an exciting atmosphere.

Over at one end of the room was a small dance floor, which I assumed would be where the dancers performed.

I couldn't help but wonder what my mother would think if she could be here and see women her age acting just as excited as the younger girls.

I followed Tina and Beth as they walked through the room and stopped in front of the bar. "What would you like to drink?" Tina asked.

"Anything without alcohol," I said.

"Come on, Trang! At least have one drink!" The girls insisted.

"Well, OK. I saw something on TV once that looked really good. It was made with strawberries, whipped cream and was served in what looked to be a champagne glass," I said.

"That's a strawberry daiquiri. Those are *really* good!" Tina said.

With our drinks in hand, we walked to an empty table. I took a small sip of my drink and it was, just as Tina said, really good!

As time went by, more and more women showed up until the club was completely packed.

Just over half of my drink was finished and the alcohol was already turning my face red.

Tina leaned over and whispered in my ear, "Are you ready? The strippers will be coming out any minute now."

"Yeah, I'm ready," I said with a smile.

Moments before the guys came walking out, some of the women began to go crazy. When the lights and music changed, you could feel the excitement filling the room. Everyone began looking toward the stage with great anticipation, including me.

With the song "American Woman" playing, the first guy walked onto the stage. He was dressed as a fireman and smoke was blowing everywhere.

A second guy came out in a green suit looking like Jim Carrey from the movie "The Mask". After gyrating around from one end of the stage to the other, the guys began ripping off their shirts.

All the women in the club began screaming with excitement, and when the dancers started to slowly pull their pants down, the screaming became almost unbearable.

Never having been exposed to anything like this before, I really didn't know what to think. A part of me felt ashamed for being there, while another part was embarrassed. To complicate matters, I was also feeling just as excited as the rest of the women in the room.

Trying to make the prudish side of me feel a little at ease, I told myself, "This is no big deal; they'll only be walking around in their underwear."

At that very moment, the guys completely removed their pants.

Oh my goodness!

With only a string covering their buttocks, and a small piece of material covering the front, it left little to the imagination! My face turned completely red.

A short while later, the guys stepped off the stage and started going around the tables dancing. I didn't understand the routine until I saw a woman stuff money under the dancer's string.

The guys were very handsome, but the one who pretended to be Jim Carrey was the best looking.

Suddenly, the Jim Carrey dancer walked directly toward our table. I was sure he was coming to dance for Tina and her friend because they were both holding money in their hands.

Before reaching Tina, he stopped and said, "Hi!" to me.

He had the biggest blue eyes with a killer smile! He grabbed my hand and placed it on his chest so I could feel his muscles flex.

I was so embarrassed! It was definitely a lesson in American culture and the only time I've ever been happy my mom was 8,000 miles away!

What an awesome girl's night out!

During our drive back home, all we could talk about was *the hot and sexy stripper who was at our table*.

I really loved spending time with Tina and felt honored to call her my friend. Sadly, she moved away for college a few months later.

Chapter Thirty

In 2000, Mom's new home was completed. That same year, we returned to Viet Nam for another visit.

My family met us at the airport and Mom constantly gave Rick and Melissa kisses for the entire bus ride back.

Once we had our luggage unloaded and on the back of motorcycles, Mom went on ahead to prepare something for everyone to eat. She knew people in the market would insist we stop and visit, giving her plenty of time before we made it home.

After working our way through the market and taking the ferry across the river, I caught my first glimpse of Mom's new home from a long distance away. Its beautifully colored cement walls made it stand out from the surrounding landscape. Most people in that area were still living in the old style huts, which made Mom's house even more noticeable.

Mom's new home

I couldn't wait to see the inside so I made everyone walk faster.

As we approached the house, I couldn't believe just how beautiful it really was. The front entrance greeted everyone with fancy steel French doors, each fitted with a large pane of glass. Beautiful red tile covered the entire porch floor and all sides of the large posts supporting the porch roof. Narrow concrete slabs, stacked one on top of another with spacers in between, gave the porch railing a very special appearance and every window in the house had two framed glass panels that swung outward when opened.

I stopped for a moment to relish the fact that I made this happen, then rushed inside.

As we stepped through the door, Jay immediately pointed to a kitchen sink installed on a tile countertop. "Look! Running water," he said.

Looking in that direction, I was completely caught off guard seeing Mom standing in front of a gas stove. It was an amazing sight! All my memories of her cooking were on a dirt floor, burning rice straw.

While Jay continued to check out the kitchen, my brother showed me around the rest of the house. The moment I looked at the bathroom, I had to yell for Jay to come and see it for himself.

"Wow! An inside toilet," he said with a bright smile.

"And look! It even works!" I said while pushing the lever to make it flush. "No other houses around here have a toilet. I didn't think local builders would know how to install one."

While we were busy going from one room to the next, Ricky and Melissa were receiving lots of attention from other family members. Ricky eventually found his way back outside to play with his cousins while Melissa showed her love of animals by chasing after the chickens and ducks.

The kids were celebrities everywhere we went. People couldn't keep their eyes off them, as if nothing else existed in this world.

For the first two weeks during our visit, Mom's home was like a major event. So many people from the local village were coming by to visit and constantly surrounded Ricky and Melissa.

Everyone seemed so joyful, even when there was no place to sit down and they had to squat down on the floor or remain standing.

I overheard women taking turns whispering, "I don't think I could ever get tired of looking at these two kids, they're so beautiful!"

On more than one occasion, I had people tell me, "I bet that Melissa will be a beauty queen when she gets older."

A small group of teachers with sweet, young voices were laughing and saying, "If they were my kids, they'd probably die a death by kisses."

Mom's house was getting fuller by the hour. While more people were continually showing up, it seemed like no one wanted to leave.

Hours later, as it was beginning to get dark outside, people finally began to leave, especially the older ones. Most people wouldn't even ask, they would just tell me, "I'm coming back again to see your kids, and I'm bringing some of my family with me."

"Why not?" I would say with half a smile.

Days later, when one group of women came back with some of their family members, they began to ask me all kinds of questions. One woman asked, "Trang, does your husband always listen to you?"

"No!" I immediately answered. "Why do you ask?"

"Because I heard that in America, the husband has to listen to his wife." She continued, but this time with a mocking tone in her voice, "It's not like it is in our country, where men think they're kings."

Everyone giggled.

"Women in our country are looked at as not being important. I'm hoping that one day, it'll change."

I quickly replied, "You're a man basher, aren't you?"

The group all began laughing again.

"Why do you think women in Viet Nam are not important?"

"You grew up here! You know how it is! Whenever there's a party or gathering of any kind, the men always get to eat first. We're always required to serve them while they're sitting up front in the living room area of the house, while we do all the cooking and are expected to eat in the kitchen. They drink whisky and chat all day, while we drink water and then hurry home to take care of our kids and housework".

My oldest sister was walking by at that moment and commented, "Women in Viet Nam have a harder life than the men. It's no wonder I look so old. But that's ok, because we're better off than our grandma or our mother ever was.

"Mom wasn't allowed to go to school because her dad always said, 'Girls don't need school. As soon as they're old enough, they'll get married and will need to stay home anyway.'" Trying to be funny, Chi Ba then added, "At least *I* went to the fourth grade."

The whole room chuckled again.

Just when I thought we were done with the questions, a woman sitting in the back shouted, "Trang! Trang!"

I popped my head up to look at her.

"I heard that in America, women are free to drink, smoke and go to the bars."

I blushed, recalling the girls' night out at the strip club, but I could never tell them *that* story!

Before I could answer, another woman jumped into the conversation, worrying her thought would be lost if she waited. "Is it true that in America, men allow their wives to give hugs to other men, and women allow their husbands to give hugs to other women?"

All the women in the room became silent and gave me their complete attention.

"Yes, it's true. They consider it normal."

"Oh my goodness! That's normal?" One woman shouted out.

The whole room came alive with everyone talking to one another, saying things like, "Can you believe that? My husband would beat the heck out of me and then kick me out!"

"Mine too! The whole neighborhood would go crazy and you'd be the talk of the town for ever and ever!"

Someone commented, "Someday, it's all going to change."

"It's never going to happen in our lifetime!" Another woman responded.

Suddenly, Jay came walking by and I stopped him. "Honey, this lady over here wants to know if you always listen to me."

I immediately translated what I asked into Vietnamese for the ladies.

Jay had no idea what was going on and looked at me as if he were asking, "Why would she ask that?"

When he heard me translate what I had just asked him and saw all the women look at him with big smiles, he knew there was only one answer.

"Yes, I always listen to Trang," He said while pointing at me and nodding.

All the women laughed because they were sure they had understood what he had said. When I translated it for them, they laughed even harder, knowing they were correct.

Jay tried to leave, but the women kept insisting I should keep him there a little longer.

"Honey, sit down. The women want to talk to you."

He smiled as usual and agreed to stay. Trying hard to squat down like everyone else, Jay ended up flat on his butt on the floor.

Of course, everyone was watching and began snickering.

One of the women was very ornery and repeatedly tapped me on the shoulder before saying, "Tell Jay I want to marry an American man and ask if he'll find me one."

Everyone cracked up. She was married and just wanted to mess with Jay.

Hearing what was going on, my brother came walking in and bailed Jay out by saying his coffee was ready.

Jay said goodbye to the women before he and Anh Hai left the room.

"I'd like to ask one question before we all leave," a woman who was quiet up to that point suddenly said. "I've heard that in America, when children reach the age of eighteen, they have to move out. That was the saddest thing I've ever heard. Is that true?"

All eyes in the room zoomed in on me. Everyone leaned forward as they waited with great interest for my answer.

"Yes and no," I said. "In America, you *can* move out when you turn eighteen, but you don't *have* to. If they have a job and can afford it, most children do move out at that age because they want to be independent and like the freedom."

Everyone seemed more relaxed once I explained.

"Oh, thank you," the woman who asked the question said. "I feel better now, but it still makes me a little sad, thinking about them moving out on their own like that. I guess I'm just not used to the idea."

While looking at a couple of my nephews standing in the far corner of the room, I yelled, "Hey! You guys are too old to be here; you need to move out tomorrow!"

Laughter filled the room once more.

ଓ ∎ ଛ

During the entire month we were visiting, Mom made it a point to never leave the house. She wanted to spend every second with our kids. She didn't understand any English, but that didn't stop her from talking to them anyway.

Both Rick and Melissa loved her cooking, especially her egg rolls.

Since it was so hot, Mom always gave them a bath in the middle of the day. Even though she had an indoor shower, she still bathed them the old fashioned way. She would put each one in a bucket and pour cold water over their heads.

Rick and Melissa taking a Vietnamese bath

The kids seemed to enjoy this more than a tub bath and would always have the biggest smiles on their faces.

I never was sure if it was the cool water, sitting in a big bucket, or simply the attention from their grandmother that made them so happy.

The one thing Mom could never get used to was Melissa wearing diapers. She always thought it was too hot for her, and every time Melissa would cry, Mom blamed it on the diaper.

Finally, I let Mom have her wish and Melissa began running around the house with just her pants on. With a huge smile, Mom looked at me and said, "Just look at her! She's running around *so* happy. I knew it was the diaper that made her cry all the time."

A few days before leaving Viet Nam, Rick had an upset stomach along with diarrhea. Right away, Mom wanted us to give him medicine to stop the diarrhea, but Jay insisted on waiting for a day or two first. He said it was our body's way of getting rid of something bad and should be given time to heal itself.

Mom didn't like Jay's idea at all.

Years before, many people in Viet Nam had died from an outbreak of cholera, and ever since, many people still panicked whenever someone developed diarrhea.

Since Mom and Jay couldn't communicate, I was caught between the two of them.

To make Mom feel better, we took Rick to a doctor.

Once we were in his office, I described Ricky's condition and relayed both Mom and Jay's points of view on how to deal with it.

The doctor said Jay was correct, but cautioned us to be sure Rick drank plenty of liquids.

He went on to explain that the fear many people have in Viet Nam is so deep that not even he can change their mind-set.

Before leaving his office, the doctor gave us an electrolyte solution to help prevent dehydration. He said it would also make Mom feel better by allowing her to see we were giving Rick medicine.

CR∎SO

A few days before our scheduled flight to America, we were so excited to once again pass out notebooks and crayons at our local school again.

As before, the students were all dressed in their best clothes while family members lined the inside and outside wall of the school yard to watch.

Jay put his arm around me and smiled. "I'm really glad we decided to do this every time we come to visit. Those kids are so happy! Just look at their faces!"

"Better than giving them candy," I said, reminding him of his original idea.

Jay sighed. "Yes, dear, you were right this time. It's better than candy."

"You actually admitted I was right for once," I joked. "Just wait until the Vietnamese women hear this one!"

CR■80

After we returned to America, I continued operating the restaurant for four more years. During that time, I saved enough money to help finance the building of three more houses in Viet Nam, one for my brother and one for each of my two older sisters. (Houses in Viet Nam were very cheap to build at that time.) I also saved enough to help one of my nieces and two nephews with college expenses.

While trying to accomplish too much in a short period of time, I unwittingly let myself get burned out. Working all those hours, seven days a week, without taking enough time off to relax and be with my family, had taken its toll.

I decided to sell the restaurant and pursue something that would be far less demanding of my time.

Chapter Thirty-One

When I was young, I always had the desire to cut and style hair. The only real experience I had was the time I talked my younger sister into letting me cut hers.

The way you learned cosmetology in Viet Nam was by paying a fee to a salon that was looking for a trainee. The salon would require you to work for free until they felt your training was complete. If you were a good stylist, you were given the opportunity to become a paid employee. You were also free to go work for someone else or start your own business.

A license was never required; anyone could open a salon any time they desired. However, if you didn't know what you were doing and gave lousy service, word traveled fast and nobody would ever come to you.

For me, becoming a stylist in Viet Nam was only a dream. Mom never had enough money to pay the salon's fee, and working without being paid would only add another burden on my family.

When I started looking for a new career—one that would be less demanding and take less of my time—I started to consider cosmetology. It was something I had always wanted, and now I could afford to do it. It would be easy, right?

Honestly, the thought of school scared me. I spoke English well, but could only read and write words found on a restaurant menu.

After spending a few days thinking it over, I made the decision to not let the language barrier- or any of my fears- stop me from achieving my dreams.

I stopped at a local beauty school to learn what would be required of me to attend classes and what I should expect once I started.

The owner of the school had her doubts. "I'm worried that since English is your second language, it will be too difficult for you to pass the state board Examination. I had one Asian student who did very well in class but failed her state boards at least a dozen times. All that hard work, and she never did pass.

"I'm not trying to discourage you, Mrs. Moreland. I just want to be upfront and honest about the difficulties you might face."

I wanted to go ahead and sign up for the class, but the owner's warning stopped me from making an immediate decision.

I asked, "Do you have an extra textbook that you use in your classes I could borrow? I want to look it over and see if it's too much for me. I promise I'll bring it back."

"Yes, we have a couple of them in the back. Let me get one for you," the owner replied.

As soon as I got home, I sat down at the kitchen table and began looking the book over from front to back. It only took a few minutes to fully realize what the school owner was talking about.

The book was so overwhelming! It contained so many words I couldn't read or even attempt to pronounce.

I had a few days to keep the book and make a decision. There were moments when I became really depressed and started thinking I should choose another path.

Those moments were short lived after I reminded myself I wasn't letting anything stop me from going after my dreams.

I went back to the school three days later, returned the book, and signed up for the course.

As I was sitting at my desk during the first day of class, I couldn't help but feel I didn't fit in. I was the oldest student and the only Asian there. Sitting in front of me, was the thick textbook, full of words and definitions far above my present level of understanding.

I became a little relaxed when a nice lady walked into the classroom and pleasantly introduced herself as one of our instructors.

After her brief introduction, the instructor immediately dived into the first chapter of our textbook. She went over the chapter so fast that I didn't understand half of what she was talking about.

I tried highlighting the main points like everyone else in the room, but couldn't keep up. While I was working on the second page, the rest of the class had all twelve pages completed. I started flipping through the pages while pretending to use the highlighter so I wouldn't look stupid.

"There will be a test on the first chapter tomorrow morning. Spend the remainder of this afternoon studying everything we discussed," the instructor announced as we were breaking for lunch.

Being tested so soon really took me by surprise. I was fortunate to be sitting beside a girl who introduced herself at the beginning of the class as "Cathy". She let me borrow her book to see everything she highlighted and looked on as I marked the same lines in my book. We became good friends as we ate and studied together.

Returning to class after lunch, everyone quieted down and began reviewing chapter one. I tried hard to do the same, but didn't understand anything.

Later that evening, when supper was finished, dishes were done, and the kids had their baths, I opened up my textbook and started to review chapter one.

After a little coaxing from me, my husband, who was passed out on the couch after a long day of work, got up to help me. Because I knew very few of the words in the book, he read each page out loud and frequently stopped to explain what everything meant.

After finishing only half of the chapter, we both fell asleep.

The following morning, I took the test and failed.

As I was sitting in the break room, feeling horrible, the owner walked over to me and asked how I had done.

With a disappointed voice I answered, "I got a 64 percent and failed."

"Don't feel too bad," she said, trying to make me feel better. "This *was* your first test. Besides, we've had other students do worse."

Just as the owner was turning to walk away, I mentioned not having enough time to prepare for the test.

"Don't worry," she replied. "You'll have plenty of time starting with the next chapter. The first chapter was mainly about cosmetology history and considered to be the easiest."

Easy? I thought. *Not for me it wasn't. I just failed!*

CR∎ΨϽ

The next morning, we were all greeted by a new instructor. She had the biggest smile when she walked in and said, "Good morning everyone! My name is Lynn, and I'll be instructing you on the remainder of your bookwork."

Lynn was an amazing teacher. Not long after class started, she noticed I couldn't keep up with everyone else. Instead of ignoring me while I struggled, she walked over and stood beside me for practically the entire class. She pointed out all the words in the book that needed to be highlighted and made notations for me along the edges of each page, all while teaching the class.

Before dismissing the class for the day, Lynn urged us to spend much of our free time studying to prepare for a test in one week.

Every night after putting our two kids in bed, my husband would stay up late helping me with my homework. Having to explain almost every word to me really slowed things down.

A Vietnamese friend suggested I try using an electronic translator which she had used before with much success.

She was right!

With help from my husband and the translator, I passed every test from that time forward with mostly A's and an occasional B.

After a month into the class, we started the hands-on portion of our training while at the same time, continuing the textbook studies.

One part of the hands-on training was everyone taking turns working at the front desk, answering the phone.

When the day arrived for me to take my turn, I approached the instructor and asked, "Are you *sure*, you want me to answer the phone?"

"Yes, I'm sure. Why?" she asked, acting surprised.

"Because of my accent. People won't always understand me."

"You'll be fine, I promise. Just be sure to remember, when first-time clients request an appointment for hair color, you must inform them a *patch test* needs to be performed to check for an allergic reaction to the color dyes."

I did really well at the desk until a first-time client called and wanted her hair colored. I remembered my instructions and informed her of the need for a *patch test.*

The lady immediately hung up the phone.

I couldn't understand why she would be so rude.

After setting the phone down, I walked over to a couple of girls in my class and expressed my confusion over the lady hanging up on me.

"What happened?" one of the girls asked.

"I don't know! The moment I told her she needed a *patch test,* she just hung up!"

The girl just stared at me with a big smirk on her face, and then responded, "No! You didn't tell her that, did you?"

"Yeah. Why? I thought we were required to tell all first-time clients that," I said while feeling really confused.

Both girls began laughing so hard they couldn't talk. After finally regaining some of their composure, one of the girls explained, "Trang! Because of your accent, when you say 'patch test' it sounds like you're saying 'pap test'. It isn't any wonder the lady hung up on you!"

Their howling once again echoed throughout the room.

CR ■ SO

School seemed to get a little less stressful, though I'd never say it got "easy." The year flew by, and, before I knew it, it was time to graduate.

Finishing cosmetology school and passing the state board test was a major milestone for me. I felt like nothing could stop me from achieving anything I wanted to do.

Once I received my hard earned license, I eagerly went to work at a beauty salon at our local mall. I was grateful for the job and used every opportunity during the next two years to learn about the business.

Confident with the knowledge I had just acquired, I took my next leap of faith. I still wanted to be like that kind and beautiful woman back home who had owned her own salon.

In 2006, I opened my own shop and named it, "Trang's Family Salon!"

My employee, Karryn, and I

Chapter Thirty-Two

Over ten amazing years have sped by since I opened my salon, and life in America keeps getting better every day.

Located in a small, eastern Ohio town, the salon is situated on a pie shaped lot bordered by a city street and railroad tracks. An American flag is proudly displayed as it flutters in the breeze and casts a shadow over a gorgeous bed of flowers. Squirrels often play on the sidewalk, and sometimes they pause, sit up, and look at passing cars as if saying, "Stop in and visit!"

One beautiful spring morning, I came to work early, like usual, to have plenty of time to prepare for my first client.

A few minutes later, my employee, Karryn, came crashing through the door with a large sweet tea in one hand and her oversized purse in the other. Everyone always teased Karryn by telling her she carried everything but the kitchen sink with her.

"Good morning, Trang!" she sang out in her usual chipper voice. She went into the back room to unload her belongings.

My first client arrived right on time. "Hello, Heather!" I said as she entered the shop. I tried to offer her something to drink like I did all my clients, but she was too excited about something.

"I saw your picture and the nice article about you in the newspaper today!" she said as she sat in my chair. "I didn't realize you had done all of those things! You are amazing!"

I blushed a little and politely replied, "Thank you."

She went on. "My favorite part was about all the note-books you've given out back home. Are things still that bad in Viet Nam?"

We then took a moment to discuss what we were going to do with her hair and what colors she wanted. As I left to mix the dyes, she said, "Don't forget to tell me about Viet Nam when you get back."

"Trang? Forget to talk about home?" Karryn said sarcastically. "Never!"

"Poor Karryn," I joked. "She has to listen to the same stories all the time. I feel bad for her!"

I returned a few minutes later and started working on Heather's hair.

"I'm just so amazed by your story, Trang. We're about the same age, and I honestly didn't know when I was growing up, people were living like you did. Is it still that way?"

"Things are improving," I explained. "After our trip back in 2000, we made it a point to return as often as we could afford. Because students still struggle to buy school supplies, we continue to donate notebooks. A lot of my customers have asked how they can help and they've ended up donating too. Over the last ten years, with their help, we've been able to supply over 5000 notebooks during each visit."

Notebooks for the students at my old school

"Wow!" Heather said again. "That is great!"

I kept the stories coming as I continued to work on her hair.

"My family has been doing really well and Mom is still overjoyed with her new home. My brother's family keeps growing, so we built another house near the river beside my uncle's place. That way, we have a place to stay whenever we go to visit and don't need to worry about crowding anyone."

"Your own vacation home!" Heather interjected.

"Yes, we are very lucky.

"Viet Nam has changed a lot in recent years. With more foreign investors and manufacturing coming in, the unemployment rate has dropped and the standard of living is slowly getting better.

"However, poor people living in the country are being left behind while everything is improving. They are either unwilling or unable to become better educated or considered too old.

"The factories only hire workers between the ages of 18 and 28, and most technical jobs require the higher education. The only jobs for the elderly and uneducated are farming or heavy labor, and these don't pay as well."

Karryn added, "I guess there's a little bad with the good, no matter where you go."

"There's a lot of good things happening in Viet Nam, though, that are making it better for everyone. In the cities, five star hotels are being built; streets and roads are being widened and updated; modern shopping centers are popping up; and there's even restaurants like KFC, Subway, and McDonalds."

"McDonalds? Really?" Heather asked. "I guess I shouldn't be surprised; they seem to be everywhere."

We paused for a moment as I finished putting dye on her hair. I offered her a drink and she accepted a bottle of water.

Resuming my story then, I told her, "Even where my Mom lives, the once narrow dirt path has been replaced with a gravel road wide enough for a car to travel on. Modern homes like Mom's are popping up everywhere, and everyone has electricity now."

Heather looked up and smiled. "I don't know what I like most about coming here, Trang: the great job you do on my hair, or the wonderful stories you tell!

"You truly amaze me. You started with nothing; came to a country where you didn't speak the language; ended up owning an operating a restaurant; learned a trade, and now own a very successful salon."

"Yea, and we just received the Local Business of the Year Award!" Karryn added proudly.

"On top of that, you own several rental properties and are a motivational speaker. Yet you've never forgotten your roots, and you're still giving back to your family and your homeland."

Speaking at Women's Success Series

"Awe, thank you, Heather! Your words are very kind, but I don't think I've done anything most people couldn't accomplish themselves. If you insist on learning everything there is to know about your interest before you begin, you'll never get started. Just jump right in and you'll learn along the way. By daring to reach out, you will find yourself around people and in circumstances that will help you."

The time came to rinse Heather's hair. As I did, I shared a funny story with her. "A lot of people think I'm smart, but when it comes down to it, there's a lot I don't know.

"Like, just driving around this area confuses me still. One time, when I was on my way to Wal-Mart, I came up on a detour. I didn't see all the signs and I wasn't sure where I was. I started freaking out and then figured some of the cars in front of me had to be going to Walmart. So I decided to just start following some random car.

"The first car pulled into a driveway. So I picked a second and he went to some part of town I knew wasn't right. The third car went straight to the store. I thought, *Who knew? One out of every three cars in this town is going to Wal-Mart!*"

I thought Heather was going to fall out of the chair from laughing so hard.

Karryn chuckled, "Going anywhere with Trang is an adventure!"

I finished drying and styling Heather's hair. On her way out, she stopped to give me a hug.

"I am so proud of you, Trang. I can't imagine myself living in a country and not knowing anything, especially the language. How did you do it when you first came?"

"Oh, learning English was easy!" I exclaimed. "The hard part was finding Wal-Mart!"

CR■SO

Karryn and I worked almost non-stop that day, like many of the days we spent together in my little salon. There were times we barely found a minute to get something to eat. But the satisfied customers and friends we gained made it worth every hard-working second!

When our last two customers of the day left, Karryn and I cleaned up the shop. We were both exhausted and made little small talk as we locked up.

I was looking forward to a relaxing drive home in my new Nissan Altima. I had just purchased it two weeks earlier and I was still learning which buttons to push and what knobs to turn.

My new Nissan Altima

There was no need for a key to start the motor—just push a button while having the small remote nearby. This kind of technology amazed me!

Even the headlights came on automatically when the switch was placed in the correct position, which I was pretty sure I had done. For some reason, that had been difficult for me to remember. It was almost dusk and I knew my headlights were needed for safety.

Before starting the motor, I took a moment to slowly ease myself into the seat and close my eyes. I took a deep breath and inhaled that new car smell I loved so much.

Feeling a pleasant spring breeze rush through the open window and brush my face, I thought about how blessed I truly was. From a poor farm girl in Viet Nam with nothing of material value, to running a successful American business, driving a new car, and carrying a high-tech smart phone!

But my biggest blessing would always be my family: the one back home and the one I had made in the United States. Life was nothing without the right people to spend it with!

As I pulled away from the salon, I continued to enjoy the warm air by leaving my windows down while still within the city limits. Once I reached the two-lane highway that lead to my house, I put the windows up and turned on the air conditioner.

I relished the peaceful drive in the twilight of the day!

About a mile from my destination, a truck suddenly caught my attention as it sped up behind me with lights flashing from its roof. My first thought was that it must be the police, but I quickly dismissed the idea because the only police I knew drove cars, not trucks, and besides, I wasn't speeding.

Perhaps the vehicle was an ambulance. But then again, there wasn't a siren.

I then decided it must be a tow truck. Yes, that was it! Tow trucks flash their lights when on their way to pick someone up.

I thought the truck, whatever it was, must be in a hurry because it was following me rather closely. So as I approached a wide area along the highway, I put on my right turn signal and slowed my speed so I could pull over and let him pass.

But the area wasn't as roomy as I had thought. Convinced the truck didn't have enough space to slide between me and the oncoming traffic, I continued forward.

I searched the berm for a better spot to pull over. Seeing a place that would give the truck plenty of room, I turned my right turn signal on again.

That's when I realized I was only about 500 yards from the first entrance to the horseshoe road my house sat on. I figured I'd just go home and be out of the way of the truck and not have to worry about pulling back out into traffic.

I cancelled the signal for that turn and advanced to the entrance of the road, turning on my left signal.

However, there was a very long string of traffic coming, and I began to worry I was keeping the truck from someplace important.

I decided to proceed to the second entrance of the same road and, by the time I got there, the traffic should have cleared and I could make my turn.

I sped up, saw a break in the cars, and made a quick turn onto my home road. The truck followed me with its flashing lights and now, a siren.

I pulled off the right side of the road and looked back at the truck.

The police! How could I not know! But I wasn't doing anything wrong!

"State Highway Patrol! Get your hands in the air!" yelled the angry trooper as he sprang from his vehicle with his weapon drawn.

Oh, please don't shoot me! I remember pleading in my head as I obeyed his orders.

I was terrified. Unsure of what I had done wrong in the first place, I knew I had only worsened the situation by prolonging the "chase". I had upset the officer enough for him to draw his gun. I was so scared, my life literally flashed before my eyes . . .

Back to Vietnam . . .

. . . My thoughts returned to the present.

This could be it, I told myself. He could shoot me dead right here, right now.

That's when a famous quote suddenly popped into my head: *I didn't come this far to only come this far.*

I would not let my wonderful life come to an end like this! I had to do something to change the irate officer's opinion of me and fast!

He demanded I roll down my tinted window. As I obeyed his order, I did the only thing I could think of doing: I smiled and meekly said, "Hello."

I was still half scared to death and the smile was forced, yet it seemed to be working.

His stern look softened when he saw me, yet he kept his gun aimed at me. "Why did you run from me?" he shouted.

"I'm sorry!" I explained. "I never knew cops drove trucks like that, and I wasn't doing anything wrong! I'm really sorry."

He lowered his gun but his voice remained firm. "Not doing anything wrong? Ma'am, it's nearly dark and you don't have as much as a parking light on. You're an accident waiting to happen!"

I closed my eyes and moaned. "Oh no! The lights! I don't have the switch in the right position! I'm sorry, Officer, but it's a new vehicle and. . ."

"Your license and registration, please. And, ma'am, you can put your hands down." He sounded nicer this time.

Again I did what he asked.

He went back to his truck and ran my information through the computer. He returned with a written warning. I couldn't believe he wasn't even going to give me a ticket after all this hassle!

"If I can make a friendly suggestion, Mrs. Moreland, you need to familiarize yourself with new vehicles before attempting to operate them. And if you see those lights come on behind you, pull over right away! Not a mile or two down the road."

"I will! I will!" I promised. I wondered if his computer told him I had made the same mistake with the lights on my last new car, 13 years ago.

I signed his pad and waited for my copy of the warning.

As he handed it to me, he told me, "You know, I wasn't sure what I was going to find when you finally pulled over—a drunk, a druggie, or a fugitive. It really threw me to find such an innocent young lady with a smile. Keep smiling, and please drive carefully."

As I drove the remaining 500 feet to my driveway, I thanked God for the safe ending to this crazy experience.

Pulling into my garage, I recalled the officer's parting words, and I thought to myself, *You know, Mom, you were right about America: just smile and say, "Hello!" and everything will be alright!*

My mother and I

About the Author

Trang Moreland grew up in southern Viet Nam. At age 21, she immigrated to the United States.

After overcoming language and cultural barriers, she was able to finish trade school and become a successful business owner.

Her present business, *Trang's Family Salon*, has received much recognition in the community, including the Twin City Chamber of Commerce Business of the Year award in 2011.

Trang is also a published author, inspirational speaker, and Vice President of the Tuscarawas County Writers' Guild.

Besides providing supplies for school children in her native country, she also donates to many local benefits and charities.

Trang and her husband, Jay, live in Ohio and have two adult children.

Email: trangsfamilysalon@yahoo.com

Follow Trang Moreland-Author On

My husband and I

My two sweet kids, Rick and Melissa

Reader's Feedback

This was the most interesting book that I have read in a very long time. My wife did not quit talking about this book till I took the time read it. It was very hard to put down. This is a very inspirational book to read.

∞∞∞∞∞∞∞∞∞∞∞∞∞

Absolutely loved this book!! Once you start reading Trang's story it is nearly impossible to put the book down. This book is clearly written from the heart. Can't wait for the next book to see how her story continues!!

∞∞∞∞∞∞∞∞∞∞∞∞∞

This wonderful book has it all. There is a hero, a heroine, intrigue and inspiration. It's a quick read, but filled with laughter, tears and most of all joy. I love watching the story unfold and seeing God's timing and preplanning make it all happen. Trang is a true inspiration.

∞∞∞∞∞∞∞∞∞∞∞∞∞

Recently finished this book and I'm in awe of Trang's inspiring story. Her spirit of determination and hope for something greater had me rooting for her after every chapter! A must read!

∞∞∞∞∞∞∞∞∞∞∞∞∞

What an awesome book...I laughed, I cried, but most of all I smiled! I'm very lucky and thankful to have met you!

Reader's Feedback (cont.)

Hi Trang! WOW!!! I just finished your book. I'm not really a book reader, but once I started reading your book I didn't want to put it down. When I reached the last page, tears came to my eyes. Your story is so captivating and inspirational! Thank you for sharing your story!

∞∞∞∞∞∞∞∞∞∞∞∞

I bought your book at the flea market yesterday. When we got home today, I sat down to read it. You were so right!! I could not put it down until I finished reading it. What an awesome book! You should be so proud! So inspiring!!

∞∞∞∞∞∞∞∞∞∞∞∞

I am speechless after reading your book!! You are such an inspiration and I thank you from the bottom of my heart for sharing this book with me. It gives me a great appreciation for all the things I have.

∞∞∞∞∞∞∞∞∞∞∞∞

This is the first true story about a person's life I have ever read. I typically read psychological thrillers but your book has opened a new library for me. Thank you for being an inspiration to others.